Campus Legends

Campus Legends

A Handbook

Elizabeth Tucker

Greenwood Folklore Handbooks

GREENWOOD PRESS
Westport, Connecticut • London

Library of Congress Cataloging-in-Publication Data

Tucker, Elizabeth, 1948–
    Campus legends : a handbook / by Elizabeth Tucker.
        p. cm.— (Greenwood folklore handbooks, ISSN 1549–733X)
    Includes index.
    ISBN 0–313–33285–1
    1. Universities and colleges—Legends. I. Title. II. Series.
LA23.T77 2005
378′.002—dc22   2005021999

British Library Cataloguing in Publication Data is available.

Library of Congress Catalog Card Number: 2005021999
ISBN: 0–313–33285–1
ISSN: 1549–733X

First published in 2005

Greenwood Press, 88 Post Road West, Westport, CT 06881
An imprint of Greenwood Publishing Group, Inc.
www.greenwood.com

Printed in the United States of America

The paper used in this book complies with the
Permanent Paper Standard issued by the National
Information Standards Organization (Z39.48–1984).

10 9 8 7 6 5 4 3 2 1

Copyright Acknowledgments

The author and publisher gratefully acknowledge permission to cite passages from the
following sources:

Excerpts from Andrea Greenberg, "Drugged and Seduced: A Contemporary Legend." *New
York Folklore Quarterly* 29:2 (June 1973): 155–156. Reprinted with permission of the New
York Folklore Society.

Excerpts from Michael Taft, *Inside These Greystone Walls: An Anecdotal History of the
University of Saskatchewan.* Saskatoon: University of Saskatchewan, 1984. 174–175.
Reprinted with permission of Michael Taft.

Excerpts from the Folklore Archives, Western Kentucky University. Reprinted with
permission of the Folklore Archives, Department of Library Special Collections, Western
Kentucky University, Bowling Green, Kentucky.

Contents

Preface

It has been a delight to work on this volume. Ever since my undergraduate days at Mount Holyoke College, I have heard legends about the fun, horror, and perplexity of college life. I vividly remember how terrifying it was to hear "The hatchet man is coming!" in the fall of 1968. At that point, knowing nothing about the field of folklore, I worried that the hatchet man might actually visit our quiet campus. In graduate school, I studied folklore while listening to fellow students tell hair-raising stories about ghosts, witches, exams, murders, and suicides. While taking a break from higher education to work as a Peace Corps Volunteer at the University of Abidjan in the Ivory Coast, West Africa, I heard campus legends that expressed the needs of students in a rapidly developing nation. Later I learned many legends from my own students and collected hundreds more from folklore archives and Internet sources. This large corpus of legends is richly diverse but also remarkably consistent. Although contexts change and cultures evolve, student life has maintained some important commonalities.

Since the earliest universities began, students have told stories about their studies and daily lives, often emphasizing extraordinary, surprising, and baffling events. Many of these stories focus on the freshman year, when students discover a new way of life away from home. Whether or not students join a fraternity, sorority, or other organization with initiatory rituals, the freshman year provides an initiatory experience. Legends dramatize certain hopes and fears, showing how stressful and exciting the first year of college can be.

This book focuses primarily on legends, although some related forms of campus folklore—especially rumors, pranks, and rituals—provide context for legend analysis. Chapter 1 traces the development of universities, examining early legend patterns, representations of the campus landscape, campus power structures, and modes of recording legend texts. Chapter 2 defines the legend and other genres to which it is closely related. Chapter 3 presents 50 legend texts from a broad range of colleges and universities. An overview of legend scholarship follows. Chapter 5 puts campus legends in the contexts of literature, film, psychology, parapsychology, anthropology, and political protest. The list of Internet resources at the end of the book provides enough information about folklore archives, journals, and legend Web sites for the reader to begin research on campus legends.

In collecting legends for this volume, I have received valuable help from archivists, friends, and colleagues, all of whom I thank very much. My first folklore teacher, Lydia Fish at Buffalo State College, helped me launch this project, and my mentor at Indiana University, Linda Dégh, offered important advice. Others who provided valuable assistance were Alan Dundes and Kelly Revak at the University of California at Berkeley, Janet Langlois and Margaret Raucher at Wayne State University, Patricia Hodges at Western Kentucky University, Rebecca Fitzgerald at Mount Saint Mary's University, John McDowell and Ruth Aten at Indiana University, Pamela Dean at the Northeast Folklore Archive of the University of Maine, Randy Williams at the Fife Folklore Archive of Utah State University, Joseph Goodwin at Ball State University, Donald Allport Bird at Long Island University, Rosemary Hathaway at the University of Northern Colorado, Simon J. Bronner at Penn State Harrisburg, Bill Ellis at Penn State Hazleton, James P. Leary at the University of Wisconsin, Elizabeth Tricomi at Binghamton University, Nancy DeJoy at Millikin University, and Elissa Henken at the University of Georgia. I want to thank my father, Frank. H. Tucker at Colorado College, for his insights into college traditions. I also want to extend warm thanks to my students at Binghamton University who have, in sharing and collecting legends, helped me understand the campus legend's dynamics. Last but very importantly, I want to thank my husband, Geoffrey Gould, whose wonderful photographs bring this book to life, and my son, Peter, who told amazing stories about his freshman year in college.

Although I will never again believe that the Hatchet Man is coming, I remain alert to the campus legend's possibilities. I hope that this book's readers will enjoy the richness of campus legendry as much as I have myself.

One

Introduction

LATE ONE NIGHT ...

Ever since higher education began, students have gathered to share stories of amazing events, horrors, ghosts, and atrocities. These stories, developing from common experiences, hopes, and fears, are known as legends. In *Legend and Belief* (2001), eminent legend scholar Linda Dégh says that the legend can be "a story, a narrative, a communicative act, a social event, a performative genre, a narrative response to a stimulus, a cultural universal, an emergent form, a poetic response" (24). British folklorist Gillian Bennett calls the legend an "elusive butterfly" whose form and content resist definition (34). Nevertheless, it is possible to identify certain key features of this verbal art form that give students an enhanced sense of life's possibilities as they study and prepare for future careers.

Setting

The campus legend tells of occurrences so startling that the listener asks, "Can this be true?" One reason for asking such a question is the legend's real-world setting. Often, though not always, campus legends describe things that happened late at night, when darkness and fatigue alter people's perceptions. Usually these events are alleged to have happened years, months, or at least weeks before the time when the story is told.

A typical legend setting emerges at the beginning of "The Ax," collected by Western Kentucky University student Brian R. Loader from Wallace Wolfe in 1971:

Late one night years ago a fraternity in a small college had a hell session for their pledge class. They made the pledges climb one at a time to the floor in the attic of an alleged haunted house. Each one was to carry a candle and each time they went round the stair well the candle would glow through the glass windows. The building had three floors (10).

Here, late at night, a fraternity holds a "hell session": a term for hazing that promises trouble. We learn that this incident happened "years ago"—within historical time but comfortably far from the present—at a "small college": a term that could apply to many institutions of higher learning. Pledges climb "one at a time" to the haunted attic, feeling isolated and vulnerable. Precise architectural details—three floors, windows in the stair well through which candles glow—give the reader or listener the sense that this is a real place.

Hero

The campus legend's hero is generally a student: often a freshman uneasily trying to adjust to college life. According to folk narrative scholar Max Lüthi, the legend's hero is "suffering man" (24). At the mercy of unfathomable forces, the legend hero struggles to survive. Folktales like "Cinderella" guarantee magical help and assurance that the hero will live "happily ever after." Unfortunately, the legend hero has no such protection. Even if he or she is a kind, innocent person, an undeserved tragedy may take place. Such an outcome seems likely for the hero of Brian Loader's story, introduced as follows:

There was one particular pledge that was absolutely terrorfied [sic]. He was begging not to go. But the actives thought they would be cute and sent this guy up first.

The "actives" are the fraternity members in good standing who direct the hazing. Since hazing tries to wear candidates down, how can the young men resist picking on this abjectly vulnerable pledge? He has done nothing wrong—with the possible exception of showing too much weakness in front of his peers—but seems destined to suffer.

Suspense

A slow sequence of frightening events can make the listener's heart beat faster. Loader's story continues:

When all the pledges were up there they were supposed to have a meeting. So the first scared pledge started towards the house. He walked in and they all watched the windows as the candle passed from floor to floor. But a strange thing happened as he reached the top floor, the candle went out. So everyone thought that the pledge had been teasing them and was up there to scare the rest of the pledges. So the next pledge went up and they all watched the windows. When the second one got to the third floor, his candle also went out. So then about four more pledges went up one at a time and all of their candles went out on the same floor. The actives thought that there was something weird about the whole thing so they got all their flashlights and went up together. They turned on some of the lights as they went up.

Artfully repeating key details, the teller of this story makes the listener feel nervous. One by one, the pledges go upstairs, and their candles go out. Darkness, movement toward the haunted attic, and uncertainty about what may be found there add to the story's somber mood.

Climax

As Mark Twain explains in his classic essay *How to Tell a Story and Other Essays* (1900), a story's climax is all-important. The last line's delivery—sometimes with a pause beforehand, sometimes not—makes the difference between a memorable, successful story and a story that falls flat. Here is the climax of Brian's story:

As they got to the trap door of the attic they flashed their lights up towards it as they opened it. And there was the pledge that went up first standing with an ax over his head and all the pledge bodies were laying on the floor next to him with their heads cut off. The pledge had gone hysterically insane and had killed all the rest of the pledges. The boy is reportedly still in an insane asylum.

What a horrifying tableau! The poor, innocent victim of hazing has been transformed into an ax murderer. Not only is he insane; he is "hysterically insane," reportedly "still in an insane asylum."

Note the teller's emphasis on the word "insane" here. Because of his fraternity's pressure, the hapless pledge loses his mind, victimizing others as he has been victimized. Insanity is a common theme in legends of college campuses, where academic and social pressures can erode the self-control of even the most confident freshman.

Like many other legends told by college and high school students, this one culminates in a moral: hazing is dangerous, and too much pressure can lead to tragedy. The story also suggests that joining a group may have consequences more horrible than anything the joiner has ever imagined.

Variation

Brian's story can be classified under motif Z510*, "The fatal fraternity initiation," found in Ernest Baughman's *Type and Motif-Index of the Folktales of England and North America* (606). Many variants of "fatal initiation" stories have been collected from college campuses over a long period of time. While the stories follow a certain basic plot—the initiate undergoes hazing, comes to grief, and dies and/or kills others—some details vary substantially. The initiation may take place in a graveyard, a house, or another location; the weapon in question may be an ax, a knife, or something else. No folk narrative text exactly matches another; oral narration always varies. Only when texts are printed and published do they become standardized; even then, printed texts serve as stimuli for new oral and written narratives.

EARLY LEGENDS

Ancient Greece and Rome

The earliest institution of higher learning was probably Plato's Academy, founded in Athens in about 387 B.C.E. Plato taught in a grove of trees sacred to the hero Akademos; since then, college and university professors have called their workplace "the groves of academe." Socrates, Plato's teacher, who died in 399 B.C.E., had developed the habit of walking and talking with his students, asking them questions and expecting them to ask questions in return. Dedicating his life to the Socratic method of teaching, Plato established an academic tradition that profoundly influenced future education.

Although we have limited knowledge of legends told in Plato's time, we do know that the death of Socrates, movingly described in Plato's *Phaedo*, became the subject of an often-told story. Having been asked by Athenian officials to comply with the Sophist philosophy, which he believed to be untrue, Socrates refused. After the Athenian government condemned him to death, he swallowed hemlock and died, as he had lived, according to firmly held principles. We might say that this is the first academic suicide legend. It is true that Socrates drank hemlock and died, but the story of his death has been told in different ways, for varying purposes. Socrates also had a reputation for being an absentminded professor. In his play "The Clouds," Aristophanes shows Socrates up in the air in a basket, literally "up in the clouds" pondering immortal truths.

In ancient Greece and Rome, ghost stories circulated actively. The Greek biographer Plutarch, who died about 120 C.E., reported that, in his native city of Chaeronea, the ghost of a bandit named Damon haunted the bathhouse where he had been murdered (Felton, *Haunted Greece and Rome* 37). Plautus, Pliny, and Lucian all told stories of haunted houses. Although the available records from classical antiquity are sparse, it seems clear that both young people and their elders enjoyed telling supernatural legends.

Africa and Asia

Since the definition of "university" varies according to culture area and educational philosophy, there are different answers to the question "Which university was founded first?" Al-Azhar University in Cairo may be the oldest, as it was founded in A.D. 975, shortly after the Al-Azhar mosque opened in 972. The first classes were religious seminars, followed by more general academic studies. Visiting faculty members supplemented the offerings of regular instructors. In 1961, schools of medicine and engineering were added to the more traditional forms of learning.

The Malian University of Timbuktu began to attract students from various parts of Africa in the twelfth century. In the early fifteenth century, when the Malian empire was declining, students gathered in courtyards of the Sankore mosque to study the Koran. On graduation day, they received turbans as symbols of knowledge. This center of advanced learning deteriorated because of the Moroccan invasion of the 1590s.

Higher education also developed early in medieval China, where scholars of the Sung dynasty (960–1269) worked closely with students to prepare them for civil service exams. Based on the Confucian classics, these exams demanded a high level of scholarly achievement and performance. The intricacies of Confucian philosophy required long and careful instruction, with much memorization by students.

In medieval Japan, Buddhist monks helped students pursue higher learning. Students concentrated on Confucian and neo-Confucian texts between the seventeenth and the nineteenth centuries, when private academies became common. Large, Western-style universities did not become part of Japanese education until after Japan opened to the West in the late nineteenth century.

Europe

European tradition suggests that the first university was either the University of Paris or the University of Bologna. Both began early in the twelfth century, and Oxford University was founded shortly afterward; Cambridge came next. A list of the establishment of some of the earliest universities follows:

- about 1140, University of Paris, France
- about 1140, University of Bologna, Italy
- 1167, Oxford University, England
- 1209, Cambridge University, England
- 1217, University of Salamanca, Spain
- 1225, University of Naples, Italy
- 1364, University of Kracow, Poland
- 1386, University of Heidelberg, Germany
- 1411, St. Andrew's University, Scotland
- 1460, University of Basel, Switzerland
- 1501, University of Valencia, Spain

It is important to understand what gave an academic institution the designation of "university." Samuel Eliot Morison, author of *The Founding of Harvard University* (1935), says, "As distinctive a product of the middle ages as Gothic architecture, the university bore a part in medieval life comparable only to that of the Empire and the Church" (5). "University" (from the Latin *universitas*, meaning "a whole") signified a corporate body that brought together students and/or faculty members for the purpose of learning. The learning structure itself, called, in Latin, *studium generale*, often included study of law, medicine, and theology as well as the seven liberal arts: the *Trivium* (grammar, rhetoric, and logic) and the *Quadrivium* (music, arithmetic, geometry, and astronomy). In the Renaissance, philosophy and literature joined the curriculum. The terms "Faculty of Arts and Sciences" and "liberal education" refer to this early program of studies, the point of which was to properly educate a *liber homo*, or free man (Morison 9).

In medieval Europe, "college" meant a place to live and eat. Students without enough money to set up their own dwelling places would rent houses and eat communally. The Sorbonne, founded in Paris in 1257 by Robert de Sorbonne, Chaplain of Saint Louis, began as a residence for students who were working toward their doctorates in theology. There were many such colleges in Paris. The first college at Oxford was University College, established in 1249; Balliol College followed in 1263. Cambridge University's colleges also began operation in the thirteenth century. The British college tradition was so strong that the founders of Harvard, Yale, and other early American colleges set up similar systems. At Emmanuel College at Cambridge, a memorial window in the chapel honors alumnus John Harvard, the founder of Harvard University. Elder William Brewster, who came to America on the *Mayflower*, graduated from Cambridge's Peterhouse College.

Some of the earliest university legends describe Peter Abelard, an early twelfth-century teacher at the University of Paris who relinquished his inheritance as the son of a Breton nobleman to pursue higher learning. A charismatic rebel, Abelard provoked controversy. A legend found in a sermon of Jacques of Vitry explains that when the French king told Abelard he could not teach on his lands, Abelard started to lecture from a tall tree near Paris while students sat on the ground below. When the king told him he could not lecture from the air, Abelard lectured from a boat on the Seine to students seated on the riverbank. Finally, persuaded by Abelard's persistence, the king gave him the right to teach wherever he chose (Ferruolo 21). Probably the best-known story about Abelard is the tragic account of his love affair with a beautiful young student, Heloise; after her uncle discovered them together, Abelard was castrated, and Heloise entered a convent. Later she became an abbess, and they worked together for the good of the church. They were buried together in Père Lachaise Cemetery in Paris.

Oxford University has so many legends about distinguished professors and alumni that it would be impossible to recount them all here. Some of the most amusing stories describe the poet Percy Bysshe Shelley, who was expelled from University College in 1811 because of his "strange and fantastic" pranks. He frequently broke rules, conducted smelly scientific experiments, charged his doorknob with electricity, and spilled acid on the rug of a tutor who chastised him (Gribble 21–31). Although Shelley's publication of a pamphlet called "The Necessity of Atheism" furnished the official reason for his expulsion, other incidents, such as his snatching a baby from its mother to test Plato's doctrine of the soul's preexistence, also contributed to the university's decision to let him go (25).

The founding of University College at Oxford has two explanations: one legendary, the other factual. Some people have claimed that Alfred the Great founded this college. Unfortunately, the evidence for this claim came from a forged deed, and the actual founder proved to be William of Durham. Balliol College also cherishes a colorful story about its origins: Robert of Balliol, from the north of England, drank too much one day and insulted the Bishop of Durham so badly that the Bishop told him he had to do penance. Balliol's choice was to found a college for 16 impecunious scholars in Oxford, giving each scholar eight pence per day for expenses (Gribble 36–37). Since Balliol was founded in 1263, this legend has had plenty of time to evolve over the years.

Tomb of Heloise and Abelard, Père Lachaise Cemetery, Paris. Photograph by Geoffrey Gould.

Another famous Oxford legend vividly describes the Battle of Saint Scholastica's Day in 1354, when scholars at Merton College complained that townspeople had sold them bad wine and stinking fish. Enraged, some of the townspeople got out bows and arrows and began to shoot at the students, who responded boisterously. Although no one was killed, this "town versus gown" battle was so wild that it claimed a permanent place in Oxford's oral history. Today, visitors to Merton College can hear the story of the Battle of Saint Scholastica's Day from tour guides.

Both Oxford and Cambridge have treasure troves of college ghost stories. A "Haunted Oxford" Web site tells of such ghosts as Archbishop William Laud,

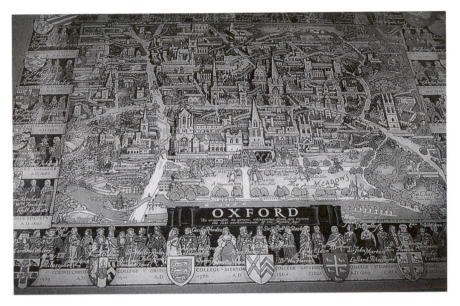

Map of Oxford University. Photograph by Geoffrey Gould.

beheaded on Tower Hill in 1645, who kicks his head around on the floor of the library of St. John's College; Obadiah Walker, the Catholic Master of University College who was imprisoned when he fled to France; and Colonel Francis Winderbank of Merton College, who was shot after surrendering to Oliver Cromwell; he walks through the library on his knees because the level of the floor has been raised. Those who wish to seek out comparable stories at Cambridge can consult Yates's *Cambridge College Ghosts* (1994), which provides an account of paranormal events for almost every residential college.

In Germany, the most sensational academic legend tells of Dr. Johann Faustus, who was so eager to learn that he could not resist summoning the devil for assistance. The chapbook *Historia von D. Johann Fausten,* published in 1587, explains that Faust signed a pact with the devil in his own blood. After 24 years of wine, women, and unlimited learning, he had to let the devil claim him. His body was found on a manure pile, still twitching. One legend tells of Faust conjuring up figures from the *Iliad* and the *Odyssey* to entertain his students; another says that Faust's book explaining how to control spirits (including the devil) was buried under a bush behind Chemnitz Castle (Ashliman, "Faust").

United States

American college traditions date back to 1636, when Harvard University became the first institution of higher learning in the New World. A list of some of the dates when colleges began provides a sense of the growth of American education:

- 1636, Harvard College
- 1701, Yale University (Collegiate School)
- 1746, Princeton University (College of New Jersey)
- 1769, Dartmouth College (for education of Indians)
- 1785, University of Georgia (first state university)
- 1789, Georgetown University (first Catholic college)
- 1795, University of North Carolina (first public college)
- 1802, West Point (first military academy)
- 1804, Ohio University, Athens (federal land grant)
- 1824, Rensselaer Polytechnic Institute (first technical school)
- 1833, Oberlin College (first to admit women, in 1837)
- 1836, Wesleyan Female College of Georgia (first women's college)
- 1837, Mount Holyoke College (first "Seven Sisters" women's college)
- 1854, Ashmun Institute, Chester, Pennsylvania (later Lincoln; first college for black students)
- 1855, Michigan State University (first agricultural college)
- 1868, Cornell University (both public and private)

Harvard University's early days are rich in folk tradition. Its first president, Nathaniel Eaton, lost his job for cruelly beating students. His wife, Mistress Eaton, fed the students loathsome food. Part of her confession shows how bad the food was:

And for bad fish, that they had it brought to table, I am sorry there was that cause of offence given them. I acknowledge my sin in it. And for their mackerel, brought to them with their guts in them, and goat's dung in their hasty pudding, it's utterly unknown to me; but I am much ashamed it should be in the family, and not prevented by myself or servants, and I humbly acknowledge my negligence in it (Morison 232).

Goat's dung and mackerel guts rival modern "fast food" legends in the degree of disgust that they inspire. From this account and others, it seems clear that

Gate of the Master's lodge at Peterhouse College, Cambridge. Photograph by Geoffrey Gould.

America's first college students enjoyed telling stories that highlighted—and probably exaggerated—the most shocking details of their miserable meals at college.

Writing about Harvard's early days, Samuel Eliot Morison emphasizes the importance of the college's setting "in the very midst of Cowyard Row, where the ammoniacal steams emanating from yarded cattle mingled not inappropriately with odors from Mistress Eaton's cooking" (204). Herds of cows, goats, and swine went out to pasture in the nearby Cow Common or grazing land. Today, Harvard University, a premier institution of higher learning in the United States, is hardly a "cow college," but its legends keep memories of the early days alive.

While Harvard and other colonial colleges were built around a central yard, Princeton, originally known as the College of New Jersey, was the first to use the Latin word "*campus*" (meaning "field") so that its layout would seem distinctive. Princeton's early history mirrors America's birth as a nation. When Princeton students heard about the Boston Tea Party in 1744, they held their own tea party, confiscating the college's supply of tea and burning it in the center of their campus. Later, when the Revolutionary War came to Princeton, the college chapel was struck several times by cannonballs. John Maclean, author of the *History of the College of New Jersey* (1877), describes what happened:

It is known that the building was struck in different places by cannon-balls during the affair at Princeton; and one may have entered the chapel, where the portrait of his Majesty was hanging and destroyed it. But, be this as it may, the portrait was destroyed, and the frame, regilded, now contains a full-length portrait of General Washington (337).

Since this story has been told in variant versions, it is clearly a legend. With its substitution of George Washington's portrait for the cannonball-shredded portrait of George III, this delightful story epitomizes college spirit at the time of the Revolutionary War.

In the same era, the founding of Dartmouth College generated another campus legend. Dartmouth's motto, "*Vox clamatis in deserto*" ("A voice crying out in the wilderness"), comes from the college's original mission: to bring the Christian gospel to Indians in the wilderness of the upper Connecticut

King's College, Cambridge. Photograph by Geoffrey Gould.

River valley. Eleazar Wheelock, Dartmouth's first president, worked with Indian minister Samson Occom to raise money for the new college. In the summer of 1770, Wheelock's family moved to Hanover, New Hampshire, bringing along a barrel of rum, wine, apple brandy, tobacco, pipes, and a slave named Exeter. The story of their journey became part of Dartmouth's history, ripe for inclusion in campus folklore.

Sometimes legends of a college's founding inspire jocular songs. In the late 1800s, Dartmouth student Richard Hovey wrote the following drinking song:

> Oh, E-le-a-zar Wheelock was a very pious man;
> He went into the wilderness to teach the In-di-an
> With a Gradus ad Parnassum, a Bible and a drum
> And five hundred gallons of New England rum.

This enormously popular song has kept the memory of Wheelock fresh, as has speculation about the meaning of the weathervane at the top of the tower of Dartmouth's Baker Library. Called "Wheelock and an Indian under the Pine," this copper weathervane includes a protuberance that might, students say, be the famous keg of rum, although it might also be the weather vane's pivot point. Students have also remarked that the green light shining from Baker Library's Tower should be called the "money light," as it is used to attract donations to the college ("Baker Library Bell Tower").

Another connection between college legend and song emerges in Frank R. Brackett's history of Pomona College, *Granite and Sagebrush* (1944). Pamona, founded in 1888, had been in session for only two years when two young professors, camping in the southern California desert with their families, happened to witness a performance of the war dance of the Coahuilla Indians. Brackett says, "It was an intensely dramatic scene, never to be forgotten by the two whites who witnessed it, and the music also was indelibly stamped upon their memories." The refrain of the war dance, "He-ne-terra-toma-he-ne-terra-toma," was unforgettable (34–35). As a stunt at a Halloween celebration, one of the professors performed the dance and sang the song. Over time, this became the song the Glee Club sang on special occasions; new verses joined the others, as did new variants of the story of the two professors' experience.

Stories about founding a college under challenging circumstances can be found on the Web site of the Historically Black Colleges and Universities Network (http://www.hbcunetwork.com). In 1867, Talladega College began when two former slaves met at a convention of freedmen in Mobile, Alabama. The two former slaves, William Savery and Thomas Tarrant, wanted to found a new educational institution where the children of former slaves would learn to preserve their freedom. That same year, Morehouse College was founded as Augusta Institute in the basement of a Baptist church in Augusta, Georgia. Spelman College in Atlanta, founded in 1881, also got started in a church's basement. With less than a hundred dollars between them, Miss Sophia B. Packard and Miss Harriet Giles ambitiously planned to establish a college for the education of Black students. Their determination led to the beginning of one of the premier historically Black colleges in the United States.

Legends about the founding of Native American colleges also emphasize the importance of not giving up, even if the chance of success seems slim. Chief Dull Knife College, located on the North Cheyenne Reservation in southeastern Montana, bears the name of a leader who refused to yield to American soldiers. Chief Dull Knife, also known as Chief Morning Star, courageously led his band of Northern Cheyenne people to their homeland under heavy fire. For information about other Native American colleges, see Stein and AhNee-Benham, *Renaissance of American Indian Higher Education: Capturing the Dream* (2002).

THE CAMPUS LANDSCAPE

In *Mapping the Invisible Landscape* (1993), Kent C. Ryden suggests that "there is an unseen layer of usage, memory and significance—an invisible landscape, if you will, of imaginative landmarks—superimposed upon the geographical surface and the two-dimensional map" (40). College campuses inspire the creation of such landscapes. Their physical landmarks—towers, chapels, gymnasiums, statues—become more than mere buildings and sculptures. Through legend telling, the campus landscape transforms itself into a place that is strange and exciting, uncanny and terrifying—not always comfortable but seldom dull.

When students first arrive at college, they respond sensitively to new stimuli. As Grady Clay explains in *Close-Up: How to Read the American City* (1973), "We do not merely react and respond to environment; we actively represent and construe it—and thus build alternative constructions on it" (13). In the early 1920s, students at the Women's College of the University of Delaware called their new temporary residence halls Topsy, Turvy, and Boletus. Students at the University of California at Berkeley have given their campus buildings new identities through some impressively creative nicknaming. The Central Dining Facility is "Super DC" or "Crossroads," Dwinelle Hall is the "Freshman Maze," Evans Hall is "Fort Evans" or the "Vertical Basement," and Soda Hall is "The Soda Can," the "Inside-Out Bathroom," or the "Emerald Palace." Three Berkeley buildings—Evans, Barrows, and Webster—have the dubious distinction of being known as "Big Ugly Concrete Boxes" ("Alfred Twu's Cultural Tour of Berkeley"). Such marvelously irreverent nicknames redefine campus landmarks as monuments to confusion, inversion, and lack of aesthetic standards.

Sometimes campus topography becomes part of folk prophecy. In the spring of 2003, a Syracuse University senior said,

It's a tradition to tell all the Syracuse University freshmen that Nostradamus predicted that a "large cross-shaped building overlooking a cemetery" will experience a horrendous event (fire, earthquake, flood . . . something) in the present year. Surprisingly, one of the largest freshman dorms on campus is cross shaped and overlooks a huge cemetery.

Buildings shaped like an "X" or cross fit prophecies of disaster well; the crossroad traditionally belonged to Hecate, Greek goddess of the dead. On July 25, 2001, a student at the University of Dayton, Ohio, said that Nostradamus had prophesied a massacre in an X-shaped building near a cemetery; this description fit the dormitory Marycrest Hall (Masterson 38). Less than two months later, after the tragic destruction of the World Trade Center in New York City, students and others spread the word that Nostradamus had predicted the Twin Towers' fall. During that sad and frightening time, students at the State University College at Buffalo called their Twin Rise building "Ground Zero."

Besides noticing X-shaped buildings, cemeteries, and towers, students see the symbolic potential of corners: tight places from which escape can be difficult. Legends about corner rooms in college residence halls have described spectral voices, demon possession, and exorcism. On some college campuses, older students say that freshmen moving into corner rooms should watch out for strange phenomena: posters may fall off the walls, and radios may turn themselves on and off. This kind of warning is typical of initiatory legend-telling for new students.

As Simon J. Bronner points out in *Piled Higher and Deeper,* the college campus "resounds with talk of the strange and wondrous" (143). Students' fondness for creating a sense of strangeness, with focus on academic stress, can be seen in the use of such terms as "Gates of Hell," identifying two columns next to Middle Path at Kenyon College in Gambier, Ohio. At the Massachusetts Institute of Technology, a bridge leading to the campus is called "Halfway to Hell." "Hell," as well as "heaven," serves as a nickname for parking lots on some college campuses.

Among the best-known features of campus landscapes are statues, often focal points of campus traditions. At Cornell University, students paint red and white footprints between the statues of Ezra Cornell and his old friend Andrew White; legend says that if a virgin graduates from Cornell, the two statues will meet in the middle of their courtyard to shake hands. A similar legend exists at Rutgers University, where "Willie the Silent" is expected to start making noise if and when a virgin graduates. Two lions at Tufts in Boston will roar if a virgin graduates; the Spartan statue at Michigan State University will drop its helmet. Sometimes students paint campus statues in the school's colors. The statue of Benjamin Franklin at the University of Wyoming has been decorated on many occasions with bumper stickers, Santa hats, condoms, cigars, and other surprising materials.

Statue of Ezra Cornell (1807–1874), Cornell University. Photograph by Geoffrey Gould.

COLLEGE POWER STRUCTURES

According to Ernest Boyer, author of *College: The Undergraduate Experience in America* (1987), college campuses must continually deal with the conflict between individuals' needs and the needs of the community. Boyer explains,

The college is committed, on the one hand, to serve the needs of individual students, celebrating human diversity in its many forms, encouraging creativity and independence, and helping students become economically and socially empowered. A college of quality is also guided by community concerns. It has goals that are greater than the sum of the separate parts and reminds students, in formal and informal ways, that there is an intellectual and social community to which they are inextricably connected. (286)

This tension between individual and community has, over the years, resulted in some fascinating folklore. Students who go head-to-head with their professors, residence hall administrators, and other staff members may become folk heroes; large groups of students who dare to break the rules will almost certainly be remembered. Stories about both kinds of collisions with authority remind listeners that the community's rules benefit from periodic testing.

At medieval universities, students enjoyed a great deal of freedom. Finding places to live and eat together, they could conduct their daily lives without much supervision. Eventually, as colleges formed and rules tightened, the degree of freedom changed, but students continued to assert themselves. At the University of Salamanca in Spain, for example, administrators of the Trilingual College discovered that two students had lent their academic robes to strolling actresses, then invited them to come over for chocolate and sweets. Forbidden to entertain the actresses in their rooms, the students brought them food outside the college. Their punishment was demotion to freshman status; the most incorrigible student, who went out again without permission, had his head shaved (Addy 54).

Students at American universities have rebelled against the power structure by organizing festive rituals, usually in the spring, that rebel against campus rules. The Massachusetts Institute of Technology students have held three-day steer roasts in their residence hall courtyards, with mud wrestling and other activities not approved by their administration. At Warren Wilson College in Asheville, North Carolina, students have held bonfires called "bubbas" in cow pastures. Princeton students have stubbornly refused to give up celebrating Newman's Day, designed for the consumption of 24 beers in 24 hours (Randall 23–24). These large-scale celebrations imply that it will be impossible for the university to punish a huge group of students. Sometimes this implication proves to be true; other times it doesn't.

Within American residence halls today, those who enforce the rules are usually known as resident assistants (peer counselors) and resident directors (heads of one or more buildings). Up to the late 1960s, it was common for houseparents to be in charge of buildings. The educational policy "*in loco parentis*" ("in the place of parents") gave houseparents the authority to keep an eye on students as their parents would, although frequently their supervision was minimal. Student uprisings in the late 1960s and early 1970s resulted in a change in philosophy at many colleges; rules for daily living became less restrictive. Four Princeton students sent a letter to the *Wellesley News* in the spring of 1968, protesting the "growing student disobedience and immorality at Wellesley as evidenced by radical changes in parietals and dress" (Horn 19). Parietals, rules for men's visitation, became more flexible at many women's colleges toward the end of the 1960s, and other rules loosened up as well.

Relationships between students and their professors also involve an important balance of power. Early legends from European universities tell of students being beaten at the hands of their professors. More recent folklore seldom depicts the professor as a person who physically abuses students, but there are stories about professors who are devious, arrogant, and negligent, especially with regard to grading papers. Stories of students who outwit their professors are very popular, and scholarly studies of students' names for college courses show how much students delight in subverting the professors' own course names. "Rocks for Jocks" (Introductory Geology), "Drugs for Thugs" (The Drug Culture), "Seed and Breed" (Advanced Livestock Production), and "Nuts and Sluts" (Abnormal Psychology) are typical rhyming names for college courses (Eschholz and Rosa 72).

Other noteworthy campus figures are those who keep order: the policemen and policewomen, sometimes called "campus cops," and the custodians, who keep things clean. While members of the police force occasionally appear in legends, custodians make frequent appearances. Their residence in the local community and familiarity with secret tidbits of information make them significant characters in college lore.

HOW SHOULD WE PRESENT LEGEND TEXTS?

Legends vary so much in form, content, and style that deciding how to present them on the typed or printed page is a challenge. While some texts look like smoothly worded stories, others look disjointed and awkward. Should collectors change the stories they have collected for the sake of making these stories readable? While the obvious answer would seem to be a resounding "no," there are reasons both for and against making changes.

The Grimm brothers, pioneering collectors of folktale and legend texts in the early 1800s, routinely rewrote the texts they had gathered. D. L. Ashliman's *Folk and Fairy Tales: A Handbook* (2004) includes a line-by-line comparison of the Grimms' original text of "The Frog King; or, Iron Heinrich" and the revised story in their 1857 edition (97–102). Wilhelm Grimm rewrote the first version of the story to make it more poetic in accordance with high literary style. As a result of his rewriting, the Grimms' stories are stylistically consistent and aesthetically pleasing. They have enchanted generations of child and adult readers and become canonical representations of folktale texts.

Legends, however, tend to be rough and variable. In *American Folklore and the Historian* (1971). Richard M. Dorson says,

The formula requires that the legend be told as if it were a straight forward, consecutive, smooth-flowing narration. And this of course is the style of writing that appeals to readers. But it is false to the nature of oral folk legend. No one individual knows the whole legend, for by definition it is a communal possession (161).

Dorson's point about the legend's communal nature is an important one. The more variants of a legend we collect, the better we can understand the legend itself. The most true-to-life portrait of a legend is a set of texts that can be compared with each other; many such portraits have appeared in folklore journals. One good example of multiple-text presentation in a college setting is Helen Gilbert's "The Crack in the Abbey Floor: A Laboratory Analysis of a Legend" (1975), discussed in chapter 4.

Often, authors compile collections in which only one variant of each legend is included. Ruth Ann Musick's *The Telltale Lilac Bush, and other West Virginia Ghost Tales* (1965) presents 100 texts collected from informants in the late 1940s, 1950s, and 1960s. Among these stories is an intriguing account of a premonitory dream, narrated by Mrs. Kathryn Heenan. Mrs. Heenan explains that her father, a student at Glenville Normal School in 1900, roomed with a friend named Will. One weekend, while her father was at home on a weekend visit, he had the following dream:

At midnight Daddy awoke from a horrible dream, in which he had seen his roommate open the door to their room in the hotel in Glenville and walk to the top of the stairs. At that instant a shot rang out from below, and Will tumbled head over heels to the bottom of the steps. He was dead when he landed at the bottom (49).

The next day, Mrs. Heenan's father learned that his roommate had died exactly as he had dreamed. This early "roommate's death" story pre-dates the better-known legends of roommates stabbed outside their own locked doors (see chapter 3). The text is stylistically pleasing and easy to read, as are the other texts in Musick's collection. There are no offensive terms, no pauses, no struggles to find the right word or phrase. In her introduction, the author freely admits that she changed the texts. Such changes certainly improve readability, but they do not provide a true-to-life sense of the narrator's performance.

In *Aliens, Ghosts, and Cults* (2003), Bill Ellis recognizes five forms or "half-lives" of the typical legend. The first identifies or names an unusual experience, the second translates the experience into language, and the third becomes a finished narrative in performance. The fourth is a "kernel narrative," and the fifth is a "legend report": just a summary of a story that no longer interests members of a group (63–64). Ellis suggests that folklorists' efforts to capture legend texts word for word, with a complete record of nonverbal elements, is "quixotic in every sense of the word" (73). Since a legend moves through many stages, no one recorded text fully conveys its complexity.

Here is an example of a legend report solicited by a student collector. Doug Shoback collected this story about a haunted theater from a male student at the University of Northern Colorado in 1999:

The ghost in Langeworthy. Like, this guy—he was a set designer and he had a heart attack on stage in Langeworthy . . . and he died. And, uh, then like, that show, they dedicated one night to him—of the show—and his wife came, and she came up and she said a few words and she sat down, in the middle of the show the . . . the . . . the fire curtain came down, and it like almost hit somebody and then it happened the next spring again when his wife came—on the night that his wife came, the fire curtain came down. And almost hit someone.

The collector of this story, showing admirable attention to nuances of performance, indicates a short pause with a double dash (—) and a longer pause with an ellipsis (. . .); he makes no changes in word order or content. This is a very fine text for the purpose of presenting authentic folklore, but if it were included in a book for a mass audience, an editor would probably make changes for the sake of readability.

When people collect texts online using Instant Messenger, the results look different from the narrative texts usually published in legend collections. Here is an excerpt from a story collected by Binghamton University student Justin Phillips (matrix72) from a female student at the same university (butterflygirl947) in the spring of 2003:

butterflygirl947 (12:55:13 AM): yeah I have heard some
butterflygirl947 (12:55:16 AM): about a girls' campus

butterflygirl947 (12:55:19 AM): something about a girls' dorm being burnt down a long time ago

butterflygirl947 (12:56:25 AM): when they used lamps for light

butterflygirl947 (12:56:32 AM): and she was making chocolate with a burner thing

butterflygirl947 (12:56:44 AM): or something

matrix72 (12:56:48 AM): cool

This is an intriguing text, rich in descriptive detail. Looking at the Instant Messenger times, we can see exactly when each line was written. But how important is it to measure narration in seconds? When the speakers' screen names and times are included on each line, the text becomes difficult to follow.

A clearer mode of presentation leaves out the screen names and times and puts the collector's comments in parentheses, as follows:

> yeah I have heard some about a girls' campus
> something about a girls' dorm being burnt down a long time ago
> when they used lamps for light
> and she was making chocolate with a burner thing
> oil lamp
> or something
> (cool)
> and it burnt down and she was killed
> and now she haunts the girls' dorms
> and she appears in the girls' rooms and bathrooms
> and sometimes people hear screaming
> (what school is this?)
> and also there is this door that looks like it has a face in the woodwork
> (that's creepy)
> and it keeps coming back

Once this story frees itself from its surrounding identifiers, its poetic structure emerges. Short, rhythmic lines tell the story in a clear, straightforward way. Six lines in a row begin with the word "and," which provides a smooth flow. The final line, "and it keeps coming back," marks the end of this story and the beginning of other possible legends.

The identity of the story's main character—the ghost of a student who died while making chocolate—is not clearly identified. The narrator remembers key sounds and sights—"screams" and "a face in the woodwork"—but not the name of the school. However, anyone adept at Internet usage can identify this ghost without too much trouble. A visit to the University of Montevallo's ghost story Web site ("The University of Montevallo") reveals that this is the ghost of Condie Cunningham, a student who died while making fudge at the University of Montevallo in Montevallo, Alabama, in 1908. For many years, students have marveled at the outline of Condie's face on the door of her room in Main Hall, and pictures of her door on the Internet have made the ghost nationally famous.

In preparing legend texts for this volume, I have avoided making any changes except for a few necessary corrections of spelling and punctuation. Because the narrators told their stories in a lively way, their texts are highly readable. Except when collectors and narrators have specifically asked to be identified or fully released their stories to an archive, I have changed their names, and I have changed the screen names in texts obtained through Instant Messenger. Above all, I have tried to be true to these legends' form and content. Legends represent real life, with entertaining, surprising, supernatural, and horrifying twists; it is only fair to present texts as truthfully as one possibly can.

WORKS CITED

Addy, George M. *The Enlightenment in the University of Salamanca.* Durham: Duke University Press, 1966.

"Alfred Twu's Cultural Tour of Berkeley." 23 Mar. 2005 <http://www.ocf.berkeley.edu/~atwu/firstcultural/berkeleyguide.html>.

Ashliman, D. L., ed. and trans. "Faust Legends." 1999–2001 <http://www.pitt.edu/~dash/faust.html>.

———. *Folk and Fairy Tales: A Handbook.* Westport: Greenwood, 2004.

"Baker Library Bell Tower" <http://www.dartmouth.edu/~libcirc/bells.shtml>.

Baughman, Ernest. *A Type and Motif-Index of the Folktales of England and North America.* The Hague: Mouton, 1966.

Bennett, Gillian. "Legend: Performance and Truth." *Monsters with Iron Teeth: Perspectives on Contemporary Legend III.* Ed. Gillian Bennett, Paul Smith, and J. D. A. Widdowson. Sheffield: Sheffield Academic Press, 1988. 13–36.

Boyer, Ernest. *College: The University Experience in America.* New York: Harper and Row, 1987.

Brackett, Frank P. *Granite and Sagebrush: Reminiscences of the First Fifty Years of Pomona College.* Los Angeles: Ward Ritchie Press, 1944.

Bronner, Simon. *Piled Higher and Deeper.* Little Rock: August House, 1995.

Clay, Grady. *Close-Up: How to Read the American City.* New York: Praeger, 1973.

Dégh, Linda. *Legend and Belief.* Bloomington: Indiana University Press, 2001.

Dorson, Richard M. *American Folklore and the Historian.* Chicago: University of Chicago Press, 1971.

Ellis, Bill. *Aliens, Ghosts, and Cults: Legends We Live.* Jackson: University Press of Mississippi, 2003.

Eschholz, Paul A., and Alfred F. Rosa. "Student Slang for College Courses." *American Speech* 45 (1970): 85–90.

Felton, D. *Haunted Greece and Rome.* Austin: University of Texas Press, 1999.

Ferruolo, Stephen C. *The Origins of the University: The Schools of Paris and Their Critics, 1100–1215.* Stanford: Stanford University Press, 1985.

Gilbert, Helen. "The Crack in the Abbey Floor: A Laboratory Analysis of a Legend." *Indiana Folklore* 8.1–2 (1975): 61–78.

Gribble, Francis. *The Romance of the Oxford Colleges.* London: Miles Boon, 1910.

Horn, Miriam. *Rebels in White Gloves: Coming of Age with Hillary's Class—Wellesley '69.* New York: Times Books, 1999.

Loader, Brian R. "College Horror Tales." Folklore Archives, Western Kentucky University, 1972:62.

Lüthi, Max. "Aspects of the Marchen and the Legend." *Folklore Genres.* Ed. Dan Ben-Amos. Austin: University of Texas Press, 1976. 17–34.

Maclean, John. *History of the College of New Jersey.* Philadelphia: Lippincott, 1877.

Masterson, Justin. "'At Least That's How I Heard It': Rhetorical Devices as Clues to a Narrative Agenda in Conversational Legend Performance." *Midwestern Folklore* 28.2 (Fall 2002): 28–41.

Morison, Samuel Eliot. *The Founding of Harvard College.* Cambridge: Harvard University Press, 1935.

Musick, Ruth Ann. *The Telltale Lilac Bush, and Other West Virginia Ghost Tales.* Lexington: University Press of Kentucky, 1965.

Randall, Laura. "Things You Do Only in College." *New York Times Education Life* 1 Aug. 2004. 23–24.

Ryden, Kent C. *Mapping the Invisible Landscape: Folklore, Writing and the Sense of Place.* Iowa City: University of Iowa Press, 1993.

Shoback, Doug. "Oh the Stories They Tell: Legends about the University of Northern Colorado as Told by Students." Unpublished student paper, Spring, 1999.

Stein, Wayne J., and Maenette K. AhNee-Benham, eds. *Renaissance of American Indian Higher Education: Capturing the Dream.* Mahwah: Lawrence Erlbaum Associates, 2002.

Twain, Mark. *How to Tell a Story and Other Essays.* Hartford: American Publishing Company, 1900.

"The University of Montevallo." 18 Mar. 2005 <http://www.cob.montevallo.edu/StuddardAL/um.htm>.

Yates, Geoff. *Cambridge College Ghosts.* Cambridge: Seven Hills Book Distributor, 1994.

Two
Definitions and Classifications

FOLKLORE

Folklore is both process and product: communication of stories, proverbs, jokes, customs, beliefs, and other traditional material from one person to another and from one generation to the next. Since 1846, when William J. Thoms first used the word "folklore" in England, scholars have debated its meaning. The *Standard Dictionary of Folklore, Mythology, and Legend* lists 21 definitions of folklore, and others have developed since the dictionary's publication in 1949. Dan Ben-Amos defines folklore as "artistic communication in small groups" (13); Henry Glassie says that folklore is "human creativity in its own context" (9). In contrast to elite or academic learning, which uses fixed texts, folklore is highly variable; no one tells a story exactly the same as someone else does. Through storytelling, music making, weaving, house building, and other artistic processes, people share their traditions with each other. Before mass communications became such an integral part of our everyday lives, folklorists often said that folklore was transmitted face-to-face, in a primary and personal way. Now, however, folklorists recognize that television, radio, film, and electronic communication function as vital means of folklore transmission. As Barre Toelken explains in *The Dynamics of Folklore*, "All folklore participates in a distinctive, dynamic process" (10). Constantly growing and changing, folklore helps people articulate their values, needs, and concerns.

FOLK

All of us belong to the folk: the human community that shares various forms of traditional learning. According to Alan Dundes, author of *The Study of Folklore*, "The term 'folk' can refer to *any group of people whatsoever* who share at least one common factor" (2). The italics in this statement emphasize how important it is to go beyond earlier definitions, which identified the folk as rural, geographically isolated people with limited education. We can chart our participation in folk culture by examining our membership in folk groups. Occupation, avocation, age, ethnicity, religion, and place of residence are some of the variables that bring people together.

LEGEND

As Gillian Bennett says, the legend is an "elusive butterfly" that resists definition ("Legend" 34). Since the legend adapts swiftly to changing times, it is difficult to define this genre in clear-cut terms. Nonetheless, folklorists have done their best to clarify the legend's form and function.

Legend classification began with the Grimm brothers, whose research in the early nineteenth century ignited the enthusiasm of others. Their *German Legends* (first published in 1816; see Ward, *The German Legends of the Brothers Grimm* 1987) examines historical, supernatural, and etiological legends. In *Legend and Belief*, Linda Dégh makes the point that these three categories are not mutually exclusive; for example, a supernatural legend can take place in historical time and explain the origin of a related phenomenon (51).

Although some legends have a stronger connection to history than others, all of them suggest the possibility of truth. Because it is often difficult to tell whether a legend is true, this genre makes people worry and wonder. Is a maniac with a hook on one arm really murdering college students? Can witches cause a student to hang himself in a graveyard on Halloween? Can a ghost make its presence felt by bringing up words on a computer screen? We know that terrible tragedies happen; murderers and suicides often appear in the news. Ghostly phenomena do not usually make news headlines, but many people take them seriously. Polarities of safety and danger, ease and unease, make the legend highly applicable to what matters most in our own lives.

Legend tellers frequently attribute their stories to friends of friends (FOAFs). In college, where students develop complex friendship networks, FOAFs often make credible sources. Even when students question the validity of a particular legend, they may wonder if something like it actually happened to an acquaintance of people they know.

If someone tells a legend in the first person ("This happened to me . . ."), the term "memorate" fits the text. Carl Wilhelm von Sydow, who introduced this term, made a distinction between the memorate and the fabulate, a clearly fictional story (65–80). While some folklorists call memorates personal experience stories, most legend specialists view memorates as part of the legend genre.

Legends that have traveled to different parts of the world can be called migratory legends. Typically, these legends have broad appeal, with themes of universal interest such as death, disaster, and sudden wealth. One of the best-known migratory legends is "The Vanishing Hitchhiker," whose progress around the world has been traced by a number of scholars (Beardsley and Hankey, "A History"; Goss, *The Evidence for Phantom Hitch-hikers*). "The Vanishing Hitchhiker" has traveled to many college campuses, as have "The Hook," "The Roommate's Death," and "The Suicide Rule."

In contrast to migratory legends, local legends tend to stay in one place. There is, however, some blurring of legend categories since local legends tend to be influenced by well-known stories. In turn, stories known locally can make their mark on more broadly circulating narratives.

One good example of a local legend is the story of Isabella at Northwestern State University in Natchitoches, Louisiana. Students at Northwestern say that Isabella, who lived before the Civil War, loved a young man who was killed in a duel. She became a nun and lived in a convent located where a campus building stands now. Miserable and antisocial, Isabella came out only at night. Late one night, after a terrible storm, she stabbed herself through the heart, leaving a bloody handprint on the wall. Students living on campus during the mid-1980s have written about hearing Isabella play music and losing track of objects that she moved or took.

The term "urban legend" became popular when Jan H. Brunvand published his first collection of legends for a general readership, *The Vanishing Hitchhiker* (1981). This collection and others by Brunvand, including *The Choking Doberman* (1984), *The Mexican Pet* (1986), *Curses! Broiled Again!* (1989), and *The Baby Train* (1993), include numerous campus legends.

Another term, "contemporary legend," has found favor with legend specialists. This term avoids reference to urban areas since legends can appear in a variety of contexts; it also accentuates the importance of tracking legends as they emerge. The International Society for Contemporary Legend Research, founded in the early 1980s, publishes a journal, *Contemporary Legend*, and a newsletter, *FOAFtale News*.

FOLKTALE

In contrast to the legend, which focuses on our own world, the folktale takes its listeners to a faraway realm where events happened "once upon a time." Stith Thompson, author of *The Folktale*, explains that people have often used the term "folktale" in reference to "the whole range of traditional oral narrative" (21). However, folklorists generally view folktales as narratives with the kinds of characters and plot sequences chronicled in the Aarne-Thompson (A-T) index, *The Types of the Folktale*. Some folktales are simple, others complex.

One of the most popular forms of the folktale is the *Märchen*, or magic tale. No matter how much the *Märchen* hero suffers, magical aid ensures a happy ending. Max Lüthi explains how the *Märchen* differs from the legend:

The Märchen outlines the narrow road of the hero walking through the world and does not dwell on the figures meeting him. But the legend looks fixedly at the inexplicable which confronts man. And because it is monstrous—war, pestilence, or landslide, and especially often a numinous power, be it nature, demons, or spirits of the dead—man becomes small and unsure before it (24).

In other words, the folktale hero moves toward the fulfillment of a glorious destiny, while the legend hero suffers unexpected, sometimes devastating perils. While the folktale satisfies our need for wish fulfillment through the hero's achievements, the legend reveals strange and difficult dimensions of our own daily lives.

INDEXES

Type Index

The Types of the Folktale, by Antti Aarne and Stith Thompson (1928/1961), has three sections: Animal Tales (types 1–299), Ordinary Folktales (types 300–1199), and Jokes and Anecdotes (types 1200–2499). Within the second section, Tales of Magic (types 300–749) form a major category. The tale type for "Cinderella" is A-T 510A; "Sleeping Beauty" follows A-T 410, and "Jack and the Beanstalk" follows A-T 328.

For the study of campus legends, two important tale types are A-T 326, *The Youth Who Wanted to Learn What Fear Is*, and A-T 366, *The Man from the Gallows*. The first, based on tale number 4 in the Grimm brothers' *Kinder- und Hausmärchen,* tells what happens when a young man spends a night in a haunted house. This framework fits some legends about fraternity initiations and experiences in haunted places. The main thrust of the second tale type, *The Man from the Gallows*, is ghostly retribution for theft of human body parts. Campus legends about pranks involving severed limbs and searches for lost body parts follow A-T 366 in intriguing ways.

Motif Index

This six-volume index, compiled by Stith Thompson between 1932 and 1936, presents a broad range of motifs: small units of folklore that can be traced cross-culturally. Organized alphabetically, Thompson's motif categories are the following:

- A. Mythological Motifs
- B. Animals
- C. Tabu
- D. Magic
- E. The Dead
- F. Marvels
- G. Ogres
- H. Tests
- J. The Wise and the Foolish
- K. Deceptions
- L. Reversal of Fortune
- M. Ordaining the Future
- N. Chance and Fate
- P. Society
- Q. Rewards and Punishments
- R. Captives and Fugitives
- S. Unnatural Cruelty
- T. Sex
- U. The Nature of Life
- V. Religion
- W. Traits of Character
- X. Humor
- Z. Miscellaneous Groups of Motifs

All these motif categories are relevant to campus legends, although some apply more specifically than others. For example, some motifs found in campus ghost stories are E402, "Mysterious ghostlike noises heard"; E422.4.3, "Ghost in white"; and E599.6, "Ghost moves furniture."

According to Thompson, the main function of a motif index is "to display identity or similarity in the tale elements in all parts of the world so that they can be conveniently studied" (*The Folktale* 416). While not all folklorists believe in the importance of motif classification, many of them carefully document traditional motifs. For example, in *Shadows and Cypress* (2000), which includes some very interesting legends told by college students, Alan Brown lists the motifs occurring in each story at the end of the volume.

The Migratory Legends

In 1958 Norwegian scholar Reidar Thoralf Christiansen introduced a new index: *The Migratory Legends: A Proposed List of Types with a Systematic Catalogue of the Norwegian Variants.* Beginning with type number 3000, Christiansen outlined eight major categories of migratory legends: The Black Book of Magic (3000–3025); Witches and Witchcraft (3030–3080); Legends of the Human Soul, of Ghosts and Revenants (4000–4050); Spirits of Rivers, Lakes and the Sea (4050–4090); Trolls and Giants (5000–5050); The Fairies (5050–6070); Domestic Spirits (7000–7020); and Local Legends of Places, Events and Persons (7050–8025).

Christiansen's types, based on Norwegian legends, have not been widely used by folklorists; however, *The Migratory Legends* is an important demonstration of how legends travel. While the terms "urban legend" and "contemporary legend" commonly designate legends in circulation now, "migratory legend" still comes up sometimes in scholarly discourse.

For campus legends, the first three parts of Christiansen's type index have the greatest relevance. Type 3000, Escape from the Black School at Wittenberg, applies to stories of black magic, as does Type 3030, Inexperienced Use of the Black Book. In the 1960s and 1970s, when American students were responding to cultural change, legends about dangerous campus witches were very common. Some of the most popular college legends describe ghosts, sometimes called revenants (spirits that come back from the realm of the dead). Christiansen's types 4000, The Human Soul Free from the Body, and 4030, Dead Mother Revisits Her Children, apply to college legends.

Baughman's Type and Motif Index

In 1966, Ernest W. Baughman published his *Type and Motif-Index of the Folktales of England and North America.* Under the new motif Z500, "Horror stories," Baughman included several that come from college lore: Z510, "The fatal fraternity initiation"; Z511, "Fraternity initiate, tied to a chair and abandoned, tries to crash through window, beheads himself," and Z512, "The initiate dies mysteriously while tied to tombstone in graveyard. He is found with bonds loosed but he has long scratches on his face, and he is dead." A legend based on motif Z510 is included in chapter 3.

CAMPUS LEGEND CATEGORIES

Origins

Many colleges and universities cherish legends that explain their origins. Sometimes these stories describe moments of discovery that led to the college's construction. For example, an Oberlin University legend says that the campus was built in 1833 on a spot "where two small bear cubs scampered down a large tree at one corner of what is today the campus" (Sherman 58). Like the legend of Romulus and Remus that describes the founding of Rome, this story gives the campus a sense of historical depth and a connection to nature.

One pattern in origin legends is the death of a child: a poignant loss that makes the new institution's beginning all the more meaningful. The best-known story of this kind is "The Rejection That Led to the Founding of Stanford University," identified on http://www.truthorfiction.com as fiction. According to this Web site's summary, two "country hicks" tell the president of Harvard that they would like to donate a building to Harvard in memory of their son, who was a Harvard student before his accidental death. When the president discourages them, mentioning how much buildings cost, Mr. and Mrs. Leland Stanford decide to build a school of their own in their son's honor since Harvard does not seem to care about him. The truth, also given on this Web site, is that Mr. and Mrs. Stanford's son died at the age of 15 from typhoid fever during a family trip to Italy. After their son's death, Leland Stanford said to his wife, "The children of California shall be our children."

When freshmen come to college, they hear legends about the origin of college buildings, statues, and other landmarks. These legends accentuate the strangeness of the students' new environment while providing an entertaining form of mock history. For example, students entering the University of Pennsylvania learn that the designer of Irvine Hall was a student who flunked

Sather Tower, University of California at Berkeley.
Photograph by Geoffrey Gould.

out of the university's school of architecture; his wealthy father commissioned the building to give his son another chance. Legends on a number of different campuses explain that college architects followed blueprints for prison design to make sure that student riots could be controlled. At the University of Arizona, for example, the designer of one residence hall is said to have been the architect of the state prison. Plans for mental hospitals also overlap with college design, according to campus legends. When Mountainview residential community opened at Binghamton University in Vestal, New York in the fall of 2003, students decided that its architects had followed designs for state mental hospitals. Such legends remind students that institutions of higher learning are, like prisons and hospitals, institutions.

Sometimes origin legends encapsulate national history. At the University of Arkansas in Fayetteville, for example, freshmen learn that Old Main's North Tower is taller than South Tower because the designer of both buildings supported the North during the Civil War (Parler 26). Similarly, students at Michigan State University in East Lansing explain Beaumont Tower's significance in creative ways. In 1965, Michigan State student Marlyn Lisiaus said, "There are three short points on top of Beaumont Tower; the fourth spire is larger and taller than the others. The shorter spires represent the idea that education is never complete. I have also heard that the fourth spire is larger because Beaumont Tower was built during the war, and the fourth spire is a tribute to those students who never returned from combat" (Newland 13).

Origin legends have also become part of the protest tradition on college campuses. In "On the Rhetorical Use of Legend: U.C. Berkeley Campus Lore as a Strategy for Coded Protest" (1998), Kimberly J. Lau examines stories told by tour guides to prospective students. The legend of Dwinelle Hall, a labyrinthine edifice with hidden staircases and uneven floors, explains that the architects were two brothers who insisted on building their own sides of the building in radically different ways. Dwinelle, Lau says, serves as a "metaphor for the university's administration and bureaucracy" (7). Another Berkeley legend about administrative peculiarity describes plans to build a reflecting pool under Sather Tower, known to most people on campus as the Campanile. According to this legend, a plaque with the words "*fiat lux*" in reverse was supposed to stand next to a reflecting pool, but campus benefactor Jane Sather canceled construction because she feared that male students would use the pool to look up women's skirts. A variant of this story is included in chapter 3. Lau makes a persuasive case for the subversive nature of such legends, pointing out the irony of the fact that legends told by campus tour guides "seem to have an official air about them" (17).

Ghosts

College ghost storytelling is complex and fascinating. Some of the most prominent ghosts on college campuses are suicide victims, reflecting intense academic and social pressures. On campuses with bodies of water, bridges, and towers, suicide legends grow. For example, students at Vassar College tell stories about a girl who put on her white graduation dress and jumped in the lake. She drowned and became a ghost that haunted the shoreline. Another Vassar legend describes Edna St. Vincent Millay's unsuccessful suicide leap from the top of a residence hall. At Indiana University, students tell stories about jumps from the top of 14-story Eigenmann Hall, known as "Suicide

Tower." Students at the University of California at Berkeley say administrative officials have placed a "suicide alarm" on the tenth floor of Evans Hall, from which students have leapt to their deaths. And at Mansfield University in Mansfield, Pennsylvania, students talk about Sarah, who threw herself down the stairs of North Hall after being dumped by her boyfriend.

Not all suicide legends involve water and high places. At Ball State University in Muncie, Indiana, students remember a male student who killed himself on the fourth floor of Elliott Hall. His ghost haunts the floor and provides a focal point for activities on Halloween ("Fact and Folklore" 20–21). Robie-Andrews Hall, a residence hall at the University of Southern Maine in Gorham, also has legends about a fourth-floor ghost. Some variants say that a woman killed herself early in the twentieth century; others say that she committed suicide in the 1800s. While reasons for the suicide vary, the most common explanation is that the woman's boyfriend rejected her because she was pregnant. Signs of the ghost's activity include footsteps in the attic, cold spots, and machines that turn themselves on and off.

More pleasant ghost stories tell of benevolent older women whose spirits linger. At the Dacie Moses House at Carleton College in Northfield,

Robie-Andrews Hall, University of Southern Maine. Photograph by Martha Harris.

Minnesota, for example, students say they can feel the presence of the kind woman who used to welcome students to her house for cookie baking and conversation. Dacie Moses left her house to Carleton College, along with a fund to make it possible for students to keep on baking cookies.

Among the "most haunted" buildings on college campuses, libraries rank high. Since libraries hold reams of old books, it is not surprising that they provide settings for stories of earlier eras. McKeldin Library at the University of Maryland in College Park has a reputation for being haunted, as does Louis Jefferson Long Library at Wells College in Aurora, New York. Most library ghosts materialize quietly, following rules for proper library behavior, but some are noisy and disruptive. Cazenovia College in Cazenovia, New York, has a ghost that has hurled books at students. The wild library ghost in the popular movie *Ghostbusters* (1984) showed viewers that not all library ghosts had to be quiet and well behaved.

Many campus theaters have such well-known ghosts that student actors expect to encounter them. At Montana State University in Bozeman, a blonde-haired young woman wearing clothing of the late eighteenth or early nineteenth century has appeared on stage. A drama teacher surmised that she was a 1940s actress playing a woman from an earlier time period (Munn 55–56). At Wayne State University's Jessie Bonstelle Theatre in Detroit, students say that they can hear the footsteps of the theater's founder, Jessie Bonstelle (1872–1932), and feel a comforting sense of her presence (Van Fleteren). Similarly, at Buffalo State College in Buffalo, New York, students have reported unusual sounds, sights, and feelings connected to the theater in Rockwell Hall, which was closed up for a number of years. One narrator said that the lights in Rockwell Hall once turned themselves on and off and a mysterious figure appeared in a window. When a university official checked the hall, he found a full-course meal cooking in a kitchen in the basement (Speanburgh). At the Annie Russell Theater at Rollins College in Winter Park, Florida, students say that the ghost of Annie Russell will appear between midnight and 1:00 A.M. the Wednesday before a play's opening, if the play will be a success (Norman and Scott 114–15). Because theater ghosts have power, it is not uncommon for student actors to give them gifts. The ghost of the Albert Taylor Theatre at Millikin University in Decatur, Illinois, likes to have actors leave three pieces of candy before performances. Plain M&Ms are the ghost's favorites, but peanut M&Ms are not allowed (Taylor 53–58).

Certain interior spaces seem to encourage ghostly activity. Passageways of all kinds—including elevators, hallways, and tunnels—offer good settings for ghosts that travel from the realm of the dead to the land of the living. In bathrooms, reflections in mirrors and startling sounds have resulted in

Witherill Library, Cazenovia College. Photograph by Geoffrey Gould.

ghost stories. Some residence hall basements have also developed reputations as haunted areas. Suggesting an underground realm like Hades in Greek mythology, the basements of large buildings furnish favorable environments for supernatural events.

Witches

Legends about witches on college campuses have not received as much attention from folklorists as some other kinds of campus legends have. Perhaps this is because witch legends tend to be local, not part of widespread cycles such as "The Roommate's Death" and "The Hook." Witch legends express attitudes toward social deviance and power, both in and outside of college.

What is a witch? According to Rossell Hope Robbins, author of the *Encyclopedia of Witchcraft and Demonology* (1959), witchcraft was heresy against Christian belief between 1450 and 1750. People suspected of witchcraft, most of whom were women, took the blame for a wide range of mishaps. For example, a cow's milk drying up, threatening a farm family's subsistence, could lead to an accusation of witchcraft. European "evil eye" beliefs became part of this sequence of fear and retribution. In tough times, witches served as scapegoats for community members' distress.

Medieval stereotypes of witches as workers of evil magic have had remarkable staying power. However, the witchcraft revival of the 1950s and 1960s has encouraged people to view witchcraft as a benevolent, nature-oriented religion. Gerald Gardner's *Witchcraft Today* (1954) made readers aware of the Wiccan revival in England, which occurred after laws mandating severe punishment of witches were repealed. Gardner describes Wicca as a religion whose followers worship the Mother Goddess and her consort, the Horned God. Closeness to nature and respect for others are central precepts of this religion. Margot Adler's *Drawing Down the Moon* (1979) offers an overview of some of the forms of Wicca and Paganism, including feminist groups. Sabina Magliocco's *Witching Culture: Folklore and Neo-Paganism in America* (2004) explains how anthropology and folklore contributed to the development of Wiccan and Pagan culture. Her study makes the important point that Pagans and Wiccans find meaning in sacred and mystical experiences that combine old traditions in new ways.

College students' legends describe two kinds of witches: people outside the college community and fellow college students. Legends about witches outside the campus generally describe strange, deviant women who have offended society by committing murder or other crimes. On-campus witch figures also represent social deviance. Although many college students of the twenty-first century understand Wicca, legends tend to preserve older ideas of witchcraft as malicious magic whose practitioners deserve to be kept on the margins of society.

"The Legend of Stepp Cemetery," by William M. Clements and William E. Lightfoot (1972), explores legends about a witch or female ghost wearing black clothes who sits on a stump called "The Warlock's Seat." Old, grim, and obsessed with grave decoration, she seems eager to welcome young visitors to her macabre realm. This witch plays much the same role as frightening figures in public "haunted houses" on Halloween, introducing visitors to the horrors of death. However, young people can visit a place like Stepp Cemetery at any time of year, not just in late October.

Witches of college age play a different role in campus legends. Young and full of energy, they subvert the established order by experimenting with their supernatural power. According to legends told at Ohio University, two young female witches horrified fellow students by sacrificing animals in their residence hall in the 1970s. Ever since that time, their residence hall has had a reputation for being haunted. During the late 1960s and early 1970s, American college campuses went through major changes and periods of upheaval. Feminism, the hippie movement, and the war in Vietnam brought about changes in behavior. Representing subversion and social disorder, witches symbolized changes that some people feared.

Jessie Bonstelle Theatre, Wayne State University. Photograph by Elizabeth Tucker.

Another kind of campus legend characterizes professors as witches. In the early 1970s, female students on one campus of the State University of New York told stories about a female professor with long hair who lived in an apartment with towers, gables, and several cats. Surely she must be a witch, the students said, because everyone knew that cats could carry witches' souls. Her eyes looked witchlike, too, they said. This was one of many situations where students, speculating about an interesting professor, wondered if the supernatural could have something to do with her appeal. J. K. Rowling, the best-selling author of *Harry Potter and the Sorcerer's Stone* (1998) and its sequels, has made all the professors at Hogwarts witches and wizards. This is an amusing extension of a form of storytelling that has entertained college students for many years.

Initiation

Freshman year, fraught with excitement and stress, inevitably provides an initiatory experience for entering students. Many legends describe rites of passage that make students feel like full-fledged members of their campuses. For example, students at Newing College at Binghamton University tell stories about the Lake Lieberman Monster, to which a virgin must be sacrificed each fall. These stories come to life in rituals in which female freshmen, called Vestal Virgins, get dunked in the lake while other students clap and cheer. Since Binghamton University is located in Vestal, New York, the term "Vestal Virgin" makes students smile (Tucker 39).

The most notorious, well-traveled legend about college initiation is "The Fatal Initiation," in which hazing leads to the death of at least one initiate. Since students have died during fraternity hazing on a number of college campuses, the stories have an unfortunate ring of truth. Some initiation legends do not specify the college, but others do. One legend told by a 19-year-old male freshman at Alfred University in Alfred, New York in 2003 explains why Greek life was banned on that campus. Putting this story in context, the narrator says, "Like many other fraternities at other schools there is one night where the pledges get blindfolded in a car and are dropped off in an unknown location without phones, money, credit cards or other means of help and are expected to find their way home somehow." Only 13 of the 14 pledges return. When the others go back to search for their missing companion, they find only "a red bandana from the blindfolded car ride." In some variants of this legend, the ghost of a student wearing a red blindfold wanders around the Alfred University campus, desperately hoping to find his way home.

Murder

Legends about gruesome murders epitomize college stress. Some murder legends circulate only locally; one of these, "The Murder at Franklin College," is discussed in chapter 4. Chapter 3 includes a legend about a murder in a bathroom at the University of Alaska at Fairbanks. Local murder legends typically draw students' attention for a while, then fade into obscurity.

Migratory legends last longer in the public imagination. Three very popular murder legends—"The Hook," "The Boyfriend's Death," and "The

Roommate's Death"—have traveled from campus to campus. Linda Dégh has traced "The Hook," a legend of near murder by a hook-handed maniac, back to 1955 ("Speculations about 'The Hook'"). "The Hook," "The Boyfriend's Death," and "The Roommate's Death" were extremely popular in the 1960s and 1970s and continued to circulate through the 1990s, toward the end of which the movie *Urban Legend* (1998) satirized all three. In "The Boyfriend's Death," a young woman's date is murdered when his car suddenly runs out of gas. "The Roommate's Death" describes two female students staying alone in their residence hall. One student leaves the room to check on some mysterious noises. The roommate who has stayed inside their room hears screams, then scratching on the door. In the morning, she discovers her roommate dead beside their door, an ax or knife protruding from her head.

In campus legends, the ax or hatchet is a familiar weapon. Rumors about an ax or hatchet murderer began to move from one American college campus to another in the fall of 1968. At Mount Holyoke College in South Hadley, Massachusetts, female students heard that a hatchet man was traveling across the Northeast and might stop at a women's college with the initials "M" and "H." That same fall, women at the State University of New York in New Paltz heard that a machete man was on his way to kill a group of 13 female students. Developing other local variations, this rumor spread quickly from campus to campus.

Jan H. Brunvand traces the evolution of campus rumor panics in *The Baby Train* (116–119), mentioning that the first wave of such rumors and legends began in 1968. It is noteworthy that legends of this kind began to circulate after Richard Speck's murder of eight student nurses in their Chicago dormitory on July 14, 1966. This shocking mass murder frightened college students and their families. Campus unrest in the late 1960s and early 1970s, including demonstrations against the war in Vietnam and Cambodia, increased students' awareness that the world was a violent and unpredictable place.

Since the rumor panic in 1968, rumors and legends of dormitory massacres have waxed and waned. The largest resurgence took place in 1998 after the movie *Urban Legend* was released. Rumors spread across the country that a killer dressed as Little Bo Peep or wearing a "Scream" mask would kill a certain number of female students with an ax, hatchet, or knife. Some versions warned students at Big 10 universities starting with an "M" or "W" (Minnesota, Michigan State, and Wisconsin, for example) to watch out for the killer. While the details always varied, the message stayed the same: students, especially women, should worry about their safety on college campuses, far from home.

Gate of Mount Holyoke College. Photograph by Geoffrey Gould.

Pranks

Pranks—outrageous practical jokes—frequently occur on college campuses. While folklorists would often classify pranks as customs or rituals, some pranks are so amazing and creative that they become part of campus legend telling.

For example, a legend at the University of Hawaii at Hilo describes what happened when a student visiting from the University of Hawaii at Manoa stayed in a residence hall with her friends. During the night, she heard loud scratching on the screen of the window above her head. Believing that the goddess Pele was making the noise, the student, with her eyes tightly shut, quietly left the room. Later she admitted that the scratching might have been a prank, but she continued to believe that Pele had been trying to enter her room. Of course, there was no proof one way or the other (Zahaczewsky).

College pranks follow certain patterns. Bringing farm animals into a college building ranks high, as does greasing toilet seats, rearranging furniture, and trapping students in their rooms by sticking pennies between the door and the wall. Putting objects up on high places can be great fun, especially around Halloween. Students at the University of California at Berkeley have succeeded in hoisting various objects, including a large pumpkin, to the top of their beloved Sather Tower. At Easter time, some Berkeley students once decorated the tower with an enormous Easter bunny.

Some pranks succeed beautifully, but others have damaging or even tragic consequences. Legends about pranks that go too far warn students to set limits on their frivolity. The most notorious legend of this kind is "The Cadaver Arm," in which male medical students leave a pickled arm in a female student's room. She goes insane and gnaws on the arm. In *The Baby Train*, Jan H. Brunvand notes that this legend became popular when few women attended medical school (315). Ernest Baughman's *Type and Motif-Index of the Folktales of England and North America* gives the legend its own motif number: N384.0.1.1.

Sometimes pranks become vehicles of protest. In the early 1920s, Colorado College president Clyde Augustus Duniway angered women students by forbidding them to go on dates on Sundays. He also infuriated both alumni and students by firing a popular football coach. In response, students held protest rallies, shouting "Do away with Duniway!" Large stuffed animals from the museum in Palmer Hall, including an enormous whale, appeared around the campus. One morning a live cow had to be removed from Palmer Hall. Hydrogen sulfide gas was released in Perkins Hall, disrupting morning chapel. Because of the many protests and pranks, President Duniway announced his resignation in June 1924 (Loevy 113).

Drugs

Students' legends about drugs reflect the kaleidoscopic patterns of recreational drug use on college campuses since the 1960s. When marijuana first became available to students, some saw it as an opportunity for mind expansion, while others spurned it. By the end of the 1960s, a number of students had tried marijuana, and some had experimented with "harder" drugs like LSD.

Serious injury, death, and date rape are the three main concerns expressed in students' drug legends. Jan H. Brunvand summarizes one of the most alarming legends of the 1960s: "Supposedly, a group of college students, high on acid, sat on a hillside and stared straight into the sun until they went blind" (*Baby Train* 109). Brunvand also mentions legends about PCP (Angel Dust) in which people pull out their own eyes. Citing a study of PCP stories by two physicians, Brunvand notes the mythic quality of such legends (Morgan and Kagan). Ever since people in ancient Greece told the story of Oedipus destroying his own eyes, horror legends about self-blinding have fascinated readers and listeners. There is, of course, a moral message in legends of this kind. Oedipus blinded himself after realizing that he had killed his father and married his mother. For college students experimenting with recreational drugs, the offense seems less serious, but the story shows that reckless self-indulgence may lead to disaster. Other legends in which drug use results in death make this point even more firmly.

Students' fears of drugs leading to date rape emerge in Andrea Greenberg's article "Drugged and Seduced: A Contemporary Legend" (1973). Greenberg's transcripts of interviews with Indiana University students include legends about Spanish fly and LSD, some of which emphasize the shame of withdrawal from school. Students' explanations of how they learned the stories clarify chains of transmission from mother to daughter and from older sister to younger sister as well as from friend to friend.

Later legends from the 1990s and the early twenty-first century focus on "roofies," date-rape drugs that make young women lose consciousness and control. The settings of many such legends are clubs, favorite gathering places for college students. While these stories emphasize sexual predation, they also highlight the importance of women staying alert and in control at all times.

Although most drug legends carry serious messages, some celebrate the excitement of experimentation. Stories about students on LSD joyfully

Palmer Hall, Colorado College. Photograph by Elizabeth Tucker.

jumping off rooftops into snowdrifts suggest that sometimes it is all right to take a chance. A legend about a Berkeley student taking drugs and jumping out of a residence hall window without sustaining any injuries is included in chapter 3.

AIDS

Legends about AIDS began to circulate in the mid-1980s, when concern about the HIV virus took narrative form. According to Jan H. Brunvand, "AIDS Mary" was the first legend that spread internationally. In this story, a man meets a beautiful, seductive woman in a bar and stays overnight with her. When he wakes up the next day, he finds a message in lipstick on the bathroom wall or on the mirror: "Welcome to the world of AIDS" (or "Welcome to the wonderful world of AIDS"). Police confirm that the beautiful woman is an AIDS patient who wants to seduce as many men as possible (*Encyclopedia of Urban Legends* 6–7).

Around 1990, Brunvand explains, "AIDS Mary" became "AIDS Harry" (*Encyclopedia of Urban Legends* 5–6). This legend describes a young, innocent woman who falls in love with a handsome young man while on vacation at a resort in the tropics. After a whirlwind romance, the man drives the woman to the airport, presenting her with a beautifully wrapped package and telling her not to open it until the plane takes off. Inside the box is another box or coffin containing the message "Welcome to the world of AIDS."

This second legend spread rapidly among college students. With its focus on a tropical resort, "AIDS Harry" described a situation that could possibly become a student's worst nightmare during spring break. For many years, college students have spent spring break in Florida, Mexico, and other tropical locales, meeting new friends and enjoying a more relaxed lifestyle than they have on their home campuses. The story of a dangerous, seductive stranger giving female college students AIDS fits the horror legend pattern of victimization of women. It also conveys the message that women who become involved with men they don't know will always regret their lack of caution.

Diane E. Goldstein's *Once upon a Virus: AIDS Legends and Vernacular Risk Perception* (2004) examines various forms of the AIDS horror legend, including stories about pinpricks in condoms, infected needles, and contaminated food. Goldstein explains that while some legends focus on "the contamination of food, objects, or spaces," others involve "a more amorphous general kind of contamination achieved through close contact or through a kind of 'contagious magic'" (39).

One legend about food contaminated with the HIV virus is analyzed by Janet L. Langlois in her article "Hold the Mayo: Purity and Danger in an AIDS Legend" (1991). In this story, a male employee of Burger King or another fast-food franchise tests positive for the HIV virus. Not wanting to be the only person in his community who suffers this terrible fate, he puts his semen into the mayonnaise. Usually a customer who has eaten the mayonnaise gets sick, showing that the vengeful employee has gotten the result he wanted. Langlois notes that semen misplaced in mayonnaise becomes "a particularly potent symbol configuring the gendered body, the body politic and social crisis" (160).

Other legends have emphasized college students' vulnerability to HIV. Mariamne H. Whatley and Elissa R. Henken describe a legend circulating in Athens, Georgia, in 1996 in which 35 percent of the donors at a student blood drive test positive for HIV. Whatley and Henken point out the positive impact of understanding that members of one's own group can get the virus while noting that such legends have negatively influenced blood donations (76).

Food

Campus food legends fall into two subcategories: migratory legends about "fast food" from national or regional franchise restaurants and local legends about food produced at the college itself or at non–fast-food restaurants nearby. Fast-food legends are usually more sensational, exciting, and horrifying than local narratives. However, legends about the campus's own food have an important function of their own. They draw new students together in a spirit of benign disgust, helping them find common ground while adjusting to college life.

As Simon J. Bronner explains in *Piled Higher and Deeper*, students jocularly express contempt for college food by using such terms as "mystery meat," "garbage barges," and "griddle pucks" (189). Sometimes this playful spirit leads to an all-out "food fight," where meals become missiles: the messier, the better. In *Cambridge from Within* (1913), Charles Tennyson recalls the time when two students "engaged in a gargantuan war with ham- bones, onions, legs of mutton, cauliflowers, trussed fowls, and all the other accumulated provision for a forthcoming banquet" (112–13). While food fights have not inspired migratory legends, the film *Animal House* (1978) recognizes their traditionality on college campuses.

Susan Domowitz's "Foreign Matter in Food: A Legend Type" (1979) offers 12 variants of legends collected from students at Michigan State University between 1948 and 1955. The core legend follows a certain sequence. Someone goes out to eat at a restaurant or buys food in a can or package. Soon, something "horrifying or disgusting" is found in the food. The foreign matter comes from either a human body or an animal. At the end of the legend, the teller gives evidence for or against the incident's credibility (86).

Some of the stories in Domowitz's sample focus on members of ethnic minority groups: for example, a little finger appears in a dish of chop suey in Lansing, and the body of a Mexican with his throat cut is discovered inside a vat in a pickle factory in northern Michigan. Two legends tell about the ashes of a dead relative being mistaken for flour and made into a cake. The horror of discovering that one has eaten human flesh is a major theme in legends told by both children and adults.

Fast-food legends convey complex messages about food produced in large quantities. In his article "The Kentucky Fried Rat: Legends and Modern Society" (1980), Gary Alan Fine discusses 115 versions of the popular "Kentucky Fried Rat" legend, finding that people worry about exchanging home cooking for food of uncertain origin. Rodents make especially horrifying meals. Bengt af Klintberg's *Die Ratte in der Pizza* (The Rat in the Pizza, 1990) analyzes a number of European legends about rats found in pizza and chicken; some of his texts come from college students. A wide-ranging study that helps put food legends in perspective is Eric Schlosser's *Fast Food Nation: The Dark Side of the All-American Meal* (2001). Tracing fast food to its beginnings after World War II, Schlosser links its proliferation to classism, obesity, global imperialism, and environmental devastation.

Professors

Legends about professors run the gamut from sensational stories of murders to gently humorous descriptions of eccentric behavior. Brilliant, strange, absentminded, arrogant, and capricious, professorial legend characters represent the mysteriousness of scholarly learning. The power to give good or poor grades makes these characters especially interesting to students.

Since grade giving may seem like a "life or death" situation, it is not surprising that some legends tell of professors who kill or try to kill their students and others on campus. Historical murder cases have increased the popularity of this kind of story. The most notorious academic murderer was Dr. John Webster, a professor of chemistry at Harvard, who had a visit from his friend Dr. George Parkman, a socially prominent Boston physician, on November 23, 1849. Webster owed Parkman money and did not want to pay his debt. When Dr. Parkman disappeared, police suspected that an Irish immigrant had murdered him. However, a janitor at the medical school thought Webster might be guilty. Tunneling under Webster's basement laboratory, the janitor found hidden body parts. Arrest followed, and a jury convicted Webster of murder. His public hanging took place in August 1850. Simon Schama's *Dead Certainties: Unwarranted Speculations* (1992) dramatizes this murder case, combining historical fact with legendlike fiction. The documentary film *Murder at Harvard,* based on Schama's study, was broadcast on television in 2003.

While murders create high drama, academic grading procedures generate their own kind of tension. Richard M. Dorson describes professors' strange grading practices in "The Folklore of Colleges" (1949). The professor who throws a pile of bluebooks downstairs, giving As to those that land at the bottom and Fs to those that stay at the top, is well known on college campuses, as is the professor who lets his children grade papers. Dorson identifies the lazy professor who lets his children assign grades as a chemistry professor at Harvard. He also describes a professor who disregards errors by good students, saying, "He knows better than that," and refuses to accept correct answers from poor students, saying, "He couldn't have meant that" (673).

James T. Bratcher analyzes another amusing story about a drunken, embittered professor who can't get his grades in on time. Following the professor to a bar, his dean reads the names of his students aloud, hoping to get a list of grades. Instead, the drunken professor makes comments like "Hell, flunk ol' Gibson, the bastard!" (121). Noting that professors who pay no attention to practical matters can be traced back to Socrates, Bratcher explains that humorous situations of this kind have a broad appeal on college campuses.

Some legends give professors credit for both physical agility and mental cleverness. In "Folklore in Academe: The Anecdote of the Professor and the Transom" (1979), Oliver Finley Graves presents three variants of the legend about a professor who reassures his students that he will only give pop quizzes on days when he enters the classroom through the transom. Believing that their professor will never crawl through a small opening at the top of a classroom door, the students are horrified to see him do just that, clutching a quiz in one hand. This legend warns students to expect the unexpected, especially where professors are concerned.

Legends about absentminded professors have circulated so widely that they require little explanation. Suffice to say that the classic absentminded professor concentrates intensely on subject matter in his own field, disregarding food, clothing, transportation, and all other practical matters. Even his wife and children get little attention. Although some actual absentminded professors are women, the central characters of these legends are almost always male.

Albert Einstein was known for his absentmindedness while teaching at the Institute for Advanced Studies in Princeton, New Jersey. One of the most popular legends about Einstein explains that he would often go downtown with a red string around one finger. The red string came from his wife, who wanted to make sure her husband remembered to buy groceries on the way home. While this kind of story is usually told as true, it is generally apocryphal. Professors and students all over the United States have described certain professors wearing strings on their fingers and signs on their backs saying, "I have my car! Don't give me a ride home today." Such legends characterize absentminded professors as childlike individuals who cannot handle everyday life, although they excel in their own fields.

One of the most thorough studies of absentminded professor legends is Bruce Jackson's "'The Greatest Mathematician in the World': Norbert Wiener Stories" (1972). Norbert Wiener, who taught at Massachusetts Institute of Technology (MIT) for 40 years, became famous for his research in cybernetics. Jackson explains that because Wiener was interested in "the relationship between his science and the human condition," students and faculty members found him more interesting than the "run-of-the-mill genius" (1). The many stories about his years at MIT characterize him as brilliant, self-centered, uncertain, and unable to find his way around town. One of the most entertaining stories describes what happens when his family moves to a new house. Even though his wife puts their new address on a note in his coat pocket, he forgets his coat and takes the train back to his old house. Seeing a little girl go by on a bicycle, Wiener stops her, saying, "Little girl, little girl: I'm Professor Wiener. I used to live here. But we moved today and I don't know where the new house is. Do you know where my family moved?" The little girl answers, "Mommy thought you'd forget, Daddy" (4).

Exams

Since the early days of higher education, students have told stories about strange and difficult examinations. Many exam stories focus on one perplexing question. For example, in a legend collected at the University of California at Berkeley in 1988, the exam question is, "If you could be any kind of chair, what kind would you be?" The student who answers "I would be a La-Z-Boy" gets the highest grade. Often the student who gives the boldest, most assertive answer is the only one who gets a high grade.

In a similar vein, stories about students who challenge their professors usually conclude with the student escaping censure. The classic story "Do You Know Who I Am?" features an arrogant, demanding student who gets away with an outrageous trick (see chapter 3). While students are the most frequent pranksters, professors sometimes prove their cleverness while giving an exam. In the legend "Which Tire?," which circulated actively in the 1990s, two students ask for a make-up exam, explaining that their car had a flat tire on the way to campus. Putting the students in separate rooms, the professor gives each of them an exam with only one question: "Which tire?"

Legends about students cheating on their exams often sound so extreme that the reader or listener doubts the stories can be true. For example, a male student attending a university in upstate New York in 1995 described using a black marble desk to leave encoded answers to the questions on a physics test. One fingerprint meant A, two fingerprints B, three fingerprints C, and four fingerprints D. While this is an ingenious method for cheating on a test, it sounds unreliable. What would happen if the fingerprints faded? As in many other legends, there is no way to know where the truth lies. More important than ultimate truth or falsehood is the fact that it would be possible to believe, if the listener was ready to do so.

RELATED GENRES

Rumor

Closely related to the legend genre is rumor, defined by Ralph I. Rosnow and Gary Alan Fine as "information, neither substantiated nor refuted" (4). According to Tamotsu Shibutani, circulation of rumors helps groups solve problems (227). While the legend tells a story, rumor indicates the possibility of a story worth telling.

College campuses are ideal locations for spreading rumors. In a limited space, with common interests and aspirations, students feel eager to share the latest news. An approaching blizzard gives rise to rumors: a foot of snow! Cancellation of all classes and exams! Such rumors, spread with hope and spirit, may seem more powerfully persuasive than official sources of campus news.

One case in point is the circulation of a rumor about ghostly gunshots at Syracuse University between 1967 and 1971. As an undergraduate student, Robert A. Emery learned that students heard gunshots in Slocum Hall around midnight every year on April 1. Tracing this rumor with the help of campus history books, Emery discovered that Professor Holmes Beckwith had murdered Dean J. Herman Wharton at 9 A.M. on April 2, 1921, because of the dean's failure to renew his teaching contract. Wondering why this event held students' interest for so long, Emery suggests, "Perhaps loud noises last the longest in student folk memory" (114).

Sometimes rumors about college campuses originate outside their own environs. In May 2004, as cicadas were returning to the American South for the first time in 17 years, people spread the rumor that Johns Hopkins

University would pay a hundred—possibly even a thousand—dollars for rare blue-eyed cicadas. When dozens of callers got in touch with the university's biology department, the rumor was proven false. As with most other rumors, no one could prove how this one started.

Belief

In *Legend and Belief*, Linda Dégh suggests that belief is "the given, underlying ideological foundation of legends." She identifies "believers, half-believers, hesitants, doubters, skeptics, and nonbelievers" as participants in the process of legend narration (311). Gillian Bennett offers somewhat similar categories of belief: convinced belief, some belief, don't know, some disbelief, and convinced disbelief (*Alas, Poor Ghost!* 17–25).

Dégh and her husband/coauthor, Andrew Vázsonyi, have made it clear that the quality of legend narration does not depend on the narrator's level of belief. Their articles "Legend and Belief" (1971) and "The Dialectics of the Legend" (1973) have helped folklorists understand the complex dynamics of the legend, which make good storytelling possible whether the narrator is a believer, a nonbeliever, or somewhere in between.

Custom

Folklorists have often used a pair of terms, "custom" and "belief," to describe traditional practices and the beliefs that accompany them. The word "custom" is virtually synonymous with "ritual." Calendar customs take place at a certain time of year, while life cycle customs happen at key points of a person's lifetime. On college campuses, calendar customs are associated with Halloween and the coming of springtime. Life cycle customs, within the four-year "lifetime" of a college student, include freshman initiation and seniors' celebrations before graduation.

Ritual

Repeated patterns of behavior are called rituals. These patterns may be very simple: for example, wearing a favorite shirt to a rugby game and then, if the game goes well, refusing to wash the shirt to keep its good luck from being washed away. As might be expected, there is a close connection between ritual and legend.

College life encourages ritual. Many institutions of higher learning begin their academic year with a convocation for new students and end it with a commencement ceremony that expresses the academic community's hopes for the future. Honor societies have their own rituals, as do fraternities, sororities, theater troupes, and many other campus organizations.

Sometimes local legends generate rituals for groups of students or for students, faculty, and staff members. On October 31, 2001, officials at Northwestern State University planned a "Welcoming Ceremony" for the campus ghost Isabella, who had already moved three times: in 1926, 1948, and 1982. Because of two fires and renovation in Nelson Hall, the university's administration wanted to make sure that Isabella would still feel welcome on campus. Going from one campus building to another, the ceremony concluded with a production of *The Tragedy of Frankenstein.*

In contrast to such public rituals as the welcoming of Isabella, fraternity initiations tend to be kept secret. Alan Dundes analyzes fraternity initiations in the chapter "The Elephant Walk and Other Amazing Hazing: Male Fraternity Initiation through Infantilization and Feminization" in his book *Bloody Mary in the Mirror* (2002). Taking a psychoanalytic approach, Dundes shows that removing pledges' clothes, force-feeding them, and insisting that they drink alcohol make them regress into a childlike state. Other kinds of coercion involve making the pledges dress in feminine clothes and act like women. In one hazing ritual, the pledges wear diapers, makeup, and perfume. With tongue in cheek, Dundes notes that "this is how hazing is supposed to transform uninitiated boys into mature young men" (120).

Festival

A festival is a complex ritual or set of rituals. Special foods, clothing, and decorations mark the festival as an event outside everyday time and space. On college campuses, some festivals take place at specific times of year. The festival most closely connected to campus legends is certainly Halloween, which owes its origin to All Souls' Day in Great Britain. Early legends say that on the night of All Souls' Day, the veil between the living and the dead becomes very thin. Ghosts walk, and strange, perplexing events take place.

Some colleges and university histories describe Halloween activities. For example, at the University of Winnipeg in 1906, students started their Halloween celebration by marching to the president's house, where faculty members entertained them. Then they marched back to campus for a masquerade ball, which had barely ended when medical students suddenly invaded the back stairs, throwing apples. After chasing the "Meds" away, the students enjoyed refreshments at tables decorated with red and blue ribbons, with a "pumpkin man" in the center of the room. This Halloween celebration seemed quiet compared to the 1890s, when typical pranks included putting one neighbor's buggy on top of a barn and stealing another's front steps (Bedford 67–68).

At Chowan College in Murfreesboro, North Carolina, students held a Brown Lady Festival for new students in the 1940s and 1950s. One student dressed up as the Brown Lady, who died of grief or fever after her young lover left to fight in the Civil War. Participants in the festival made their way to a local cemetery, where they celebrated Halloween together (Brown, *Stories from the Haunted South* 201–6).

More recent Halloween festivities on American college campuses have included parties, dances, and other programs organized by resident assistants. "Haunted houses" in residential areas, either for students or for visiting children, have been popular events. Corridor-decorating contests and pumpkin-carving competitions have helped students get in the mood for spooky activities. Legend telling has often provided the basis for Halloween events. For example, students at Huntingdon College in Montgomery, Alabama, have put a red light bulb in the room once inhabited by the spectral "Red Lady." Students at Montevallo University in Montevallo, Alabama, have visited the room of Condie Cunningham, who became a campus ghost in 1908 after starting a fire while making fudge.

"Ghost walks" have become popular celebrations of campus legends. On Halloween of 2002, professors from the Folklore Department at Indiana University in Bloomington led a group of more than 100 people past haunted sites while telling stories. Wearing cloaks and carrying lanterns, the professors told their group members about the "McNutt Hatchet Man," the ghost of a woman at La Casa, and other frightening figures. The walk ended at the Indiana Memorial Union, where the professors told the legend of a woman who had died in a fire in the Union's Federal Room. According to this legend, the spectral scent of the woman's perfume still lingers in the room.

WORKS CITED

Aarne, Antti, and Stith Thompson. *The Types of the Folktale: A Classification and Bibliography.* Helsinki: Suomalainen Tiedeakatemia, 1961. First published in 1928; the original type index, Antti Aarne's *Verzeichnis der Marchentypen*, was published in 1910.

Adler, Margot. *Drawing Down the Moon.* Boston: Beacon Press, 1979.

Baughman, Ernest W. *Type and Motif-Index of the Folktales of England and North America.* The Hague: Mouton, 1966.

Beardsley, Richard K., and Rosalie Hankey. "A History of the Vanishing Hitchhiker." *California Folklore Quarterly* 2(1943): 13–25.

Bedford, A.G. *The University of Winnipeg: A History of the Founding Colleges.* Toronto: University of Toronto Press, 1976.

Ben-Amos, Dan. "Toward a Definition of Folklore in Context." *Journal of American Folklore* 84.331 (1971): 3–15.

Bennett, Gillian. *Alas, Poor Ghost! Traditions of Belief in Story and Discourse.* Logan: Utah State University Press, 1999.

———. "Legend: Performance and Truth." *Monsters with Iron Teeth: Perspectives on Contemporary Legend III.* Ed. Gillian Bennett, Paul Smith, and J. D. A. Widdowson. Sheffield: Sheffield Academic Press, 1988. 13–36.

Bratcher, James T. "The Professor Who Didn't Get His Grades In: A Traveling Anecdote." *Diamond Bessie and the Shepherds.* Ed. Wilson M. Hudson. Austin: Encino Press, 1972.

Bronner, Simon J. *Piled Higher and Deeper: The Folklore of Campus Life.* Little Rock: August House, 1995.

Brown, Alan. *Shadows and Cypress: Southern Ghost Stories.* Jackson: University Press of Mississippi, 2000.

———. *Stories from the Haunted South.* Jackson: University Press of Mississippi, 2004.

Brunvand, Jan H. *The Baby Train.* New York: Norton, 1993.

———. *The Choking Doberman.* New York: Norton, 1984.

———. *Curses! Broiled Again!* New York: Norton, 1989.

———. *Encyclopedia of Urban Legends.* Santa Barbara: ABC Clio, 2001.

———. *The Mexican Pet.* New York: Norton, 1986.

———. *The Vanishing Hitchhiker.* New York: Norton, 1981.

Christiansen, Reidar T. *The Migratory Legends.* Folklore Fellows Communications 175. Helsinki: Suomalainen Tiedekatemia, 1958.

Clements, William M., and William E. Lightfoot. "The Legend of Stepp Cemetery." *Indiana Folklore* 5.1 (1972): 92–141.

Dégh, Linda. *Legend and Belief.* Bloomington: Indiana University Press, 2001.

Dégh, Linda, and Andrew Vázsonyi. "The Dialectics of the Legend." Folklore Preprint Series 6. Bloomington: Indiana University Folklore Institute, 1973.

———. "Legend and Belief." *Genre* 4.3 (1971): 281–304.

———. "Speculations about 'The Hook.'" *Folklore Forum* 24.2 (1991): 68–76.

Domowitz, Susan. "Foreign Matter in Food: A Legend Type." *Indiana Folklore* 12.1 (1979): 86–95.

Dorson, Richard M. The Folklore of Colleges. *American Mercury* 68 (1949): 671–77.

Dundes, Alan. *Bloody Mary in the Mirror: Essays in Psychoanalytic Folkloristics.* Jackson: University Press of Mississippi, 2002.

———. *The Study of Folklore.* Englewood Cliffs: Prentice Hall, 1965.

Emery, Robert A. "An Undergraduate Ghost Rumor." *New York Folklore* 24.1–4 (1998): 113–14.

"Fact and Folklore: Capturing Campus Mystique." *Ball State Alumnus* Sep. 2003: 18–24.

Fine, Gary Alan. "The Kentucky Fried Rat: Legends and Modern Society." *Journal of Folklore Research* 17.2–3 (1980): 222–43.

Gardner, Gerald B. *Witchcraft Today.* London: Rider and Company, 1954.

Glassie, Henry. *Turkish Traditional Art Today.* Bloomington: Indiana University Press, 1993.

Goldstein, Diane. *Once upon a Virus: AIDS Legends and Vernacular Risk Perception.* Logan: Utah State University Press, 2004.

Goss, Michael. *The Evidence for Phantom Hitch-Hikers.* Wellingborough: The Aquarian Press, 1984.

Graves, Oliver Finley. "Folklore in Academe: The Anecdote of the Professor and the Transom." *Indiana Folklore* 12 (1979): 142–45.

Greenberg, Andrea. "Drugged and Seduced: A Contemporary Legend." *New York Folklore Quarterly* 29.2 (1973): 131–58.

Grimm, Jacob, and Wilhelm Grimm. *Kinder- und Hausmärchen* (Children's and Household Tales). Ed. Heinz Rölleke. 3 vols. Stuttgart: Reclam, 1980. Based on the 7th edition of 1857.

Jackson, Bruce. "'The Greatest Mathematician in the World': Norbert Wiener Stories." *Western Folklore* 31 (1972): 1–22.

Klintberg, Bengt af. *Die Ratte in der Pizza und andere moderne Sagen und Grosstadtmythen* (The Rat in the Pizza and Other Modern Legends and Big-City Myths). Kiel: Wolfgang Butt, 1990.

Langlois, Janet. "Hold the Mayo: Purity and Danger in an AIDS Legend." *Contemporary Legend* 1 (1991): 153–72.

Lau, Kimberly J. "On the Rhetorical Use of Legend: U.C. Berkeley Campus Lore as a Strategy for Coded Protest." *Contemporary Legend*, new series 1 (1998): 1–20.

Loevy, Robert D. *Colorado College: A Place of Learning, 1874–1999.* Colorado Springs: Colorado College, 1999.

Lüthi, Max. "Aspects of the Märchen and the Legend." *Folklore Genres.* Ed. Dan Ben-Amos. Austin: University of Texas Press, 1976. 17–34.

Magliocco, Sabina. *Witching Culture: Folklore and Neo-Paganism in America.* Philadelphia: University of Pennsylvania Press, 2004.

Morgan, John P., and Doreen Kagan. "The Dusting of America: The Image of Phencyclidine (PCP) in the Popular Media." *Journal of Psychedelic Drugs* 12.3–4 (1980): 195–204.

Munn, Debra D. *Big Sky Ghosts: Eerie True Tales of Montana.* Vol. 2. Boulder: Pruett Publishing Company, 1994.

Newland, Donna. "College-lore." Folklore Collection, Labor History Archive, Reuther Library, Wayne State University, 1965.

Norman, Michael, and Beth Scott. "Entr'Acte—Haunts of Ivy." *Haunted Heritage.* New York: Tor Books, 2002. 63–136.

Parler, Mary Celestia. "Folklore from the Campus." *The Charm Is Broken: Readings in Arkansas and Missouri Folklore.* Ed. W. K. McNeil. Little Rock: August House, 1984. 25–29.

Robbins, Rossell Hope. *Encyclopedia of Witchcraft and Demonology.* New York: Crown Publishers, 1959.

Rosnow, Ralph L., and Gary Alan Fine. *Rumor and Gossip: The Social Psychology of Hearsay.* New York: Elsevier, 1976.

Rowling, J. K. *Harry Potter and the Sorcerer's Stone.* New York: Scholastic, 1998.

Schama, Simon. *Dead Certainties: Unwarranted Speculations.* New York: Vintage Books, 1992.

Schlosser, Eric. *Fast Food Nation: The Dark Side of the All-American Meal.* New York: Houghton Mifflin, 2001.

Sherman, Constance D. "Oberlin Lore." *New York Folklore Quarterly* 18 (1962): 58–60.

Shibutani, Tamotsu. *Improvised News: A Sociological Study of Rumor.* Indianapolis: Bobbs-Merrill, 1966.

Speanburgh, Sharon A. "Mysteries of Rockwell Hall." 17 Dec. 1982. Niagara Folklore Archive, Buffalo State College.

Taylor, Troy. *Ghosts of Millikin: The Haunted History of Millikin University.* Forsyth: Whitechapel Productions, 1996.

Tennyson, Charles. *Cambridge from Within.* London: Chatto and Windus, 1913.

Thompson, Stith. *The Folktale.* New York: Holt, Rinehart and Winston, 1946.

Toelken, Barre. *The Dynamics of Folklore.* Boston: Houghton Mifflin, 1979.

Tucker, Elizabeth. "The Lake Lieberman Monster." *Midwestern Folklore* 30.1 (2004): 36–45.

Van Fleteren, Margaret Ann. "Haunted Parameters: The Importance of Place in Ghost Stories." 11 Oct. 1991. Folklore Collection, Labor History Archive, Reuther Library, Wayne State University.

von Sydow, Carl Wilhelm. *Selected Papers on Folklore.* Copenhagen: Rosenkilde and Bagger, 1948.

Ward, Donald, trans. and ed. *The German Legends of the Brothers Grimm.* 2 vols. Philadelphia: Institute for the Study of Human Issues, 1981.

Whatley, Mariamne H., and Elissa R. Henken. *Did You Hear about the Girl Who . . . ?: Contemporary Legends, Folklore, and Human Sexuality.* New York: New York University Press, 2000.

Zahaczewsky, Theresa. "Spirits Walk on UH Campuses." *Ku Lama* 2:11, University of Hawaii, 27 Oct. 1995 <http://www.hawaii.edu/ news/kulama/1995/951027/ kulama951027.html#cover>.

Three
Examples and Texts

INTRODUCTION

Most of the following texts come from campus folklore archives. Narrated between the early 1960s and the beginning of the twenty-first century, these legends provide insight into student life and academic routines at various colleges and universities. While some texts focus on joyful experiences, many of them present stressful situations. Dangers from human and supernatural assailants, catastrophic fires, drugs, food contaminants, and illness are recurrent subjects, as are peculiar, demanding professors and difficult exams. In telling legends, students strengthen their understanding of past perils and present needs.

If the narrators of legend texts described their own ethnicities, those are included here, as are the names of narrators who wished to be identified. To facilitate finding texts, this chapter follows the same sequence as the "Campus Legend Categories" section of chapter 2.

ORIGINS

"Insane Asylum" (Miami University of Ohio)

At Miami of Ohio everybody was afraid to live in this one girls' dormitory on the first floor because it once was an insane asylum. They moved the insane people out and the students in. The insane people used to come back and stare in the windows and try to get in. One story said one did get in and he was in a girl's room when she walked in. There was nothing said about what happened when she found him.

Source

Folklore Collection, Labor History Archive, Reuther Library, Wayne State University. Donna Newland, "College-lore," July 29, 1965. Narrated by Pat Roach, a 20-year-old female student at Tufts College residing in Birmingham, Michigan, on July 13, 1965. The narrator spent one semester at Miami University of Ohio, where she learned this legend.

Commentary

This is one of many campus legends about buildings that once served a different purpose. Students have often drawn comparisons between their residence halls and hospitals for the mentally disabled, speculating about the similarities and differences between the two. Sometimes, as in this legend, a residence hall seems to have begun as a hospital; other legends explain that college authorities used blueprints from a hospital for the mentally ill to build new residence halls.

Why do college students compare themselves to patients with mental disabilities? Academic life, with its constant emphasis on demonstrating intellectual excellence, can be tense and difficult. In comparing a residence hall to an "insane asylum," students articulate the stress they feel, especially as entering freshmen.

"Light on the Mountainside" (Mount Saint Mary's College)

Mount Saint Mary's was founded by Father John DuBois in an unusual way. On one of his pilgrimages of duty he was attracted by a light on the mountainside which he thought was in a settler's cottage. He traveled towards it but never reached it. Finally, growing tired, he stopped.

While resting, he made a cross out of two sticks and secured it to a tree. When he decided it was time, he came back here to start the Mount. A century before all this, a priest passing by foretold the erection of the church right where the church was built.

Source

Archive and Special Collections, Mount St. Mary's College. Narrated by Lisa Villard, a student at Mount Saint Mary's College, in December 1976, as part of her term paper "The Legends of the Mount." Lisa learned the story from Father Dan Nusbaum, a popular professor with extensive knowledge of campus folklore.

Commentary

Mount Saint Mary's College, the first Catholic independent college in the United States, was founded in Emmitsburg, Maryland, in 1808. This story of the college's founding resembles the saint's legend in its focus on miraculous events ordained by God. According to folk tradition, extraordinary or ghostly lights indicate hidden treasure (motif N532) or the birth of a saint (motif V222.0.1.3).

The mention of a priest's prophecy 100 years before is very important. Mount Saint Mary's, one of the oldest Catholic colleges in the United States, becomes even better established in religious history through the foretelling of its origin. Hearing this legend, students can take pride in their college's long heritage of unusual events.

"Fiat Lux" (University of California at Berkeley)

Underneath the awning that is in front of the door of the Campanile on UC Berkeley's campus is a bronze inlaid inscription written in a circle which reads "Fiat Lux," which in Latin means "let there be light." The inscription, however, is written backwards. The reason for this is that originally the awning was designed to have a reflecting pool directly under it, so that when you looked down into the pool, you would read the words reflected forwards. However, in the early 1900's, when the tower was being built, women used to wear hoop skirts, and if you stand next to a reflecting pool while wearing a hoop skirt, people can see right up your skirt! Jane Sather, the benefactress of the tower, realized this, and decided to forgo the reflecting pool idea, but not before the letters had already been placed in the awning. It was too late to change it, so that is why the letters are backwards.

I work as a tour guide on campus, and first heard this story from Carrie Alexander, a senior guide who trained me. I heard it in May of 1989. We were told from the outset that this story might not be true, but a lot of people believe that it is. The Visitor's Center on campus received an irate letter from the University carillonist a while back that said this rumor was absolutely untrue, and that he was very sick of having to hear this pack of lies every day! A lot of tour guides, including myself, continue to tell this story, however,

Sather Gate, University of California at Berkeley. Photograph by Geoffrey Gould.

because it is a real crowd pleaser. People like to hear it better than any other explanation for the letters being backwards.

Source

Folklore Archive, University of California at Berkeley. Narrated by Michelle Ling, a 20-one-year-old Chinese American student at the University of California at Berkeley, on November 3, 1991.

Commentary

This charming story brings the listener back to the early twentieth century, when Berkeley's campus was under construction. Founded in 1873, the University of California at Berkeley underwent many phases of development. Students are proud of their Campanile, officially named Sather Tower, so stories of its early days make good campus legends. Mixed-up or backward features of campus design frequently come up in origin legends. Among the common patterns are accidentally reversed buildings and structures meant for one purpose whose usage gets distorted. Simon Bronner offers a good sampling of such legends in *Piled Higher and Deeper* (144–48).

This text helps us understand how campus tour guides choose which stories to tell prospective students and their families. As Michelle explains, this story is probably not true, but it is "a real crowd pleaser." Laughter from an appreciative audience can extend a legend's life, sometimes for quite a long time.

"A Fresh Pair of Legs" (Tulane University)

Tulane is a private school in the heart of New Orleans down in Louisiana. There is a statue standing outside the main library there of one of the founders of the school from when the school first opened. The statue used to stand tall but after the fire whose cause was unknown, the bottom half of the statue was burned to ashes and is now only from the hips and above. It is said to be true that every time there is something burning on the Tulane campus, the statue uses its arms to crawl and drag its body around the campus in search of a fresh pair of legs to steal from a student of the university.

Source

Narrated by a 19-year-old female student at Tulane University on October 29, 2003.

Commentary

The narrator of this story learned about the legless statue during freshman orientation. Since the statue represents one of Tulane's founders, the story is ideal for initiating new students. The gruesomeness of the search for a fresh pair of legs reminds the listener of legends told at summer camp, where counselors enjoy telling campers, "It's coming to get you!"

As in other campus legends, statues that move around and think seem suitable for the landscape. College is a world within itself where the fantastic blends easily with the rational.

GHOSTS

"Daisy's Ghost" (Sweet Briar College)

Just after the Civil War, an old Vermonter came down to Sweet Briar, Virginia and married a wealthy widow who owned a tobacco plantation. They had one daughter named Daisy. One night there was a fire in the main house. Daisy, then sixteen years old, was caught in her room on the third floor and died. Her parents were so upset that they went away and left the plantation to start a girls' college in Daisy's memory. The house was rebuilt and is now where the President of Sweet Briar College lives. Daisy's ghost comes back often, and no one will stay in her room on the third floor. At night you can see a burning candle moving in her room or across the look-out walk on the top of the house.

Source

Northeast Folklore Archive 217:13. Nola Johnson, a student at the University of Maine, collected the story from a fellow student, Nancy Townsend, on October 27, 1966. Before coming to the University of Maine, Nancy Townsend was a student at Sweet Briar College.

Commentary

Daisy Williams, the daughter of wealthy plantation owners in Sweet Briar, Virginia, died at the age of 16 in 1884. When Daisy's mother died in 1900, her will made Sweet Briar an educational institution for young women. The family's graveyard lies at the top of the Sweet Briar College campus. According to the Web site "Ghosts of Sweet Briar College," Daisy and her mother watch over the college. This Web site includes stories by faculty and students who have seen Daisy or experienced her playful tricks ("Daisy Drove My Car," "My Roving Towel," and others).

In *The Story of Sweet Briar College* (1956), Martha Stohlman explains that Daisy Williams died of pneumonia in New York City. The college's most treasured building, Sweet Briar House—the center of the original plantation—almost burned to the ground in 1927. After a fierce effort by college staff members and two fire departments, the house was saved. That evening, an instructor who wanted to view the burned house by moonlight saw a woman and a little girl, hand in hand, go up the steps and through the front door. Later that same evening, two students saw the same woman and girl come down the steps and disappear into the garden (170). Both observations, published in the *Sweet Briar News,* showed how much faculty and students cared about seeing Daisy and her mother in their beloved home.

In the nineteenth and twentieth centuries, many American colleges suffered damaging fires in which some students lost their lives. Ghost stories about fatal fires remind listeners how important it is to maintain fire safety. Although colleges today have strict fire codes, memories of catastrophic fires remain part of the oral histories of college campuses.

Monument in memory of Daisy Williams, Sweet Briar
College. Photograph by Geoffrey Gould.

"Dooley" (Emory University)

Years and years ago when Emory was starting out, one of the medical school
skeletons walked. The professors and students evidently became so frightened
at the sight of the walking skeleton that classes were dismissed. Ever since
then, for one week out of the year, "Dooley walks." A student called "Dooley"
dresses up like a skeleton and walks around campus. If "Dooley" enters a
classroom when it is in session, that class is dismissed for the day. "Dooley,"
by the way, was the name of the original walking skeleton.

Source

Folklore Collection, Labor History Archive, Reuther Library, Wayne State University. Donna Newland, "College-lore," July 29, 1965. This story's narrator was Richard Moser, 25, a Detroit engineer who had learned about Dooley from his brother, a student at Emory.

Commentary

"Dooley" describes a set of legends and rituals that Emory University has cherished since 1899, when a student's essay, "Reflections of the Skeleton," appeared in the campus literary magazine *The Phoenix*. In 1909, another article in *The Phoenix* explained that Dooley, the only son of a Virginia planter, died of alcoholism and then became a member of Emory's faculty, teaching students anatomy by showing them his bones (Hauk). Both articles show familiarity with the traditional motif E422.1.11.4, "Ghosts in the form of skeletons."

In Moser's story, Dooley announces his presence by walking down the hall of the medical school. Emory's tradition allows the skeleton to interrupt classes and dismiss them with one squirt of a water pistol. Classes can be interrupted at any time during "Dooley's Week" in the spring, which ends with "Dooley's Ball." The power to disrupt classes makes Dooley a beloved campus icon, a "Lord of Misrule" whose authority transcends the rules of professors and administrators. This tradition goes back to the Middle Ages in Europe, when students had more authority over their education than professors had. When a new president comes to Emory, Dooley takes the president's first name and middle initial. At the beginning of the twenty-first century, this incarnation of Emory's spirit was James W. Dooley.

"Hands" (Mount Saint Mary's College)

As odd as it might seem, hands have come to play a big role in the Mount's legends. Supposedly every Seminarian must take a class in the Black Mass and all the black arts. This one priest went up to the Grotto to test out his newfound knowledge on the night of All Souls' Day, which happened also to be the night of the full moon. The priest never returned to his room that night, and the following morning his shredded body was found scattered in the cemetery by the Grotto. They could not find one of his hands.

According to the story the hand has traveled from dorm to dorm and through each floor, searching for an open window. Once it finds an open window it rips open the screen and strangles the people in the room. There is another hand that roams our college. At one time, under Phillips Hall were the slave quarters. The slaves were tortured and buried here. Some say they can hear their cries and screams. There was one very unfortunate slave that lost one of his hands. This hand too crawls up the sides of the dorms looking for an open window to crawl through.

Source

Archive and Special Collections, Mt. Saint Mary's College. Lisa Villard, "The Legends of the Mount," December 1976. No informant is identified for the story of the seminarian's hand. The narrator of the story about the slave's hand was Jean Harshmen, a freshman at the college in 1975.

Commentary

Mount Saint Mary's College has a long history of folk legendry. Students have said that the archivist at Mount Saint Mary's keeps secret files of stories in a locked room that students are forbidden to enter. In reality, the archivist offers help to anyone with a serious interest in learning about the college's traditions.

The legend of the seminarian who performs a Black Mass on All Souls' Day is a Halloween horror story with a clear message: deviation from accepted religious doctrine leads to disaster. Legends about people who practice black magic make

Bradley Hall, Mount Saint Mary's College. Photograph by Geoffrey Gould.

up one section of Reidar T. Christiansen's *The Migratory Legends* (1958). Students at Catholic colleges have had a particular interest in telling legends of this kind.

It is interesting to see that the seminarian's hand takes on a life of its own after being severed from his body. Traditionally, ghosts may take the form of hands (motif E422.1.11.3). This hand's search for someone to strangle brings to mind the ghost in A-T 366, *The Man from the Gallows,* which strangles the person who has eaten part of its body. Why the seminarian's hand wants to strangle someone can be explained by the principle of metonymy. The hand that performed the Black Mass represents the renegade priest. Dedicated to black magic, the priest's ghost must pursue innocent seminarians one by one.

The story of the slave's hand also emphasizes a search for victims. Other versions of this legend say that the slave, Leander, lost his hand as a punishment for stealing, then watched the punishers bury his hand under the campus quadrangle. Like other campus legends about ghosts of slaves, this one reminds listeners of slaves' suffering in the American South.

"Girls Running" (Hartwick College)

They built our college upon a Native American burial site. I think our dorm "Smith" was haunted by a little girl. At nights, we would hear her running door to door on our floor. She would knock on the doors and ask to play outside. This happened at four in the morning, and our Resident Assistant would always yell at us, but it was never us! One night she even came into my room when I was alone and I could not move. I was really scared, and I didn't know what to do.

We also used to have a fifth floor, until it was burnt down, which killed two girls. Even though the floor was burnt, the college decided to rebuild the floor, but the spirits of the girls never left. The girls on the fifth floor say that you can hear the girls running around on the floor. They even turn off the television and mess with the heating, but luckily they stop when you say "STOP." The school was haunted!

Source

Narrated by a 19-year-old female student from Hartwick College in November 2001.

Commentary

Legends and rumors about Native American burial grounds are well known on college campuses. Hartwick College, founded in 1816 in Oneonta, New York, became the first Lutheran seminary in the United States. Like students on other campuses in areas where Native Americans used to live, Hartwick students have told stories about their campus standing on a burial ground. Most colleges where such stories circulate have very low Native American enrollments. In her study *The National Uncanny* (2000), Renée Bergland suggests that the dominance of mainstream American culture has made Native Americans seem like ghosts. When students tell stories about Native American ghosts on campus, they express curiosity and concern about past injustices.

All three ghosts in this story—the little Native American girl and the two female students who died in the fire—run around the residence hall causing trouble. Like many other college ghosts, these three torment students by making noise, turning machines on and off, and changing rooms' temperature.

Only the ghost of the little Native American girl seems to scare the teller of the story. Her statement "I was alone and I could not move" suggests the possibility of sleep paralysis, described in other campus legends. Her more cheerful response to the other three ghosts shows how much students living in residence halls can enjoy talking about their resident spirits. Laughing about strange phenomena and trying to figure out how to make the ghosts go away, students come to terms with their concerns about the supernatural.

"Dr. Stanton's Ghost" (Bates College)

Several years ago Dr. Stanton was a professor at Bates College in Lewiston (Maine). I think he was probably an English professor, but I'm not sure about that. Anyway, he was a great nature-lover. For part of Freshman Orientation every year, he used to take all the freshmen on a nature-walk through the woods, where he had a cabin.

When he had to retire he still did this for a few years and then donated his cabin to the Outing Club at Bates. He said that he always wanted the tradition to be carried on and said, "I'll always be there to meet you."

Shortly after that Dr. Stanton died. Every year the freshmen are still taken up to the cabin. On the way they are told the story of Dr. Stanton. When they reach the cabin, there is always an enormous feast laid out for them and no one around, so they believe that Dr. Stanton's ghost is there.

Source

Northeast Folklore Archive 217:12. Collected by Nola Johnson, a student at the University of Maine at Orono, on November 5. The narrator was Anne Witham, who heard the story from her mother, a graduate of Bates.

Commentary

This ghost story shows us what freshman orientation was like at Bates College in the 1940s, when the narrator's mother was a student. The initial description of a male professor who took freshmen to his cabin in the woods might sound like the prelude to a horror story. However, those were different times, when there was more trust in the benevolent motives of adult authority figures. The story makes it clear that Dr. Stanton is a kind professor who wants to share his joy in nature with new students.

One of the most interesting aspects of this text is its description of a yearly ritual. Each year, orientation leaders take freshmen into the woods, telling them that Dr. Stanton's ghost is there. Contextual notes for this story explain that Anne Witham's mother believed in the ghost, but Anne herself did not. Since Anne was not a Bates student and had not personally experienced the trip to the cabin, she had no compelling reason to believe that the story was true.

Certain traditional motifs show this story's kinship to other supernatural legends and folktales. Motif E373, "Ghost bestows gifts on living," applies here, as does D1472.1.7, "Magic table supplies food and drink." Another relevant motif is E323.1.1, "Dead mother returns to suckle child." Dr. Stanton, like other faculty members of his generation, takes the role of a parent surrogate, "*in loco parentis*." Whether or not freshmen believe in Dr. Stanton's ghost, they learn that people at their new college will protect their well-being.

"Lavender"

One night there was this girl, named Lavender, hitchhiking. Some college guys picked her up. They were on their way to a party and asked her to go with them. She said that she would. On the way she complained of being cold, and one of the guys gave her his sport jacket. They went to the party. On the way back she asked to be let out at an isolated spot.

The guys came back the next day because she still had the jacket. They found a path and followed it. They saw an old house and an old man came to the door. They told him the story and asked for the jacket. He said that she was dead and was buried out back. They found the jacket on the grave.

Source

Northeast Folklore Archive 127:18. Collected by Brenda Ellis from Deanne Kaake, a 20-year-old student at Farmington State College, on April 14, 1967.

Commentary

The "Vanishing Hitchhiker" (motif E332.3.3.1), one of the most popular ghost stories in the world, has circulated in oral tradition since the nineteenth century. Campus versions of this legend, like the previous one, describe a hitchhiking young woman who turns out to be a ghost. The most common pattern for college "Vanishing Hitchhiker" legends fits Example D in Jan H. Brunvand's *The Vanishing Hitchhiker,* which ends with the discovery of an overcoat draped over a headstone (27–28). Brunvand provides a bibliography of "Vanishing Hitchhiker" studies, including one, Lydia M. Fish's "Jesus on the Thruway" (1976), which tells of a Christ-like hitchhiker picked up by college students and other travelers.

Could this be Lavender's grave? Photograph by Geoffrey Gould.

Carl Carmer's story "The Lavender Evening Dress" was published in *Dark Trees to the Wind* (306–11). A version of "Lavender" about two students at the University of Chicago in 1948 was published in *The Little Giant Book of "True" Ghostly Tales* (Colby et al. 2002). Both oral and printed versions of familiar legends like this one have contributed to their continuing popularity in college communities.

"Eerie Orange" (University of Texas at Austin)

A large clock tower stands in the middle of campus and with every UT athletic win, the tower is lit up an eerie orange. In the 1970s, a US Marine climbed the steps to the observatory at the top of this tower. Armed with a sniper rifle, this lunatic picked off students walking to their classes. If my memory serves me, I believe he shot twelve to fifteen students before the police captured him.

This was a horrific event and for years it was not mentioned. In the late nineties, however, students began to see strange occurrences around this tower. I was one of these students. After walking back from a football game that UT had won, my friends and I decided to walk to the center of campus to eat at the late night cafeteria.

As we neared the center of campus, the tower slowly rose before us. Covered in the soft glow of the orange light, the tower looked magnificent. The observatory, that had been closed off years before, appeared to be slightly lit. As we neared, in the shadow of the orange light, we saw what looked like a barrel of a gun. Quite frightened, we quickly walked away from the tower back to our dorms.

To this day my friends and I are unsure as to what we actually saw. Maybe it was a janitor doing some late night cleaning and his shadow caused an illusion of a rifle barrel, or maybe it really was the ghost of that Marine, haunting the observatory, searching for his next target.

Source

Narrated in April 2003 by a male student who was a freshman at the University of Texas at Austin in the fall of 2001.

Commentary

The massacre of 14 students by a sniper in the University of Texas's clock tower in 1966 left a lasting legacy. After a series of suicides, the tower's observation deck was closed in 1975. A book by Gary Lavergne, *Sniper in the Tower: The Charles Whitman Murders* (1997), became very popular in the late 1990s.

Because of its illumination in "eerie orange" after athletic victories, the clock tower attracted students' attention in the fall of 2001, when this personal experience occurred. The teller of the story was not sure if he and his friends had seen an illusion or a ghost in the clock tower, but he enjoyed describing what had happened. He also mentioned that frightening stories about the clock tower sniper were part of the Texas Longhorns' tradition.

In college folklore, towers often furnish focal points for legends. Berkeley's Sather Tower, for example, has been a magnet for ghost stories and other legends. Even if no tragedy has taken place, students tend to create stories about sad events, especially suicides, in the tower's vicinity. Since so many students lost their lives in the mass shooting at the University of Texas in 1966, all that was needed to make the tower seem haunted was the appearance of a ghost.

"Book-Throwing Ghost" (Cazenovia College)

Cazenovia College has had two dorm fires in the same residence hall over the years of the college's existence. After the first fire the dorm was rebuilt so that it looked exactly like the one that was lost to the fire. The second fire killed a girl who couldn't get out of the building in time. When the building was rebuilt the dimensions of the building were changed. The floors were now a foot higher than they were in the original building. The residents of the new building over the years have reported hearing a girl crying through the halls at night.

Also in the new building there is a common area with book shelves, and it has been reported that the girl can be seen throwing books off the shelves, but over there, her feet are not present because she died in the old building where the floors were a foot higher than they are now. Some residents also reported that they woke up in the middle of the night (during the winter) to find their windows wide open; one of the girls got up and closed the windows (and locked them) only to wake up an hour later with them open again.

About 8 or 9 years ago I was working with a group who was doing a fundraiser by reenacting ghost stories throughout the town. I was doing the ghost story at the college and one night while we were sitting around talking about how to make the story scarier and while we were sitting there talking, one of the display cases that was firmly mounted on the wall fell onto the girl who was playing the ghost.

Source

E-mailed by a female student in Cazenovia, New York, to Brandon Leonard, a student at Binghamton University, on March 29, 2004.

Commentary

This legend provides three kinds of proof for the existence of a campus ghost. The narrator describes two fires in a Cazenovia College residence hall, identified by other students as Hubbard Hall. After the second fire, in which a young woman tragically dies, the college erects a new building with different dimensions. The first proof of supernatural activity is an apparition with no visible feet. Windows that mysteriously opened in the middle of the night during the winter provide the second proof. The third and most convincing proof is an eyewitness account of books falling on a female student playing the part of a ghost for a fund-raiser.

Libraries are common settings for campus ghost stories. Old books, musty tomes from the past, seem to encourage appearances of the dead. This female ghost makes her presence felt repeatedly both by throwing books and by opening windows. What message does this story convey? Its most obvious moral is to beware of causing fires, but there seem to be other layers of

Hubbard Hall, Cazenovia College. Photograph by Geoffrey Gould.

meaning. Should the college guard against forgetting the loss of one of its students? Should women be more aware of dangers in a college environment? Is the ghost expressing contempt for learning by throwing books? In any case, this legend makes the point that people should take ghosts seriously.

"Logan's Lyric Theatre" (Utah State University)

One summer, about five years ago, a gal was with the Lyric Company and was taking tickets. Her assignment was to be there in the afternoon taking tickets for the show and the ticket booth is situated so that you can look out the door into the booth and look directly up the stairs on the right.

She saw a figure at the top of the stairs just as clear as a bell. She described it as being some kind of a strange costume. Her first reaction when she heard someone up there was to call out and ask who was there. There was no response, but she could see the figure.

She said something like, "You're not supposed to be here, you know." When she got out to where she could see the figure disappear, she ran very distraught over to Glauser's restaurant across the street and called the police. The police went down and searched but could see nothing. She would never be down there alone after that.

Source

Fife Folklore Archive, Utah State University, 83–039. John P. Worthington, the student author of "Logan's Lyric Ghost Legends," collected this text from Farrell J. Black, a theater department faculty member at Utah State University, on March 1, 1983.

Commentary

The Lyric Theatre in Logan, Utah, has one of the best-known campus theater ghosts in the United States. Purchased by Utah State University in 1962, the theater has a long history of memorable performances. According to legends told at Utah State University, a famous Shakespearean troupe sometimes came to Logan after putting on performances at the Orpheum Theatre in Salt Lake City. Some narrators of Lyric Theatre ghost stories have described a specter in Shakespearean garb, suggesting that one actor killed another and buried his body in the basement.

Like other theatre ghost stories, this one emphasizes a mysterious figure that briefly materializes, then fades away. Since actors often make quick exits after their appearances on stage, this kind of ghost seems just right for its setting. Actors on college campuses learn about a rich array of theater traditions: not only ghost stories but also customs and beliefs. In some campus theaters, students say that a light left burning all the time represents the theater's spirit. Strict prohibitions against saying "Macbeth" or "Good luck!" reinforce the impression that bad luck imperils those who are careless. Hearing ghost stories, student actors discover that some victims of the worst kind of luck keep enacting their own tragedies, startling viewers of their entrances and exits.

"Elevator Ghosts" (University of Idaho)

In the residence halls at the University of Idaho, most of our ghost stories deal with elevator ghosts. For example, my good friend, Mary, who's also a native of Moscow, Idaho (the town which contains the U of I), told me about how male ghosts haunt the elevators in the Theophilus Tower, which is currently an all female residence. She told me that when men used to live in the Tower, they would find some way to get themselves caught in the elevator shaft which led to their demise and their ghosts would haunt the Tower. I'm not sure of the accuracy of the information, but it is a nice legend.

Then, this year, one of my friends, Gina, who casually studies ghosts, told me that there was a ghost in the Gooding Wing of the Wallace Complex. She told me you could feel his presence because there was a spot of cold air that moved at random. I actually felt for this cold air and she was right, there was a decrease in air temperature. Since I am not a ghost expert, all I could do was smile and nod. However, the presence of a specter might explain why the elevator doors in the Gooding Wing randomly open when someone passes by without pressing the directional buttons. I don't believe this is a natural function of elevators because I've never seen any other elevators open at random.

Source

E-mailed by Marie Reed, student and Residence Hall Association secretary at the University of Idaho, to Elizabeth Tucker on January 29, 2003.

Commentary

This text is an example of what Bill Ellis calls a "legend report": a familiar part of a group's repertoire that no longer needs to be told in a vivid, immediate way (*Aliens, Ghosts, and Cults* 62). While she enjoys and values elevator ghost stories, this student/staff member knows them so well that she provides their details in summary form. She does not exactly believe in ghosts but pays attention to changes in temperature and unexplainable openings of elevator doors. These pieces of evidence, coming through the eyes and skin, seem more convincing than details about people who died years ago.

Since the female students of Theophilus Tower worry about male ghosts in their elevator shaft, this text seems appropriate for Freudian analysis. "Elevator Ghosts" also shows how much people in a residential community can become attached to their ghosts. These nonthreatening, familiar supernatural phenomena offer students a comfortable level of participation in the world of the supernatural.

Stories about haunted elevators, often connected to memories of tragic accidents, are told on a number of college campuses. The prevalence of films and television shows about dangerous elevators has encouraged the telling of stories of this kind.

"Running Water" (University of Alaska at Fairbanks)

One time I was about to take a shower and I forgot something in my room. When I came back to the bathroom I heard the water running in the last stall. I hadn't seen anyone in there before and the door looked open. I went to go see who was there, but there wasn't any water in the bathtub and no one was there. I told someone on my floor and they said that someone died in there a few years ago. I think they were murdered or something. Now people hear running water in the bathroom.

Source

Narrated by a 20-year-old female student at the University of Alaska at Fairbanks on April 16, 2003.

Commentary

This is one of many bathroom ghost stories told on college campuses. Jeannie B. Thomas's article "Pain, Pleasure and the Spectral: The Barfing Ghost of Burford Hall" (1991) explores how pain intersects with perceptions of spectral phenomena. In this legend, the teller asks whether sounds heard in an empty bathroom are related to a murder several years before. While the description of the murder seems vague, the sound of running water (motif E402, "Mysterious ghostlike noises heard") suggests that someone has suffered in this bathroom.

On April 26, 1993, a 20-year-old female student was shot to death in a residence hall bathroom at the University of Alaska at Fairbanks. Police found her body in a bathtub. Nine years later, on the anniversary of the murder, a student found a riddle written in ink on a stall in one of the men's restrooms. Police said that the riddle revealed fresh information about the murder, but no definitive solution was shared with the public at that time.

"Haunted Hoover" (San Jose State University)

It was a quiet night in Hoover. All of a sudden, a scream was heard, followed by the sound of someone running down the stairs. It was a girl running down, screaming for help. A man was after her with a knife in his hand. She was running for her life. She reached the phone booth and started dialing 911. The man got to her and stabbed her in the phone booth. She was unable to finish dialing 911. She bled to death in that phone booth.

Ever since the incident, anyone who went into that phone booth hasn't been able to dial anything but the digits 9 and 1. That has freaked out many people over the years and the phone booth was finally boarded up.

Source

E-mailed to Elizabeth Tucker by Melissa Hatteyer, resident director of Hoover Hall at San Jose State University in California, on February 7, 2003.

Commentary

In this legend about a haunted phone booth, the ghost of a murdered student reminds residents of her death by preventing them from dialing any digits but 9 and 1. Unusual sounds also bring the murder to mind (motif E 402, "Mysterious ghostlike noises heard"; E231, "Return from dead to reveal murder").

Campus legends have given phone booths a bad reputation. In particular, legends about people contracting AIDS from needles in public phone booths scared college students in the 1990s and the early twenty-first century. The adolescent legend of "The Babysitter and the Telephone," in which a murderer repeatedly calls his victim, has also contributed to the telephone's mystique.

"The Roommate Who Wasn't There" (State University of New York at Buffalo)

This happened in Buffalo. My friend who goes to Buffalo heard this from his RA. Well, supposedly many years ago, there was a transfer student who moved into a room. On the day that he moved in, his roommate was not there. So he just unpacked and went to bed. When he woke up, he found his roommate there unpacking. They started talking and they instantly became friends. It is the first day of classes and the guy proceeds to go to class. Finally, at the end of the day he goes back to his room and bumps into his RA in the hallway. He tells his RA how he enjoyed his first day of classes, and that he really got along with his roommate. The RA turns ghastly pale, and carefully breaks the news to the transfer student that he lives in a single dorm—and that a male student had committed suicide in that room years ago.

Source

Collected by Susan Ng, a student at Binghamton University, from a 23-year-old man from Brooklyn, New York, on March 15, 2004.

Commentary

This legend is a classic piece of initiatory folklore. Mentioning that the events in the story happened "many years ago," the narrator explains that it came from his resident assistant (RA). There are only two living characters in the story: the transfer student and his RA. Only the RA can tell the difference between real and ghostly roommates. For the student, trying to adjust to a new place, this distinction is difficult to make. Busy starting classes and getting settled, he does not expect his new roommate to be a ghost.

Many campus ghost stories feature two contrasting students: one who lives and another who dies. In this case, the spectral roommate died years ago. His reappearance, boding no good, frightens the student and his RA. Will the transfer student follow his ghostly roommate's example and commit suicide? Nobody knows. The first weeks of college are stressful; sometimes it isn't easy to distinguish reality from illusion. Inscrutable and strange, the ghostly roommate initiates entering students into their new way of life.

"Hanging from the Pipe" (Wayne State University)

I was told a girl used to be in my room, a student and unhappy. Kind of strange. Anyway, she was supposed to have killed herself in the room. One morning they came in and found her hanging from the pipe. I believe it happened about two or three years ago. She was supposed to have the other side of the room and keeps coming back pulling things from the cupboard and making a pest of herself. I guess her spirit never rested, she was so unhappy.

I heard it from Sheri [her suitemate] and Jeananne and Jan, she's been here the longest, so I guess she'd know. They said several girls had to move out because of it.

We started telling ghost stories one night and then I heard every sound that night. I hadn't noticed them before. To top it off I was told "I wouldn't want your room for anything" by Sheri. I sort of believed it at first but later I just forgot about it.

Source

Folklore Collection, Labor History Archive, Reuther Library, Wayne State University. Rosemary Kreston, "Folklore in Helen Newberry Joy Residence for Women," winter 1973. The narrator was Beverly Dinham, a 23-year-old student from Jamaica, who had lived in the United States for a year and a half.

Commentary

This legend gives gruesome details about the suicide of a former student. For the student who currently lives in the room (in this case, a student who recently came to the United States from Jamaica), such a story is frightening. Saying that the suicide happened "two or three years ago," Beverly explains how sensitive she became to every sound in her room. She mentions the cupboard as a place of ghostly activity, while the student fieldworker, Rosemary Kreston, uses the word "closet." Both in children's folklore and in the folklore of adolescents, closets are prime locations for disturbance by ghosts.

Note that Beverly listens closely to what she hears from suitemates Sheri, Jeananne, and Jan, who have lived in the Helen Newberry Joy Residence longer than she has. In college residential communities, students come and go within relatively short periods of time, so those who have lived in a building for at least a year become experts in the building's history.

"Jumped off the Bridge" (Cornell University)

This story took place by a bridge that is on campus at Cornell. There was once a student who could not take the stress of school and the family issues he was said to have so he jumped off the bridge, killing himself. From that day on, it was said that every year on the anniversary of his death, he is seen standing on that same bridge at intervals of a few minutes throughout the day. Every few hours or so there is also a loud scream, which is thought to be his scream as he jumped his way to death.

Helen Newberry Joy Residence for Women, Wayne State University. Photograph by Elizabeth Tucker.

Source

Narrated by a male Cornell University student on April 20, 2003.

Commentary

Cornell University's suspension bridge is a campus landmark. Perhaps because Cornell is high up in the hills, with a deep gorge and steeply angled paths, stories about fatal jumps have appealed to student storytellers. There have been some suicide attempts around the bridge, but not as many as the plethora of legends suggests.

Among various versions of Cornell's suspension bridge suicide legend, the detail emphasized most often is an image of the student at the time of his death (motif E334.4, "Ghost of suicide seen at death spot or nearby"). This text also includes a scream (motif E402.1.1.3, "Ghost cries and screams"), which serves as a partial reenactment of the tragic death (motif E337.1.2, "Sounds of accident reenact tragedy"). The student's reason for jumping off the bridge is usually academic stress. Sometimes, as in this text, family problems are mentioned. Still another reason for the fatal jump is a traumatic fraternity initiation that shatters the student's peace of mind and makes him decide that life is not worth living.

"The Pregnant Nun" (Nazareth College)

There was a rumor that when Naz was still an all-girls' Catholic school (full of nuns) that there was one particular nun who lived on the fourth floor in Medaille Hall that committed suicide because she had an affair with one of the priests and became pregnant. It is rumored that her ghost still roams the fourth floor of that building, and freaky stuff happens.

We just recently expanded Naz—the infirmary (which is one of the buildings we just bought from the nuns this past year) was converted into a dorm. Since the infirmary is where most of the nuns went when they were sick and really old, there were a lot of deaths in that building. Now that kids are living in there, they say that it is haunted by the nuns' spirits. It is even rumored that the school hired a Catholic priest to come in and do an exorcism.

Source

Collected by Irene Strong, a student at Binghamton University, from a 22-year-old student at the State University of New York at Albany in February 2004. The story was sent by e-mail.

Commentary

At Catholic colleges, students' speculation about secret liaisons between nuns and priests has stimulated legend telling. In this story from Nazareth College in Rochester, New York, the nun becomes pregnant and kills herself. This suicide of a woman who is supposed to set a good example for her students has high shock value. Its emphasis on forbidden sex subverts the idea that instructors are chaste and high minded; it also reflects students' own interest in sexuality.

The second part of this story is harder to interpret. Why would it be necessary for a Catholic priest to exorcise the spirits of dead nuns? Malevolent haunting is vaguely indicated here. As for the reason why nuns would want to cause trouble at their last dwelling place, the story provides no answer.

Suspension bridge, Cornell University. Photograph by Geoffrey Gould.

"The Ghost with Red Eyes" (Hong Kong University of Science and Technology)

This one is in Hong Kong University of Science and Technology, there is a dorm, the left hand is female and the right hand side is male, a guy always saw a beautiful gal with long hair, but all the time he could only see her back and during that time, there was a rumor in the dorm that there was a female ghost with red eyes in the dorm since the guy saw the girl many times but still could only see her back, one day, he tried to follow her, he followed her until the girl went into her room, there was a peep hole on the door, then after the gal went inside, he looked into that hole and then the only thing he saw was red.

Source

Collected by Beatrice Yung at Binghamton University from a 23-year-old female Binghamton University student on March 23, 2004.

Commentary

This legend sent by Instant Messenger lacks conventional punctuation and capitalization. Because of its free form, the story's flow is smooth and poetic.

Red symbolizes death and danger in Asian culture and in other cultures as well (motif 422.2.1, "Revenant red"). This young woman's red eyes prove that she is a ghost, but the male student cannot see her eyes at first. Irresistibly drawn to the beautiful woman with long hair, the young man follows her until she enters her room. Looking through the peephole, he discovers her true nature.

Women and men live in separate parts of this residence hall at Hong Kong University of Science and Technology. This legend dramatizes what can happen when a male student comes too close to a female student's living space. There is certainly a warning here: if you don't keep the right distance, you may be horrified by what you find.

WITCHES

"A Coven of Witches" (Kirkland College)

A coven of witches made up of students lives on at Kirkland. They meet three times a year to celebrate their high holidays. In the beginning years they invited spectators to their festivities in the Glen.

As each witch graduates (supposedly they were often theater majors), she finds a replacement. Nowadays it is an underground organization. This is due to the witches being blamed for a Hamilton student's death (he hung himself from a tree in the graveyard on Halloween of 1972).

Source

Collected by a 20-year-old female Hamilton-Kirkland alumna from a 23-year-old graduate of Kirkland College in September 1977.

Commentary

Founded in 1812, Hamilton College established Kirkland College for women in 1968; the two colleges merged 10 years later. This story about Kirkland witches causing a Hamilton student's death seems to suggest tension between students at the two colleges. Since witches have been blamed for many tragic events, it is not surprising to hear that students say Kirkland witches caused the young man's untimely death. Students on other college campuses have told similar legends about Halloween hangings.

Worries about witchcraft found their way into campus legends in the late 1960s and 1970s. Since the Middle Ages, when Europeans told stories about witches teaching apprentices their craft, initiation into witchcraft (G286) has been a prominent motif. Films such as *Rosemary's Baby* (1968) have bolstered interest in witches' dangerous behavior.

"A Coven of Witches" shows more familiarity with the folktale's conventions than with contemporary witchcraft. "They meet three times a year" follows the folktale's rule of three rather than the sequence of four high holidays celebrated by witches in the twentieth and twenty-first centuries.

"The Shorb Sisters" (University of California at Berkeley)

Did you hear what happened in this house? Well, there were three sisters that used to live in this house, and they were accused by the townspeople of practicing witchcraft. So the townspeople came and hung the three sisters outside the entrance way.

And only one of the sisters died, and so they took the two remaining sisters—and this was before Berkeley had paved roads—and they tied the two sisters behind a horse carriage and dragged them up and down the street. And only one of the sisters died.

And so they took the last sister, and they burnt her in front of the house, and that is why there is that steam that comes out of the middle of the road. And that's the family that donated the house to the Campus Housing and Dining.

Source

Folklore Archive, University of California at Berkeley. Told by Monica Nguyen, second-generation Vietnamese American student, in November 1996. Collected by Shia Michele Levitt, age 20.

Commentary

Before 1995, Shorb House was known as "Casa Italiana" on the Berkeley campus. More recently, it has served as a residence hall for single graduate students. Usually students know little about donors who gave a building or money to a university. This intriguing legend satisfies people's curiosity about the identity of the Shorb family.

When the student fieldworker asked Monica how this legend was told, she replied, "It's normally told to new students when they come into the house to explain the creaks in the house, and any weird things in the house, because it's an old house.... It's told your first semester, and old members try to wait until Halloween." Evidently, "The Shorb Sisters" is an initiatory legend for entering students. Explaining the jet of steam that rises from the road, it describes a horrific set of punishments for witchcraft.

Without knowing exactly how this legend originated, we can guess that upperclassmen wanted to tell a scary story for Halloween. Perhaps seeing steam rise in the middle of the road brought the burning of witches to mind. Shakespeare's *Macbeth* made three "weird sisters" some of the world's most famous witches; there are three Shorb sisters as well. The three modes of death remind readers of horrible deaths in the folktale. Some readers might also remember the men and women who died after being found guilty of practicing witchcraft in the trials in Salem, Massachusetts, in 1692.

As exaggerated and out of place as this story might seem, it reminds listeners of the pain suffered by people who were convicted of practicing witchcraft in Europe and the United States. Freshmen might take this legend seriously or discount it as an entertaining fabrication.

"Room 109A" (Pennsylvania State University, Hazleton)

Room 109A in North Hall is haunted. Supposedly two girls that practiced witchcraft once lived there. One day during their fourth semester, they died for some reason. There are reports from past residents of room 109A of strange occurrences happening in the room. One of the most common reports is that the residents would leave to go home for the weekend, making sure everything in the room was off. They returned to find things such as lights, computer and television turned on. Also, some residents reported that posters had mysteriously been knocked off the wall onto the floor.

There have also been reports that mysterious lights would flash in the walk-in closet, and even of hearing knocks on the window when the residents knew no one was outside. The interviewee who told of this legend happens to live in room 109A in North Hall. So far, he and his roommate have not encountered any strange occurrences and they hope nothing out of the ordinary ever occurs. Only the people who say they have experienced strange events in the room know for sure if the room is really haunted or not. Perhaps it is just a story to try to scare incoming students and make them believe that the room is really haunted. There is also the slight possibility that the room may actually be haunted and that the spirits of the two dead girls still roam around the room.

Source

Folklore Archive, Pennsylvania State University at Hazleton. Nate Fullme, Mike Petrocelli, Justin Rickert, and Brad Satkowski, "Campus Legends," November 2, 1999.

Commentary

At first glance, this story seems to be one of many "haunted dorm room" legends. Falling posters, flashing lights, knocking sounds, and self-activating machines are all classic ingredients of legends about haunted residence halls.

However, this story also describes two girls who practice witchcraft. No details of the girls' activities are given, but it is obvious that their practice of witchcraft, followed by their untimely deaths, explains the strange things that happen later. Other campus legends about witchcraft tend to follow a similar pattern, with vague descriptions of witchcraft and horrifying details of its consequences. Here, witchcraft signifies chaos, destruction, and lack of control: just the opposite of what happens in a well-ordered society.

While the students who wrote this paper do not exactly believe in ghosts or witchcraft, they recognize the "slight possibility" that the spirits of the two young witches may still haunt room 109A. Current residents of the room might shudder on hearing this story, wondering how much the heritage of witchcraft will affect their own lives.

INITIATION

"The Fatal Fraternity Initiation"

I was riding on the train and at the last stop a man got on and sat in the seat next to me. He saw that I had a fraternity jacket on and he got talking about his college days. He said that he would tell me about his initiation.

He said that the brothers had taken himself and two other pledges, blindfolded, way back into the woods. They had left them in this old haunted house, each with one candle.

That night it was real dark—the moon wasn't out and there wasn't any wind; in fact, he said, "I'd never seen it so calm before or since then." Anyway, they told us we had to stay there all night, and the next morning we had to find our way back to the fraternity house.

Well, we heard something move upstairs. We knew it couldn't be the wind, because it was as still as the calm before a storm. One of the guys got real brave and started up the stairs with his candle. As soon as he reached the third step, his candle went out. He came back down; then, he tried again. The candle went out again. He tried once more; the candle went out for the third time. We couldn't understand why. It went right out just like it was snuffed out. He decided to go up anyway. We heard him when he reached the top, and we yelled up and asked him what he saw. There was no answer!

The next thing we knew, we heard a blood-curdling scream and he came tumbling down the stairs. His eyes were nearly popped out of his head, his hair was pure white, and he was dead.

The two of us didn't know what to do. We listened but there wasn't a sound. We knew we had to stay there the rest of the night or we would never make fraternity. We sat down on the floor and talked to each other to get our minds off what had happened. It didn't help; we kept looking over at the body at the bottom of the stairs.

Finally the other fellow that was with me couldn't stand it any longer. He grabbed his candle and ran over to the stairs. He went up three steps. The candle went out. He started to back down but said, "By God, I'm going to find out who's up there or what's up there," and he groped his way up the stairs.

He returned a few minutes later. I thought everything was okay until I saw his eyes. He just stared at me and didn't say a word.

I started up because I knew there was something up there. My candle went out on the third step, the same as the other two had. I continued all the way up.

Three years, three days and three hours from the time the second guy went up, he died. His wife was with him and she told me he howled. One minute he seemed fine and the next minute he let out a blood-curdling scream, his hair turned pure white and he fell over—DEAD!

About this time I asked the man what he had seen when he went up the stairs.

He said—you know in three minutes, it will be three years, three hours and three minutes since that second guy died.

Again I asked him what he saw. All of a sudden his face got a wild look on it and his eyes started popping out and he let out a blood curdling scream— "AAHHhhhhhhhhhhhhhhhhhhhhhh!"

His hair turned pure white and he slumped over—dead in my arms!

Source

Northeast Folklore Archive 67:006–008. Narrated by Carol Clark, a student at the University of Maine, in the spring of 1964. Carol heard the story from a girlfriend whose cousin had recently been initiated into a college fraternity. She did not mention the name of his college.

Commentary

This long, dramatic story captures listeners' attention with a sequence of terrifying events. It follows the Aarne-Thompson tale type 326, *The Youth Who*

Wanted to Learn What Fear Is (Grimm tale 4), in which a young man spends a night in a haunted house so that he can learn how to shiver. These three young men want to join a fraternity and not experience fear, but their night in the haunted house leads to unforeseen consequences. (For a close analogue of this story, see Grider, "Dormitory Legend-Telling in Progress" 13–14.)

Motif N384.4, "Fraternity initiate dies from fright," is the mainspring of this story. One by one, the three pledges succumb to the horror of what they have seen, which the narrator never explains. It is interesting to see how much the formulaic number 3 influences the story's progression. Three times the candle goes out, always on the third step. The initiates' death occurs after three years, three days, and three hours (motif M341.1.2.4, "Prophecy: death in three years and three months"). As in some other college legends of sudden death, hair changes color (motif F1041.7, "Hair turns gray from terror").

Although this legend's formulaic quality takes it out of the realm of daily life, tragic deaths of fraternity initiates have perplexed and horrified college administrators and students. Antihazing laws have limited risks to some extent, but fraternity initiations have continued to be a source of concern at some colleges. Legends like this one warn students that if initiations get out of control, pledges may lose their lives.

MURDERS

"The Hook" (Western Kentucky University)

As the boy and girl drove along, a flash came over the radio—"Man escaped from Hopkinsville—Is dangerous and has a hook in place of his right hand." The couple didn't think too much of the report and after the movie, parked on a deserted and dark road outside of town.

After a short while, the girl thought that she heard someone walking around the car and became a little afraid. Remembering the previous report on the radio, she asked her boyfriend to take her back to the dorm. Seeing that she was jittery, he agreed to leave.

When the couple reached the dormitory, the boy got out of the car and walked around to let his girlfriend out—only to find a hook wrapped around the door handle.

Source

Folklore Archive, Western Kentucky University. June Baskett, "Folklore Collection: Scare Stories Found in Girls' Dormitories," January 24, 1965. The narrator of this story was June Baskett.

Commentary

One of the earliest campus horror legends is "The Hook," circulating in the Midwest since 1955. Folklorists have given close attention to this legend, analyzing its form and function (Dégh, "Speculations about 'The Hook'" 68–76; Ellis, "Why 'The Hook' Is Not a Contemporary Legend" 62–67) and its expression of adolescent sexuality (Dundes 21–36).

This legend teaches college students to think before making rash decisions and to avoid getting into trouble while parking. If the young couple in the legend paid attention to the report on the radio and left right away, they would not be vulnerable to the killer with a hook for a hand. They barely get away in time, finding his hook on the handle of the car door.

This text gains authenticity by mentioning Hopkinsville (Western State Hospital in Hopkinsville, Kentucky). When a horror legend includes well-known local details, its credibility rises substantially.

"Semester Break" (Western Kentucky University)

During the semester break, all but two of the girls in the dormitory went home. It was a cold, windy night and the girls, alone in the large dormitory, were afraid to leave each other.

During the night, they heard numerous dragging sounds and became even more jumpy. After talking for some time, one of the girls decided to stop being foolish and go to her room on the floor below the one in which she was staying, to get some books. She told her friend not to unlock the door until she heard three knocks.

Her friend, waiting in the room, became worried after almost an hour had passed. Later, she heard a scratching sound at the door and became terrified as it persisted. Afraid to move, she sat huddled in a corner until she finally fell asleep. Waking early the next morning, she went to the door to unlock it, planning to go after her friend.

She opened the door to see her friend lying dead in a pool of blood and several bloody scratch marks on the door.

Source

Folklore Archive, Western Kentucky University. June Baskett, "Folklore Collection: Scare Stories Found in Girls' Dormitories," January 24, 1965. The narrator is Karen Lee, a resident of Whitestone Hall.

Commentary

This narrator begins by setting the stage for a classic campus horror legend. On a "cold, windy night," two female students feel lonely and afraid. Soon they hear ominous dragging noises (motif E402, "Mysterious ghostlike noises heard"), meaning that either a ghost or an intruder has entered the building. Bravely deciding to "stop being foolish," one roommate goes off in search of books, warning her roommate not to unlock the door unless she hears three knocks. Then a "scratching sound" on the door terrifies the student who has stayed inside.

How the roommate inside the room responds to her friend's warning provides the crux of this legend. Faithfully following the advice meant for her protection, she does not open the door until morning, when all is quiet. We can imagine her horror and guilt on finding her friend "lying dead in a pool of blood." Should she have disregarded the warning and gone to her friend's aid? There is no easy answer to this question.

Folklorists have offered more interpretations of "The Roommate's Death" than of any other campus legend. Some of these interpretations can be found in chapter 3.

"Rigor Mortis" (University of Maine)

There were two University of Maine girls who lived in Balentine Hall, who, due to extenuating circumstances, had to stay in the dorm an extra night before Thanksgiving vacation. That evening they got hungry. One of the girls volunteered to go to the store for food. Just after she left, her roommate heard a flash bulletin on the radio. It said that some lunatic murderer had just escaped from the asylum and was in the vicinity of the University of Maine. The police wanted everyone to lock their windows and doors, and especially told everyone not to go outside under any circumstances. The girl left in the dorm got worried more and more about her roommate, since it kept getting later and later. Four or five hours had gone by and she hadn't returned.

Pretty soon she heard a funny scratching on the door. By this time her nerves were just about to their limit and she screamed. When she calmed down a little she said, "Jane, is that you?" There was no answer. Then she heard the scratching again. Desperately, she yelled, "Who's there?" Still no answer. She heard the scratching a third time. This was too much for her to stand. She had to see what was doing it; so, she opened the door. There was her roommate, lying on the hall floor all covered with blood. She had been beaten to death. She had been placed in such a position that as rigor mortis set in her fingers would curl, causing her fingernails to scratch on the door.

Source

Northeast Folklore Archive 67:004–005. The narrator, Carol Clark, a student at the University of Maine in Orono, included this legend in her folklore collection project in the spring of 1964. Explaining how she learned the story, she wrote, "This was told . . . one night before vacation, 1962. I don't remember who told it—by this time we were all too scared to remember who was telling what. Each of us was trying to out-do the other and make the group shiver a little bit more."

Commentary

This version of "The Roommate's Death" is much more dramatic than the one from the University of Western Kentucky. The narrator, Carol Clark, admits that she and the other storytellers were competing with each other to make their stories as scary as possible. Dramatic dialogue makes this story exciting, as does the gruesome discovery of fingers curled in rigor mortis, scratching against the door. Hearing this story just before vacation, the students must have shivered at the idea of such a tragedy taking place in Balentine Hall.

One interesting feature here is the combination of "The Hook" with "The Roommate's Death," proving Linda Dégh's point that "The Hook," "The Boy Friend's Death," and "The Roommate's Death" are related to each other in structure and function ("The Boy Friend's Death" 105). All three of these legends emphasize the horror of colliding with a maniac in the dark. If students follow the implicit warning to avoid dangerous situations, they can expect to stay safe.

"The Hatchet Man" (Mount Holyoke College)

The hatchet man is coming. He already killed a bunch of students at some other colleges, and now he's heading in this direction. Nobody knows where he's going, but he might be coming to a New England women's college with the initials "M" and "H." You'd better be careful riding back to your dorm alone.

Source

Personal recollection of hearing this rumor/legend at Mount Holyoke College in October 1968. A fellow student told the story on a moonless night, a week or two before Halloween. It was not easy to ride a bicycle across campus in the dark, thinking about the hatchet man.

Commentary

This pre-Halloween legend, told as true, frightened many college students in the fall of 1968. Richard Speck's murder of eight student nurses in the summer of 1966 had made Americans aware of students' vulnerability to serial killers, so legends about mass murderers on college campuses seemed credible. Tragedies such as Ted Bundy's killing of two young women at a sorority house at Florida State University in 1978 reinforced the legend's believability.

Students who have seen *Urban Legend* (1998) and other movies that parody campus killings understand the ludic nature of "hatchet man" legends, which dramatize people's fears. Back in the late 1960s, however, this legend was likely to shock and scare those who heard it.

"Aren't You Glad You Didn't Turn on the Light?" (University of Northern Colorado)

Hannah: Tanya once told me about this murder that happened at some school her friend went to in Colorado.

Joanne: Not UNC I hope.

Kara: For real.

Hannah: No, not UNC. Anyway, I don't remember exactly how it goes, but I'll try. So like, there's this girl who goes out to some party one night, but her roommate didn't feel like going out. Well, later that night the girl had to get something she had forgotten from her dorm room. She didn't want to wake her roommate so she found it in the dark. The next morning when she came home there were police all around and when she went into her room she found her roommate murdered. Then when she looked in the mirror she saw written in blood, "Aren't you glad you didn't turn on the light?"

Kara: Isn't that in the movie *Urban Legends?* (tone of disbelief)

Hannah: I never saw it.

Joanne: Me either.

Kara: Wouldn't that *freak* you out though?

Lower Lake, Mount Holyoke College. Photograph by Geoffrey Gould.

Source

"Aren't you glad you didn't turn on the light?" Paper submitted to Professor Rosemary Hathaway at the University of Northern Colorado by Katy Nellsch and Heather Tinnin in the fall of 1999. Following the student authors' wishes, pseudonyms are used for all speakers here.

Commentary

This version of "The Roommate's Death" was popular in the 1990s. The horrifying message on the mirror, written in the roommate's blood, tells the surviving young woman that she was wise not to turn on the light while the murderer was still in the room. What is the underlying moral of this legend? Is it that a female student should never bother her roommate, no matter what happens, or that she should protect herself by avoiding looking at the scene of a crime? The second alternative seems more reasonable. Living away from home, far from the protection of their families, young women learn ways to keep themselves safe.

In some versions of this legend, including the one shown in the movie *Urban Legend,* the surviving roommate refrains from turning on the light because she thinks her roommate is having sex with her boyfriend. If we compare this scenario to the earlier "Roommate's Death" stories from the 1960s, we see how much times have changed. Then again, the morality behind this sequence of events seems fairly consistent. If one roommate does nothing while the other appears to have sex, then discovers a gruesome death, both students are being punished for sanctioning sexual freedom.

Since this legend was recorded in dialogue form with three speakers, we get a much better sense of its meaning to than we would if we had only the story's core. Kara, who has seen *Urban Legend*, cannot accept Hannah's story as true. Nonetheless, it is Kara who says, "Wouldn't that *freak* you out though?" Even for sophisticated moviegoers, it is shocking to imagine finding one's own roommate in a pool of blood.

PRANKS

"Scratching in the Closet" (Michigan State University)

One girl, I heard, returned from a date to tell her roommate of her exciting experiences. Little did she know that two girls from down the hall were hiding in the closet. As she explained to her roommate that her date's father had flown her from East Lansing to Schullers in Marshall, Michigan for dinner there came some scratching on the closet door. The girl turned around and stared at the door as her roommate choked a smile. The noise stopped and the girl continued her story. The scratching began again and she flung herself around and said, "Who's in there!" No one answered so she walked to the door, not really expecting anything, and flung it open. The sight of two females placidly sitting on the floor caused her to scream and jump back two feet. It was too bad that it was in the middle of finals week, for the girl ended up with late minutes as did her roommate. The roommate couldn't stop laughing long enough to tell the angry R.A. just why she was laughing.

Source

Folklore Collection, Labor History Archive, Reuther Library, Wayne State University, Donna Newland, "College-lore," July 29, 1965.

Commentary

This text demonstrates the close relationship between legend and prank. The narrator, Donna Newland, joyfully remembers hearing this story while living in Gilchrist Hall at Michigan State, where she also heard the legend "The Roommate's Death." It seems clear that the two young women hiding in the closet, scratching on the door to frighten the roommate coming back from her exciting date, are acting out this popular legend. They are engaging in ostensive play: lighthearted re-creation of a story in dramatic form.

However, is this closet scratching just playful? It seems that the student who has stayed in her dorm, dateless, is paying her roommate back for having such an extravagantly wonderful date: a flight in a private plane, then dinner with a boyfriend. Enactment of "The Roommate's Death" reminds the returning roommate of the perils of college life. Since the killer is a man, this legend also brings to mind the dangers of male/female contact. The prank restores equilibrium, reminding the young women that none of them are impervious to horrors and dangers.

In this narrative, the resident assistant takes a quasi-parental role, angrily giving both roommates "late minutes" as a parent might "ground" a high school student. No matter how her resident assistant feels, the prank-playing roommate can't stop laughing. She has successfully fooled her roommate, and her prank will live on as a funny story.

"The Student Who Didn't Exist" (Georgia Tech)

John P. Barnett was an excellent student at Georgia Institute of Technology, but he didn't actually exist. He took all the exams; he joined a fraternity. He held an office in an organization. He was a popular student. Everyone knew John P. Barnett, but he never was a real person. A group of students supposedly registered him, paid his fees, took his exams, ran for an office for him, etc. From the time he allegedly entered Georgia Tech until he received his diploma, this group of students did everything for him that a normal college student would have done. That's why they use his name on all the sample forms at Georgia Tech.

Source

Folklore Collection, Labor History Archive, Reuther Library, Wayne State University. Donna Newland, "College-lore," July 29, 1965. Narrator: Jan Moser, 23, a student at Wayne State University who attended Georgia Institute of Technology for one year before moving to Detroit with her husband to study at Wayne State.

Commentary

Enrolling a fictitious student in college takes time and bravado. This narrator, a student at Georgia Tech, gives a fairly accurate account of what happened almost four decades before, although he gets the name and some of the details wrong. In 1927, Ed Smith received two Georgia Tech applications by mistake. Putting his cat's name on the second application, he successfully enrolled "George P. Burdell" at Georgia Tech. Friends helped George register for classes and take exams. George did so well that he graduated in three years and returned for a master's degree later on. Would such an elaborate prank be possible with modern university data systems? As recently as 1968, fictitious student Joseph Oznot attended Princeton University. Other nonexistent Princeton undergraduates have included Bert Hormone and Ephraim Di Kahble (Betterton 179). Since the Internet has become popular, some college students have experimented with creating fake students online. Sherry Turkle's *Life on the Screen* (1995) provides information about creation of fictitious identities in cyberspace (see chapter 4).

"Joke on the Janitor" (University of California at Berkeley)

Several years ago the students of the Anatomy department decided to play a joke on the janitor. They plugged several electrodes into a cadaver and left the switch at a place where the janitor will have to touch. The trick worked; that evening while the janitor was cleaning he touched the switch, and the cadaver sat up. The janitor nearly had a heart attack.

Source

Folklore Archives, University of California at Berkeley. Collected by Shirley Chin from Donald Yee, age 22, on November 6, 1979. Both the collector and the informant studied anatomy at the University of California at Berkeley.

Commentary

The student collector of this story questioned its validity but said that, since Donald had heard the story from the janitor himself, it might be true. While students would not usually expect such an event to happen in everyday life, their stories show that they want to explore the borderline between life and death. Ilana Harlow's article "Creating Situations: Practical Jokes and the Revival of the Dead in Irish Tradition" (1997) is useful for putting this story in perspective, as is Mary Shelley's *Frankenstein* (1993), in which a mad scientist brings a corpse to life by jolting it with electricity. Legends about medical students using cadavers to scare or shock people have been popular for many years. Stories about toll booth pranks in which a dead hand holds out money to a toll taker have been especially appealing. Jan H. Brunvand has traced toll booth legends back to 1939, when the chancellor of the medical school at the University of California in San Francisco got a call from a highway patrolman, saying that three students had given a cadaver hand to a toll taker on the San Francisco Bay Bridge (*Curses!* 300–301).

DRUGS

"Drugged and Seduced" (Indiana University)

Andrea: Can you tell me the story you said you heard?

Ana: Okay, I heard it from a friend of mine, and she's about one or two years younger, and we have older sisters who are about four years older and who are exactly the same age and who went through school, grade school, high school, together. And she had told me that when her sister went away to college, that her big story that she came home with, on Christmas break, was "Mom, you're not going to believe what goes on with those fraternity boys! They're awful!" You know, and she came back and had her big story about a girl down the hall, everybody heard that this girl down the hall went out with a guy, and that he had put Spanish fly in her drink, and that it was really . . . anyway, then they got into this thing about, oh, then her mother told her about how this girl had killed herself on the gearshift, and it just really got bad and she ended up leaving school because of that. She quit school.

Andrea: Did she believe that the girl had been given Spanish fly?

Ana: Yeah, she really believed it, and she said all the girls in the dorm were talking about it and she said they were all afraid to go out with those fraternity guys after that.

Andrea: What happened to the girl?

Ana: She never did find out, that was the whole thing. Everybody said this girl had it, but nobody really ever knew what happened. Everybody *knew* that this had happened to her, but nobody really wanted to ask about it. That was her freshman year, because she never finished her first year. That was four years ago.

Andrea: This girl told her sister, who told you?

Ana: Yeah, she really left school. It was the big scare of the dorm.

Andrea: Was that on this campus?

Ana: No, it was somewhere in Wisconsin. I think it was a girl's school.

Andrea: Was the girl who told you afraid something would happen to her?

Ana: Yeah, she was dating a guy in a fraternity at the time, that was the funny thing, these awful people. I can't understand why people pass these stories around.

Source

Andrea Greenberg, "Drugged and Seduced: A Contemporary Legend," *New York Folklore Quarterly* 29.2 (June 1973): 155–56. In this excerpt from the article, Andrea Greenberg interviews Ana R., a sophomore living in Foster Quadrangle who comes from East Chicago, Indiana.

Commentary

Because of Andrea Greenberg's thoroughness in presenting full interview data, we gain insight into how legends circulated among college-aged women in the early 1970s. Recreational drug usage increased on American college campuses in the late 1960s, stimulating the narration of legends about drugs. One drug that often came up in legends of the 1970s was the infamous aphrodisiac Spanish fly, rumored to make people lose all their sexual inhibitions. The most shocking story about Spanish fly is "The Girl on the Gearshift," briefly mentioned here, which Jan H. Brunvand discusses in *The Choking Doberman* (133–34).

Campus legend transmission is a complex process. As we see in this interview, legends do not just circulate among college students; they also come from parents, siblings, and friends in other places. Mothers warn their daughters to be careful; friends repeat shocking details that may cause a "big scare." Older sisters share information with their younger sisters, who use what they know to tell stories to friends in college.

What worries these young women most? Ana expresses concern about "awful" fraternity boys who may try to seduce unsuspecting female students. As Ana's story develops, it becomes clear that the worst thing imaginable is for a young woman to leave school because of sexual licentiousness caused by drugs. Emphasis on the phrases "never finished" and "quit school" shows how horrifying it is to imagine having a college education interrupted in this way. Because Ana's worry is so strong, the incident seems credible. It is only at the end of her story, after a question from her interviewer, that Ana says the incident happened "somewhere in Wisconsin," probably at a women's college. This is a typical "friend of a friend" (FOAF) story, told as if it were true.

"The Student Who Jumped Out of the Dormitory Window"
(University of California at Berkeley)

When I was a freshman here at U.C. Berkeley, I heard a story that someone had once jumped out of a seventh-story window in Ehrman Hall dormitory. I was living in Griffiths Hall dormitory at the time. One of my fellow dorm residents told me that the student, on some sort of drug, jumped out of the window and landed squarely on his back on the roof of a yellow Volkswagen. He got up, unhurt. However, the car's roof was totaled. I met a student in Spring 1987 who told me that he knew this student personally. In fact, the student was a Resident Assistant. He had taken the drug Ecstasy with some other students living on his floor. He walked out of his seventh-story window and landed on a yellow Volkswagen's roof. He was entirely unhurt by the incident. Thus the story I had heard was entirely unaltered.

Source

Folklore Archive, University of California at Berkeley. Narrated by a male student of Swiss descent on December 5, 1988.

Commentary

Between 1986 and 1988, when students at the University of California at Berkeley told this story, Ecstasy (MDMA) was a popular recreational drug. Known for its hallucinogenic properties, Ecstasy caused some alarming accidents on college campuses.

One of this legend's focal points is the roof of a yellow Volkswagen. In a legend unrelated to college campuses, "The Elephant That Sat on the VW," an elephant gets up on the roof of a small red car, mistaking it for the stool in its circus act (Brunvand, *Choking Doberman* 58–61). Such a mistake is amusing and unusual. This campus legend about a student landing on a Volkswagen's roof is also entertaining because the student is "entirely unhurt"; only the car's roof is damaged.

It should be noted, however, that many stories of students' jumps from dormitory windows have a darker tone. At Indiana University in the late 1970s, students living in the 14-story building for graduate students told stories about a student jumping out a window and falling through the roof of the first floor. This story and others remind the listener that stress may lead to suicide attempts.

"Midnight Yell" (University of California at Los Angeles)

During finals week, UCLA students would wait until about midnight. Then, one by one, they would each open their windows and start to scream. It was a great stress reliever, from all the quiet time during the day. The entire campus was to have silent time for a week during the finals period, except for a two-hour reprieve.

One morning during the winter final period, in 1991, the student newspaper read: "Co-ed raped during midnight yell." It told of how one of the ladies was viciously raped after taking a "roofie" drug during the midnight scream two nights before, and no one cared about her screams for help because everyone thought she was just fooling around, letting off stress, like everyone else. To this day, anyone screaming unnecessarily during finals week at UCLA is subject to expulsion from campus.

Source

Narrated by Christopher Ivey, a 19-year-old college student from Bronx, New York, on November 3, 2004. His story was collected by Kerri Johnson, a student at Binghamton University.

Commentary

In the 1990s and the early twenty-first century, roofies (Rohypnol) became known as date-rape drugs. Documented incidents of roofies slipped into drinks in bars blended with legends about horrific drug-related events. In many cases, it was difficult to separate legend from reality. In England, for example, many students have heard stories about roofies, but few have seen evidence of the drug's effects. A documentary by the British Broadcasting Corporation in the fall of 2004 attempted to separate legend from reality, with limited success.

The midnight yell at UCLA is one of many campus traditions for relieving stress at exam time (Bronner 37–38). At the University of California at Berkeley, students shout "Pedro," the name of a dog that was allegedly lost many years ago. Students at many universities, including Franklin and Marshall, have screamed or chanted at midnight (Brubaker 46). Usually, midnight noisemaking serves as a harmless stress reliever, but the legend about a rapist using roofies suggests that the campus is not a safe place when students yell. Of course, the rule that anyone screaming during finals week will be expelled has as much validity as the "suicide rule" that a student whose roommate commits suicide will get a 4.0 average for the semester.

AIDS

"Welcome to the World of AIDS"

This is a true story about this girl, a college student from upstate, who went with her friends to Daytona Beach for spring break a couple years ago. So while they were there they were having fun, and she met this really great guy. And during the whole break, they spent all their time together. He was really great, and she felt like she was falling in love. He did all these really nice things for her, and they would make really passionate love, and he seemed to really care about her. So when it was time to go, she was really upset, but you know, he gave her a kiss and said something like "I had a wonderful time with you, and I want you to have this present so you can always remember me." And he gave her this beautifully wrapped present, and she was crying. And he told her not to open it until she was on the plane. So they said goodbye one last time, and she went on to the plane. And she did as he told her, she waited until he was on the plane, and then she unwrapped the present. And it was a little black box, and she opened the box, and inside the box was a note that said "Welcome to the World of AIDS."

Source

Collected from a female member of the junior class at Binghamton University by a female friend who lived in the same residence hall in December 1994.

Commentary

In the 1980s, the AIDS epidemic started a wave of campus legends. College students, already handling the complexities of dating, had to deal with the threat of a life-threatening sexually transmitted disease. Before the outbreak of the AIDS epidemic, students knew of other sexually transmitted diseases: syphilis, gonorrhea, and herpes, among others. While all these other diseases were worrisome, none were as horrifying as AIDS.

In *Once upon a Virus* (2004), Diane E. Goldstein identifies subtypes of the "Welcome to the World of AIDS" legend that have swept college campuses. According to Goldstein, the story of an innocent young woman getting AIDS from a stranger on vacation began to circulate actively in the early 1990s Goldstein discusses a legend told by a college student in 1991 that differs from the previous one in one interesting way: on opening her gift, the girl finds a little coffin (100–101).

In this story, as in many other college horror legends, the victim is female. The setting is Daytona Beach during spring break, a week of freedom from academic work when students can enjoy going to parties in exotic locations. At first, this seems like a story of typical spring break enjoyment ("they were having fun"), but the entrance of a "really great guy" marks the beginning of a passionate love affair. Swept off her feet by this dazzling young man, the female college student thinks he really loves her. Her high hopes are cruelly replaced by sorrow when she receives a gift from him: a black box with a terrifying message.

"Welcome to the World of AIDS" is a Cinderella story in reverse. A young woman meets her handsome prince, then discovers that he brings her doom.

This death-dealing young man is a descendant of the folk ballad's demon lover, who seduces a young woman, then causes her death. The title of a popular TV show, *The Wonderful World of Disney*, shown between 1954 and 1990, may have influenced this legend's title. Another tradition that can be recognized here is the story of a "dark, dark box" from oral tradition, popular among American children.

Ironic reference to an enchanted folktale milieu is emphasized in the title of Goldstein's *Once upon a Virus*. For college students, this irony seems especially cruel. On spring break, full of hopes and dreams, one young woman meets a man who will blight her life forever. With roots in real tragedy, this legend warns students to think before leaping into disastrous relationships with strangers. It also suggests that the fabled freedom of spring break is not as marvelous as it might seem.

FOOD

"You'll Never Eat Fast Food Again!" (University of Nevada at Las Vegas)

This girl was really in a hurry one day she just stopped off at Taco Bell and got a chicken soft taco and ate it on the way home. Well, that night she noticed her jaw was kind of tight and swollen. The next day it was a little worse, so she went to her doctor. He said she was just having an allergic reaction to something and gave her some cream to rub on her jaw to help.

After a couple of days the swelling had just gotten worse and she could hardly move her jaw. She went back to her doctor to see what was wrong. Her doctor had no idea so he started to run some tests. They scrubbed out the inside of her mouth to get tissue samples and they also took some saliva samples. Well, they found out what was wrong.

Apparently her chicken soft taco had a pregnant roach in it!!! The eggs then somehow got into her saliva glands and, well, she was incubating them. They had to remove a couple layers of her inner mouth to get all the eggs out. If they hadn't figured out what was going on, the eggs would have hatched inside the lining of her mouth!!!

She's suing Taco Bell!

Source

Narrated by a 19-year-old male student at the University of Nevada at Las Vegas. Collected by Paul Lee, a student at Binghamton University, through e-mail on September 15, 2004.

Commentary

Busy college students often grab fast food on their way to class. This legend dramatizes students' fear of contamination from impersonally prepared food. Invasion of the body by insects brings to mind Upton Sinclair's *The Jungle* (1946), which graphically describes how insects, rodents, and other contaminants affect mass production. Jan H. Brunvand documents the urban food legend about spider eggs in Bubble Yum in *The Vanishing Hitchhiker* (89–90).

Medical details, especially "allergic reaction," "tissue samples," and "saliva samples," make this legend sound authentic. Suspense builds as the doctor, who has no idea what is wrong with the girl, runs some tests and discovers a "pregnant roach" in her mouth. Pregnancy seems even more frightening here than contamination from the roach. The female college student narrowly misses giving birth from her mouth: "If they hadn't figured out what was going on the eggs would have hatched inside the lining of her mouth!!!" The fact that this student is female, not male, clinches the story's meaning as a warning against both premarital sex and careless consumption of fast food.

The last line, "She's suing Taco Bell!," has become a classic conclusion for food contamination legends. Even though the student has suffered pain and humiliation, she can look forward to some reassuring financial gain.

"Genetically Manipulated Organisms" (University of New Hampshire)

During a recent study done at the University of New Hampshire, they found some interesting facts regarding the "chicken" at KFC. The company seemed to have changed their name from Kentucky Fried Chicken to just the initials KFC. At first it was thought this was because of the diet fad that discouraged people from purchasing fast foods, but the real reason it is being referred to as KFC is because they cannot legally use the word "chicken" any more.

KFC seemingly does not use real chickens. Instead, they use genetically manipulated organisms. The meat is kept alive by pushing tubes through their bodies to pump in blood and nutrients. They do not have beaks, feathers, or feet. The bone structure is reduced to make room for more meat. KFC benefits greatly from this because they do not need to pay to remove beaks, feathers, or feet. The US government has ordered KFC to change their menus so that nothing says "chicken" on it and the same with their commercials.

Source

Narrated by a 20-year-old female student at Binghamton University. Collected by Erik Dienna, a student at Binghamton University, on September 15, 2004.

Commentary

One of the best-known food horror legends is the story of the "Kentucky Fried Rat," described in detail by Jan Brunvand in *The Vanishing Hitchhiker* (81–84). This more recent legend focuses on corporate fraud and profit-mongering rather than on an individual's discovery of a disgusting deep-fried rat.

Referring to a study at the University of New Hampshire, the teller of this legend makes her story sound authentic. Phrases such as "genetically manipulated organisms" and "pump blood and nutrients" may convince the listener that the story is true. Public concern about food companies' efforts to save money may also make this story more believable. However, the idea of beakless, featherless, footless chickens seems exaggerated and unlikely. In fact, Kentucky Fried Chicken changed its name in 1991 because it wanted to highlight healthful, nonfried foods and to streamline its image. For more details on this subject, see the "Urban Legends Reference Page: Lost Legends" (http://www.snopes.com/lost/kfc.htm).

This story offers a nightmarish vision of the future. Will food production become as impersonal and mechanistic as the baby production line in Aldous Huxley's *Brave New World*? Studying and preparing to enter the workforce, college students must come to terms with people's fears of what the future will bring.

"Never Ask for Pizza Delivery" (University of California at Berkeley)

When I was living in Freeborn Hall at the Unit 1 dorms in my freshman year, 1996–97, I was told to never ask any of the local pizza parlors to deliver the pizza. This was because the deliverymen, who hate their jobs and having to walk to the dorms, would spit in the pizzas. I was also told that you could even see the white spit glob sitting on the pizza. Raj, an Indian junior who I was friends with at the time, told me this. I completely believed him and for the next year I would check my pizza for any signs of deliveryman spit. I finally stopped when I realized that I never saw anything. This story was passed along to any student living in the Units, regardless of age, gender, or ethnicity.

I also heard this story from two mutual friends, Eyal (a Jewish student) and Steven (a Chinese student from Texas), who also lived in Freeborn Hall. All three boys insisted that the story was true and avoided getting delivery whenever possible. It is true that delivering pizza to the dorms is a hassle because the delivery men would have to walk to the location rather than drive, call the person who ordered the pizza on the call box outside of the dorm, and then wait outside until the student came out to pay him. It would not surprise me at all to know that the deliverymen don't like delivering to the dorms. Also, the pizza places near the dorms serve extremely greasy pizza, so I think that someone may have mistaken a large blob of grease as a blob of spit.

However, since students are telling the legend about the deliverymen, I would say that the students do not like the deliverymen very much either. These deliverymen tend to have grungy appearances and to be large and strong looking. The perfect type to intimidate and scare any college freshman away from home for the first time. So it would not be hard to imagine a student believing that these men would actually spit in the pizza just to get revenge on the students for hassling them. Therefore, this story is the student's revenge on the pizza places and the deliverymen.

Source

Folklore Archive, University of California at Berkeley. Narrated by Kimberly Cunningham, a 20-year-old student at Berkeley, on October 25, 1998.

Commentary

Like "fast-food" legends, college stories about pizzerias question the safety of food from local restaurants. This student's self-collected legend about deliverymen spitting on pizzas reveals a certain amount of "town/gown" antagonism: deliverymen have "grungy appearances" and are "large and strong looking." This legend teller checks her pizza slices for spit, then eventually decides that she shouldn't worry. She shows some empathy toward those who deliver pizzas on campus—"It would not surprise me at all to know that the deliverymen don't like delivering to the dorms"—but suspicion overrides her fellow-feeling.

The student storyteller makes an important point: "this story is the student's revenge on the pizza places and the deliverymen." If dormitory residents stop ordering pizzas, local businesses' profits will go down. However, this narrative does not give us the impression that ordering will stop. Pizza is a college staple; it takes more than a local food legend to slow its delivery down.

"Ex-Lax in a Burger" (James Madison University)

In the cafeteria at my school, someone ate a burger that had so much Ex-Lax in it that they were in their room/on the toilet for two days. When he finally came out of his room, his roommate and suitemates had gone to sleep in their other friends' rooms and everyone on the floor had hung air fresheners outside their door.

Source

Narrated by a 19-year-old male student at James Madison University. Collected by Stephanie Holleran, a student at Binghamton University, through e-mail on September 7, 2004.

Commentary

As Simon J. Bronner explains in *Piled Higher and Deeper,* stories about colleges putting additives in students' food are deeply embedded in college folklore (189). Most commonly, these stories say that saltpeter or other aphrodisiacs in the food decrease students' sex drive; they also suggest that strategically added laxatives aid in digestion of bad food. Another complaint is that the college has deliberately added starch or another fattening ingredient so that the students will become fat and unattractive.

In this brief legend, the poor student who ate an Ex-Lax burger suffers for two days, either on the toilet or alone in his room. By the time he comes out, he discovers that his roommate and suitemates have gone to sleep elsewhere and that all the other students on the floor have hung up air fresheners. This is "fartlore" at its most extreme: both humbling and hilarious. Students who hear this legend can only hope they will continue to be the ones who laugh, not victims of such embarrassing discomfort.

"Soup Every Night" (Chinese University of Hong Kong)

I was in Chinese University of Hong Kong in one dorm, they separate girls and boys on alternate floors, there was a couple, the girl lived exactly above the boy, they were very good, but as the exam was coming, the boy studied very hard and didn't hang out with her so every night, the girl cooked soup and delivered the soup through the window (imagine fishing here) the girl used a rope to tie the bowl and then the boy got it downstairs after the exam, the boy wanted to find the girl but couldn't and people told him that his girlfriend died, he didn't believe them because he received soup every night and then when he went back to the dorm, he found that those soup materials were the girl's eyes and hair.

Source

Narrated by a 23-year-old alumna of the Chinese University. Collected by Beatrice Yung, a student at Binghamton University, through Instant Messenger in March 2004.

Commentary

Some food horror legends qualify as ghost stories. In this text, the devoted girlfriend's special soup turns out to be made of her own eyeballs and hair after her death. Why would a dead woman send such terrible soup to the man she loves? Clearly such a dish violates the taboo against eating human flesh, which is the mainspring of the slumber party story "The Stolen Liver"(A-T 366). To break this taboo, the female student must have a good reason. The most likely explanation seems to be that she is angry because her boyfriend, whom she loves very much, has neglected her while studying for exams, not even noticing her illness and death. He seems interested only in getting food from his girlfriend, and he gets it—at a terrible price.

Another way to interpret this legend is to see the girlfriend's soup making as devotion that outlasts death. Even though she is no longer alive, she persists in making soup for her boyfriend from the only ingredients available to her: parts of her own body. Chinese folklore of the supernatural includes a wide range of angry and devoted ghosts. This ghost expresses both traditions.

PROFESSORS

"The Sixth Step" (University of California at Los Angeles)

On the campus of UCLA there stands one of the original buildings high up on a hill. Years ago, when the college was first constructed, one of the custodians was known by all the students and was very well liked. However, one professor thought this custodian was playing around with his wife, and this made him very angry. One night the professor went back to the school and shot the custodian. The next day the custodian was found dead on the sixth step entering that building. Since then, no student steps on the sixth step going in or out of that building. If someone does, it is believed that this student will fail all of his courses for that semester.

Source

Narrated by a 19-year-old female student at the University of California at Los Angeles in April 1978.

Commentary

This legend about a jealous, vengeful professor fulfilled an initiatory function at UCLA in the late 1970s. The narrator, a freshman, heard the story during her first semester on campus. Since "The Sixth Step" tells of the university's early days, it is an origin legend as well as a shocking account of a professor's behavior.

Two polarities emerge here. One is "town/gown" tension between academics and townspeople, well documented since the Battle of Saint Scholastica's Day at Oxford in 1534. The other involves contrasting priorities of professors and students. Even though the custodian is "very well liked" by students, the angry professor does not hesitate to kill him. The last two lines of this story drive home its main point. If students dare to step on the place where the professor killed the custodian, they will fail all their courses for the semester. Just as one professor murdered a custodian, others can inflict "academic murder" on a student who steps out of line.

"Smarties" (Duke University)

My cousin told me about an incident that happened a few years before he was a freshman at Duke University. He said that one of the Chemistry professors and one of his students were involved in an affair. The girl's ex-boyfriend, who was the captain of the football team, was also in the class. He found out from rumors that the relationship existed, and jealousy overcame him. He confronted the two of them at the teacher's apartment and threatened to expose the affair if they didn't stop.

The next day, the football player was eating candy (I believe they were Smarties), and unbeknownst to him the professor had slipped cyanide pills into the package. Upon consumption, the mouth eroded and blood-curdling screams were let out. The entire class saw the football player crumple to the ground and lie limp. To this day, in that chemistry lab, his screams can be heard on the first Thursday of every month at his desk.

Source

Narrated by a 19-year-old female student in New York City on November 15, 2001.

Commentary

Like the professor in the previous text, this one seems sex crazed and ruthless. When the ex-boyfriend of the student with whom the professor is having an affair threatens to tell others, the professor cleverly slips cyanide pills into a bag of candy, causing a gruesome death. The candy's name, "Smarties," seems ironic. If this professor and his students followed their intellects instead of their libidos, the tragedy would not take place. Another contemporary legend, "The Death of Little Mikey," tells of a boy dying when Pop Rocks and soda explode in his stomach (Brunvand, *Choking Doberman* 103–6). Although "Smarties" is about young adults, its focus on eating candy reminds the reader that students are quite young and vulnerable to the ploys of a professor who has chosen not to nurture and guide them.

Like many other college ghost stories, this one ends with recurrent screams (motif E402.1.1.3, "Ghost cries and screams"). Because the professor's crime is so heinous, it will never be forgotten.

"Bluebooks in the Cornfield" (Colorado College)

In the old days at Colorado College, more people went back East for summer vacation. Some professors from the East Coast took jobs in Colorado Springs because its climate was so good for people with lung disease. After recovering, they could go home for long vacations.

This one professor hated grading bluebooks and would take them home with him on the train when the spring semester ended. When they had been traveling for a while, he would go out to the observation platform and happily throw the bluebooks to the winds.

One day the train was going through the cornfield of someone who was in the professor's class, and a student found his own bluebook, along with some others. None of the bluebooks had grades on them. The student reported what he'd found to the college authorities. Certainly the professor would never have reported it in any way. The dean would not have been pleased to hear that bluebooks had been found in a cornfield, with no grades whatsoever.

Source

Narrated by Frank H. Tucker, Professor Emeritus of History at Colorado College, on February 4, 2004.

Commentary

Told at Colorado College since the early 1960s, probably earlier as well, this legend describes a professor who cares very little about his students' work. On his train trip East for summer vacation, the professor "happily throw(s) the bluebooks to the winds." Unfortunately, a student finds his own ungraded bluebook in his family's cornfield. Once the student reports the professor to the college authorities, everyone knows what a careless, indifferent grader he is.

Bluebooks scattered in a cornfield. Photograph by Geoffrey Gould.

This story belongs to a legend cycle about professors who grade strangely (Toelken 319–21; Bronner 138–39). These legends reflect students' curiosity about how professors grade exams and papers. Do professors read students' work carefully, or do they assign grades arbitrarily? Legends like "Bluebooks in the Cornfield" dramatize the grading process, making it both amusing and ridiculous.

"Absentminded Professor" (University of Saskatchewan)

I'm told also that one rainy day Dr. Lightbody—he apparently had the habit of, quite a bit of the time at any rate, reading a book as he walked down the street. Which is a pretty hazardous pastime, especially if you're crossing College Drive. But he went out one morning, a rainy day, and already his book was open and he was reading it as he went out the door. This is the story that is told. It *may* be apocryphal. I don't know. And there was an umbrella stand at the front door which contained not only umbrellas but also contained Dr. Lightbody's cane. And Dr. Lightbody allegedly was seen walking down University Drive headed for the campus reading a book in the pouring rain and holding a cane over his head. And not even aware that he was getting wet. That's the kind of single-minded scholar that man was.

Source

Michael Taft, *Inside These Greystone Walls: An Anecdotal History of the University of Saskatchewan.* Saskatoon: University of Saskatchewan, 1984. 174–75.

Commentary

This amusing legend from the University of Saskatchewan describes Professor Lightbody, a local character whose name epitomizes his disregard of bodily needs. Unaware that he is getting wet or that he might get hit by a car, Professor Lightbody saunters down the street, reading a book and holding his cane over his head. Through this odd set of actions, he exemplifies two of the main characteristics of absentminded professors: obliviousness to the environment and confusion in identifying familiar things. Both of these bring to mind the traditional motif J2040, "Absurd absent-mindedness."

Although Professor Lightbody makes people laugh, he also represents the seriousness of academic work. The story's last line, "That's the kind of single-minded scholar that man was," offers unqualified admiration. Even if a professor behaves strangely, his fierce attention to intellectual issues commands respect.

EXAMS

"Why Not?" (Gonzaga University)

At Gonzaga University, there was a philosophy professor who was noted for long and boring lectures as well as long, meaningless explanations. On the final exam, the professor asked the question, "Why?" The "A" response: Why not." The "B" response: "Because." All other responses received "C's or "D's."

Source

Folklore Archive, University of California at Berkeley. Collected by Frank Motta, a 21-year-old student at Berkeley, from James Willis, a 44-year-old English teacher in Livermore, California, on November 5, 1988. Willis told the collector that he learned this legend from a philosophy major at Gonzaga University in Spokane, Washington, in September 1966.

Commentary

Ever since universities began, students have speculated about professors' exam questions. This legend offers an intriguing set of answers to a deceptively simple question, "Why?" Only the students who write "Why not?" get As, winning respect for their independent thinking. At first glance, this story just seems to be one of many campus legends about strange professors asking unusual questions. However, it is important to recognize that the story teaches students to think carefully about the kinds of answers they write. Sometimes, concise answers may succeed better than long academic diatribes.

"I Cram" (Mount Holyoke College)

Years ago, when a Mount Holyoke student was getting ready for exam week, she started embroidering a huge sampler in many colors of thread. The words on her sampler were "I cram for the damn exam." All through exam week, she put more and more fancy stitches into the sampler. It looked beautiful, with bright colors and an amazing variety of stitches. But because she was working so hard on her sampler, she didn't have any time to study. She flunked all her exams and had to leave school at the end of the semester.

Source

Personal recollection of storytelling during exam week at Mount Holyoke College in the spring of 1967.

Commentary

This story warns students not to distract themselves from studying by doing extra projects. It also shows that reliance on cramming—rapid learning of course material for an exam—can lead to academic disaster. In 1837, Mary Lyon founded Mount Holyoke Female Seminary. Previously, daughters of relatively prosperous families in the Northeast had had more limited educational opportunities, including lessons in needlework, china painting, dancing, and French. It is interesting that the student in this story avoids studying for exams by doing embroidery, once a normative activity for women of her age-group. Perhaps she finds comfort in doing the kind of sewing with which women of an earlier generation proved their artistic competence.

"I cram for the damn exam" parodies the words on traditional New England samplers, most of which show respect for religion and duty. Since tension runs high during exam week, students who hear this legend can enjoy its comic relief.

"The Cast Cheaters" (Wayne State University)

I first heard this legend at Wayne State University in Detroit, Michigan, in 1987. I was in Anthro 101 with Professor Berniece Kaplan, who told us this legend.

We were all in class about to take the midterm. Professor Kaplan was especially worried about people cheating n the test, so she was organizing us into rows so that everyone was evenly spaced and couldn't look on their neighbor's paper. While she was doing this she told us a story about two students in another professor's class at Wayne State. She said that two young men came into a final exam a few years before, one with an arm cast and the other with a head cast. Neither of these students had a cast before that day. It turned out that the casts were wired with hidden microphones that they were communicating with during the test, in order to cheat. This was a very complicated method of cheating. The telling of the story seemed to come from the professor's anxiety and worry about her students cheating.

Source

Folklore Archive, University of California at Berkeley. Narrated by Jennifer Ohno, a 19-year-old Japanese American student at Berkeley, on September 18, 1988.

Commentary

As the teller of this story points out, legends like this one express anxiety about exam taking. They also convey a warning: don't plan to cheat because you may get caught.

The "cast cheaters" entertain the reader or listener because their method of cheating is so elaborate. If they spent as much time studying as preparing casts with microphones, they would not need to cheat on the exam. This kind of irony is common in legends about beating the system. Did this incident actually happen, or did the story grow from professors' eagerness to warn their students not to cheat? While it is difficult to know for sure, the story's familiar time frame of "a few years before" makes it recognizable as a campus legend.

"Do You Know Who I Am?" (University of California at Berkeley)

Peter Jennings, while in college, was taking a large lecture course. When the professor announced that the time for the test was over, Jennings continued to work on his test. The professor then threatened to fail anyone who did not turn in their test immediately. Jennings ignored the professor and continued writing in his exam.

The professor then told Jennings that he would not accept Jennings' test and began to pack up the other tests to walk out of the lecture hall. Jennings then ran up to the professor to turn in his test, but the professor refused. Jennings then asked the professor in a condescending and threatening voice, "Do you know who I am?" The professor replied, "No." Jennings then said, "Good." He stuck his exam somewhere in the middle of the pile of exams that the professor was holding and walked out of the lecture hall.

Source

Folklore Archive, University of California at Berkeley. Narrated by Tina Yu, a 21-year-old Chinese-American student at Berkeley, on December 1, 1995.

Commentary

During the 1990s, this legend was very popular on American college campuses. Its central character is a tricky student who, by using a "condescending and threatening" voice, outwits a professor who has threatened to flunk anyone who refuses to obey. In this satisfying and humorous role reversal, the student takes charge of a difficult situation. Most variants of "Do You Know Who I Am?" feature an unnamed student, but this one identifies the rebel as Peter Jennings, the famous television news anchor for ABC. With his celebrity status, Jennings seems ideal for this role, but he dropped out of high school and started a successful career without attending college.

Some college lecture classes are so large that professors cannot know all their students' names. While this legend highlights the impersonality of a large class, it also shows that anonymity has its advantages.

WORKS CITED

Bergland, Renée. *The National Uncanny: Indian Ghosts and American Subjects.* Hanover: University Press of New England, 2000.

Betterton, Don. *Alma Mater: Unusual and Little-Known Facts from America's College Campuses.* Princeton: Peterson's Guides, 1988.

Bronner, Simon J. *Piled Higher and Deeper: The Folklore of Student Life.* Little Rock: August House, 1995.

Brubaker, John H., III. *Hullabaloo Nevonia: An Anecdotal History of Student Life at Franklin and Marshall College.* Lancaster: Franklin and Marshall College, 1987.

Brunvand, Jan H. *The Choking Doberman.* New York: Norton, 1984.

———. *Curses! Broiled Again!* New York: Norton, 1989.

———. *The Vanishing Hitchhiker.* New York: Norton, 1981.

Carmer, Carl. *Dark Trees to the Wind: A Cycle of York State Years.* New York: William Sloane Associates, 1949.

Christiansen, Reidar T. *The Migratory Legends.* Folklore Fellows Communications 175. Helsinki: Suomalainen Tiedeakatemia, 1958.

Colby, C. B., et al. *The Little Giant Book of "True" Ghostly Tales.* New York: Sterling Publishing, 2002.

Dégh, Linda. "The Boy Friend's Death." *Indiana Folklore* 1.1 (1968): 101–6.

———. "Speculations about 'The Hook.'" *Folklore Forum* 24.2 (1991): 68–76.

Dundes, Alan. "On the Psychology of Legend." *American Folk Legend: A Symposium.* Ed. Wayland D. Hand. Berkeley: University of California Press, 1971. 21–36

Ellis, Bill. *Aliens, Ghosts, and Cults: Legends We Live.* Jackson: University Press of Mississippi, 2003.

———. "Why 'The Hook' Is Not a Contemporary Legend." *Folklore Forum* 24.2 (1991): 62–67.

Fish, Lydia M. "Jesus on the Thruway: The Vanishing Hitchhiker Strikes Again." *Indiana Folklore* 9.1 (1976): 5–13.

Goldstein, Diane E. *Once upon a Virus: AIDS Legends and Vernacular Risk Perception.* Logan: Utah State University Press, 2004.

Greenberg, Andrea. "Drugged and Seduced: A Contemporary Legend." *New York Folklore Quarterly* 29.2 (1973): 131–58.

Grider, Sylvia. "Dormitory Legend-Telling in Progress: Fall, 1971–Winter, 1973. *Indiana Folklore* 6.1 (1973): 1–32.

Harlow, Ilana. "Creating Situations: Practical Jokes and the Revival of the Dead in Irish Tradition. *Journal of American Folklore* 110.436 (1997): 140–68.

Hauk, Gary. "Lord of Misrule: The Spirit of Emory Turns 100." *EM: Emory Magazine,* Winter 2000 <http://www.emory.edu/EMORY_Magazine/Winter2000/cover.html>.

Huxley, Aldous. *Brave New World.* New York: Harper and Brothers, 1946.

Lavergne, Gary. *Sniper in the Tower: The Charles Whitman Murders.* Denton: University of North Texas Press, 1997.

Shelley, Mary. *Frankenstein.* New York: Bantam Books, 1991.

Sinclair, Upton. *The Jungle.* Cambridge: R. Bentley, 1971 (1946).

Stohlman, Martha Lou Lemmon. *The Story of Sweet Briar College.* Sweet Briar: Sweet Briar College, 1956.

Taft, Michael. *Inside These Greystone Walls: An Anecdotal History of the University of Saskatchewan.* Saskatoon: University of Saskatchewan, 1984.

Thomas, Jeannie B. "Pain, Pleasure and the Spectral: The Barfing Ghost of Burford Hall." *Folklore Forum* 24.2 (1991): 27–38.

Toelken, Barre. "The Folklore of Academe." *The Study of American Folklore: An Introduction.* Ed. Jan H. Brunvand. New York: Norton, 1968. 317–37.

Four

Scholarship and Approaches

NORDIC SCHOLARS

Toward the end of the nineteenth century, folklore scholars in Scandinavia began to develop the historic-geographic method. The goal of this method was to trace narratives back through time and space, determining where and how they originated. By collecting and studying as many variants of a text as they could find, these researchers tried to determine the text's original form (*Urform*) and place of origin. This was a difficult process because, while some tale texts were available, many others were not. Scholars' efforts to re-create a tale's life history yielded much important data, but it was impossible to learn all the twists and turns of a narrative's development.

A crucial contribution from advocates of the historic-geographic method was the insistence on complete, accurate texts: not just summaries or retellings but careful transcriptions of orally transmitted stories, including dates of collection and information about storytellers (age, gender, and storytelling experience, among other facts). Previously, collectors of oral narratives had not felt compelled to record texts exactly as they heard them. In collecting their *Kinder- und Hausmärchen* (Children's and Household Tales), Jacob and Wilhelm Grimm took notes, wrote drafts, then extensively revised the drafts to give their collection an appealing, consistent style. After the historic-geographic method took root, folklore collectors cared much more about careful and accurate transcription.

One of the best-known proponents of the historic-geographic method was the Finnish scholar Kaarle Krohn, whose father, Julius Krohn, had tried to establish the origin and life history of each part of Finland's national epic,

The Kalevala. Making a similar attempt to document the derivation of Finnish folktales about the fox and the bear, Kaarle Krohn demonstrated how much could be learned from close scrutiny of individual tale texts. As the first professor of folklore at the University of Helsinki, he significantly influenced the work of other researchers.

Another Finnish scholar, Antti Aarne, made an important contribution to the field of folklore by writing the first comparative index, *The Types of the Folktale* (*Verzeichnis der Marchentypen* 1910). This index, published by the Folklore Fellows, set the pattern for future indexing. In partnership with the American folklorist Stith Thompson, Aarne published revised, enlarged editions of *The Types of the Folktale* in 1928 and 1960. Later, Thompson edited the six-volume *Motif-Index of Folk Literature* (1966): an ambitious project that made it possible for scholars to study motifs in a cross-cultural context.

Swedish folklorist Carl Wilhelm von Sydow laid the foundation for future legend study by defining important concepts and terms. His distinction between the memorate (a narrative about personal experience) and the fabulate (a clearly fictional narrative) helped folklorists envision the legend's parameters. In addition to defining the legend, von Sydow introduced the term "oikotype" (regional type). He also explained the difference between active bearers of folk tradition, who shared texts with others, and passive bearers, who knew some material but, for one reason or another, chose not to share it. Understanding the importance of both passive and active bearers helped researchers learn about legend transmission (60–85).

In the late 1950s and early 1960s, two significant legend indexes were published. The first, by the Norwegian scholar Reidar T. Christiansen, was *The Migratory Legends* (1958). This study of Norwegian legends circulating internationally showed how much could be learned by careful documentation of available texts. The second, by the Finnish scholar Lauri Simonsuuri, was *Typen und Motivverzeichnis der finnischen mythischen Sagen* (Type and Motif Index of Finnish Mythological Legends, 1961), which classified texts in the Archive of the Finnish Literature Society. Both indexes encouraged scholars to undertake more systematic and thorough study of the legend, which had, at that point, received less scholarly attention than the folktale.

These early compilations of folk legends did not focus specifically on college campuses. The first Nordic scholars did their research and teaching at universities but did not view their workplaces as distinctive environments for legend telling. That realization came later when collectors in the United States made their first forays into the field of academic folklore.

EARLY COLLECTIONS

In 1944, Rosalie Hankey wrote that college campuses hold "a large mass of true folklore largely unnoticed and unstudied" (29). Hankey enjoyed reading legends that students at the University of California at Berkeley collected. Before publishing her article on campus folklore, she coauthored, with Richard K. Beardsley, the first study of "The Vanishing Hitchhiker" (1943). Her sensitive observation of legend-telling patterns showed what treasures could be found in the academic community.

Hankey's essay on campus folklore distinguishes the "widely diffused folktale" from "folklore of small, isolated communities" (29). Characteristics of both kinds of folklore, Hankey says, appear in campus stories. She uses the term "floating legend" for narratives that migrate from place to place. Stories about "Pedro!," a cry of distress during finals week at the University of California at Berkeley, illustrate how local legends can belong to a migratory legend pattern. Pedro has been identified as a lost dog, a lost freshman pledge, a lonely man from the Philippines, and a donkey, among other explanations. Tracing Pedro stories back to their earliest apparent sources, Hankey suggests that they started in 1931 or 1932. She compares the "Pedro!" cry to "Reinhardt!" at Harvard, "Rowbotham!" at the University of Pennsylvania, and "Pigger!" at the University of Oregon. She also briefly discusses seasonal student celebrations, such as the "Spring Riot" at the University of Illinois and "Storm" at the University of Georgia.

In 1949, Richard M. Dorson's "The Folklore of Colleges" introduced readers of the *American Mercury* to a representative sample of college narratives. Some texts describe absentminded professors like Albert Bushnell Hart at Harvard, who, when giving a speech, carefully read all the pages his secretary had prepared for him, including two carbon copies. Other stories tell of surprising examinations, unusual grading practices, and cheating. The "dumb star athlete" and the clever coach are popular characters. Dorson explains that Adolph Rupp, the "wizard basketball coach at the University of Kentucky," would screen candidates for his team by checking to see whether they could walk through the six-foot-tall door without stooping. If a student didn't stoop, the coach would not shake his hand (673–74).

Dorson's enthusiastic presentation of college folklore encouraged others to collect campus stories. He explained, "The enterprising folklorist doesn't need to journey into the back hills to scoop up tradition. He can set up his recording machine in the smoke shop or the college grill" (677). Although such encouragement hardly seems necessary now, it was important in those days, when many scholars thought folklore should be collected from country people without access to higher education.

Benjamin Earl Washburn's "College Folklore at Chapel Hill in the Early 1900s" (1955) gives the reader a glimpse of southern students' stories. Although Washburn was not trained as a folklorist, he remembered many stories, songs, and rituals from his years at the University of North Carolina at Chapel Hill (class of 1906). One story describes Dr. Thomas Hume, a "classroom martinet" who always wore a stovepipe hat and a cutaway coat. What annoyed him most was students chewing and spitting tobacco. Once, catching a male student spitting tobacco, Dr. Hume held out his stovepipe hat, saying, "If you must chew tobacco and spit in this room, spit into my hat." Soon all the young men in the classroom filled his hat with fragrant tobacco juice (28).

Although Washburn's article covers a variety of campus folklore, many of his reminiscences pertain to freshman initiation. He recalls upperclassmen taking freshmen on snipe hunts (hunts for animals that do not exist) behind the "Stiff House" that contained the Medical School's cadavers. Another task for freshmen was to call on Dr. Hume and ask him for a quart of "Cream of Kentucky." This, the upperclassmen explained, meant cream from Kentucky, Dr. Hume's Jersey cow. Unfortunately for the freshmen, Dr. Hume had no such cow and was a dedicated prohibitionist. "Cream of Kentucky" was the name of a popular brand of whiskey.

Alfred B. Rollins's "College Folklore" (1961) explains how students subvert official rules and expectations. Rollins notes that "college folklore, at large, tends to poke fun at authority and establishes the student's prestige over an inevitably halting administration and blind faculty" (164). He offers many descriptions of pranks, including early Harvard students' threats to burn down the president's house, their destruction of the rope used to ring the university's bell, and their treatment of drinking water with laxatives on examination mornings. One of the most intriguing stories tells of female students at a large university using a utilities tunnel to escape from dormitory restrictions for an entire year. Like Henri Charriere's book *Papillon* (1971), which recounts an escape from prison at Devil's Island, this legend makes it clear that people in institutional settings can be much trickier than anyone suspects.

Other entertaining stories appear in Maurice A. Mook's "Quaker Campus Lore" (1961). Most of Mook's material comes from Haverford College, the oldest Quaker college in the United States. One memorable prank involved a student who broke a window while chasing a fellow student named Justice. When the window breaker received a bill, his destruction of college property was classified "In Pursuit of Justice." Another prank followed the classic pattern of bringing an animal into a college building. When several male students coaxed a donkey to follow them up to the top floor of their residence hall, Haverford's president said that "the college stables are always free if some students need special quarters for the entertainment of their closest friends" (243). The gently humorous tone of these stories contrasts with the wildness of prank stories on other college campuses.

In 1965, JoAnn Stephens Parochetti wrote "Scary Stories from Purdue." Her texts, collected from college students in 1963, illustrate legend patterns of the early 1960s in Indiana. Since 18 of the 22 informants are female, these are primarily stories about what women students "talk about and tell in the safety of their rooms on cold, winter evenings" (56). Titles of texts include "The Hook," "Cockroaches in Hair," "Dwarf's Suicide," "Women Trailed by Mysterious Car," "House of Blue Lights at Indianapolis," "The Cadaver's Hand," and "The Ghostly Hitchhiker."

Parochetti's discussion of "Two Girls Alone" (better known to folklorists as "The Roommate's Death") is especially noteworthy. She presents six versions of this legend, three at colleges and three in other settings, pointing out the adaptability of its plot to different environments. In "Two Girls Alone," an outside attacker kills one of two roommates. When morning comes, the surviving roommate discovers her friend outside the door of their room with an ax in her head. A closely related story, "Girl's Throat Cut in Dorm," involves a brutal murder with no outside attacker. Lying in bed, one roommate hears the other gurgling. Assuming that the gurgles come from "a bad case of asthma," the concerned roommate goes back to sleep. The next day, she discovers that her roommate's throat has been cut. Another female student in their residence hall, "jealous of the girl for some reason," has committed the murder (53–54). Folklorists have written less about this story than the more popular "Roommate's Death," which has attracted more scholarly attention than any other campus legend.

Daniel R. Barnes's "Some Functional Horror Stories on the Kansas University Campus" (1966) analyzes five college legends: "The Cadaver Hand," "The Boyfriend's Death," "The Hook," "The Pregnant Girl," and "The Roommate's Death." Barnes suggests considering these legends from a structuralist perspective. Three steps—interdiction, violation, and consequence—apply to the five texts. When students violate a warning, disaster ensues. Noting that hall counselors and "big sisters" tell horror stories to younger students, Barnes concludes that the stories' main function is initiatory.

Until the end of the 1960s, relatively few people knew about the study of academic lore. Folklorists had published articles in journals, but most of those journals did not have a large general readership. When Barre Toelken published "The Folklore of Academe" in 1968, that situation changed since Toelken's article was "Appendix B" in Jan H. Brunvand's popular textbook *The Study of American Folklore: An Introduction.* By the end of the 1960s, folklore archives existed at a number of universities. The climate for legend collecting had become much more favorable.

INDIANA FOLKLORE

Dedicated to presenting and analyzing legends that were "vigorously alive," the journal *Indiana Folklore* began publication in the fall of 1968. Its editor, Linda Dégh, wrote two articles about campus legends for the journal's first issue: "The Hook" (92–100) and "The Boy Friend's Death" (101–6). In her introductory statement, Dégh explained that the new journal would offer a "listing of variants, comments and analysis pertaining to their social function, meaning and distribution, the technique of their composition and variation" (11). *Indiana Folklore*'s preference for "reliable tape recorded legend texts from new collections" (9) set a high standard for subsequent legend collectors.

One of the first legends analyzed in *Indiana Folklore*, "The Boy Friend's Death," tells of a young man and woman who go out on a date. When his car runs out of gas, the young man goes in search of more, cautioning his date not to leave the car or to look outside. Although she hears screams and then scratching and dripping noises on the car's roof, the young woman follows orders and stays inside the car, not looking out. In the morning, police come to lead the young woman away, telling her not, under any circumstances, to look back. Of course, she looks anyway and sees her boyfriend strung up over the car. His fingernails are scratching the car roof, and his blood is draining from his body, drop by drop.

Dégh points out that "The Boy Friend's Death" has much the same structure and function as "The Hook" and "The Roommate's Death" ("Boy Friend's Death" 105). The characterizations vary somewhat—a young couple in the first two legends, two female roommates in the third—and the settings vary also. "The Boy Friend's Death" and "The Hook" take place in Lovers' Lane, while "The Roommate's Death" transpires in a residence hall room. However, all three legends feature a horrible scratching sound signaling danger. Whether this scratching sound comes from a car's roof or door or from the door of a room, it terrifies the listener or reader.

Dégh analyzes "The Roommate's Death" in the second volume of *Indiana Folklore* (1969). Explaining that the hatchet man symbolizes danger for young women, Dégh notes that the tellers of this legend are generally female. She finds the style and structure of "The Roommate's Death" to be "highly refined and extremely effective, with contrasts carefully proportioned as action builds tension toward the climax, the concluding tragedy" (65). What happens to

Indiana Memorial Union, Indiana University. Photograph
by Elizabeth Tucker.

the victim is never described in detail. Only the roommate's body, discovered
at the legend's climax, reveals what occurred.

Another article featuring female characters is "The Legend of Stepp
Cemetery" by William M. Clements and William E. Lightfoot (1972), which
analyzes legends about a well-preserved graveyard in Morgan-Monroe State
Forest of southern Indiana. The authors outline these legends' main features:
a woman, witch, or female ghost wearing black clothes visits the grave of her
husband or child, sitting on a stump called "The Warlock's Seat." Anyone
who sits on this stump, especially at a certain time, will die or experience
terrible misfortune within a certain period of time. Deaths and mutilations in
the area authenticate the stump's power to harm careless visitors.

One of the legends in Clements and Lightfoot's collection came from a 19-year-old male student at Indiana University in 1969. This student, his fraternity brother, and two young women drove to Stepp Cemetery on a dark, spooky night to visit the spot where "an old witch with long grey hair, dressed in a long black dress" was supposed to put flowers on her baby's grave every night. According to one of the young women, visitors' arrival would make the old witch turn her head and then disappear into the forest. Sitting in her "tree-stump chair" would bring on a rapid, untimely death. After entering the graveyard, the four visitors heard "a wolf-type howl" that made them run away (112).

Another important article on the dynamics of campus legends is Sylvia Grider's "Dormitory Legend-Telling in Progress: Fall, 1971–Winter, 1973" (1973). As a resident assistant at McNutt Quadrangle, known at that time as the "party dorm" of Indiana University, Grider learned about the legend-telling patterns of entering freshmen. Noting that students were isolated from each other in rooms along McNutt's narrow corridors, she found that storytelling offered an important means of socializing. It also gave students familiar with certain horror legends the chance to "'initiate' or scare for fun" fellow students who had not yet heard the stories (8).

In one especially interesting section of Grider's article, a female student subjects her roommate to an elaborate prank. With the help of a friend who hunts ghosts, the student tells Carol, her roommate, that McNutt was built on the site of an old farmhouse where three girls burned to death. She moves a lamp, claiming she hasn't touched it, then seriously frightens Carol by throwing a glass against a wall. Grider explains that this prank goes too far, frightening Carol so much that the process of initiation comes to a sudden end (8).

Building on Linda Dégh's statement that "horror is pacified by humor" ("Roommate's Death" 74), Grider shows how the students in McNutt use humor to defuse the horror of "Hatchet Man" legends. They write a series of notes, some signed by "The Hatchet Man" himself, which put a jocular spin on serial killing. One note addressed to Miss Smith says, "My calling card is enclosed, and, as is custom, whoever holds that card is the next to die. See you in the graveyard. Heh, heh, heh . . ." (18). The last set of notes, addressed to the most active legend teller, reveals that the Hatchet Man is really George Washington, who says, "I did it with my trusty hatchet" (25–27). Humorously focusing on the killer rather than his victims keeps the mood light enough for everyone to have a good time.

Another thought-provoking article from the same time period is James Gary Lecocq's "The Ghost of the Doctor and a Vacant Fraternity House" (1973). Talking with fraternity brothers from the recently disbanded Phi Kappa Tau house at Indiana University in Bloomington, Lecocq collected several variants of a ghost story. In some variants, the ghost is the builder of the house; in others, it is a doctor who performs abortions on sorority girls. One especially gruesome detail is the doctor's use of a coal bin or hole in the basement wall to hide the results of his illegal work. In one variant, the body of a girl who died during an operation goes into the hole in the wall and is never seen again.

Lecocq describes how the Phi Kappa Tau fraternity brothers integrate the legend into their initiation of pledges. To become full-fledged members of the fraternity, pledges must prove that they can sit in the coal bin without getting too scared. One text describes a séance in the coal bin where a candle's flame rises to the height of one foot, then suddenly flickers out. While the coal bin is the spookiest place in the house, a bedroom on the second floor represents another kind of danger. Everyone who chooses to live in that small room, called "the closet," either flunks out or moves away (194). This is a good example of a legend limited to one group of students on a university campus, with little likelihood of broader circulation. However, legends about flunking out of college because of spending time in a particular place have migrated across the United States.

One macabre and popular legend, "The Faceless Nun," appears in Michael L. Crawford's article "Legends from St. Mary-of-the-Woods College" (1974). "The Faceless Nun" has become famous for its narration at freshman orientation and on Halloween. This small Catholic college for women was founded in 1840. Students say that the Faceless Nun, once a member of the Art Department, used to paint people's portraits, always saving the faces for last. While painting her own portrait, she died, dooming her ghost to be faceless forever. Legends about students' and professors' encounters with this ghost have frightened many listeners. Crawford explains that, although he expected ghost stories to entertain and delight prospective students, "some pre-freshmen were actually scared away from the college after hearing about the Faceless Nun" (64). He also shows how building styles can influence a college's ghost stories. The Gothic buildings of St. Mary-of-the-Woods, often shrouded by fog, create a spooky atmosphere suitable for ghost stories.

Another significant contribution to college legend scholarship is Helen Gilbert's "The Crack in the Abbey Floor: A Laboratory Analysis of a Legend" (1975), which analyzes 58 versions of a local legend circulating at St. John's University and Abbey in Collegeville, Minnesota. After interviewing students and faculty members, Gilbert learned that Father Hilary, a popular English professor who enjoyed telling stories, had made the legend up himself in 1966. Based on a historical fact—the death of a young workman while building the Abbey's old church in the 1870s—the legend describes the grief of the young man's mother, who asks the abbot to compensate her for the loss of her son. The abbot adamantly refuses. At the church's dedication, the grief-stricken mother throws herself down on the church's floor, shouting that she will return. That same day, she dies in a horse-and-buggy accident. On the anniversary of the dedication, the church's door opens, and wet tracks move down the center aisle to the abbot's throne.

While Gilbert cannot see any footprints or cracks in the floor herself, she discovers that students are eager to believe that the legend's multifarious events might be true. One student-generated variant of the legend explains that a monk drowned while carrying bricks across the lake by boat for the construction of a small chapel. The monk's restless spirit makes itself known through sounds of ice cracking, bricks falling, and voices muttering. Sometimes the monk drowns instead of falling, and the mother reproves the abbot for making her son, who cannot swim, take a boat across the lake. Although this legend has many variants, its stable core is the evidence of a dead person's spirit (75). Frequently told at freshman orientation, "The Crack in the Abbey Floor" gives entering students an initiation into the "community of believers" (76).

An interesting early study of murder legends by Gerry Marie Till is "The Murder at Franklin College" (1976). Franklin, a private college near Indianapolis, was founded in 1834. Legends about a murder early in the twentieth century evolved in an intriguing way. Interviewing students, former students, and faculty members, Till heard frequent references to someone wanting to "keep the death quiet" (188). With some variations, the story says that a sorority sister murdered a pledge from an affluent family and that the pledge's dismembered body was found in a dresser drawer. All versions of this legend emphasize the horror of dismemberment.

Could such a murder have actually occurred? Till does not say, but she explains how much students care about discovering whether the murder legend is "really true" (194). Secrecy and suspected suppression of the legend make it more exciting than it would be otherwise. This pattern also surfaces in legends of other campuses where students suspect that administrators will refuse to reveal any negative information.

URBAN LEGENDS

Between 1981 and 1993, Jan Brunvand published five compilations of legends circulating on college campuses and at other locations (*The Vanishing Hitchhiker* 1981; *The Choking Doberman* 1984; *The Mexican Pet* 1986; *Curses! Broiled Again!* 1989; and *The Baby Train* 1993). Having heard legends in high school and in a folklore class at Michigan State University, Brunvand had developed an early interest in legend study. After folklore graduate study at Indiana University, he became a leading proponent of legend collection and analysis.

Brunvand uses the term "urban legends" to signify "popular belief tales found in contemporary storytelling, such as those about hitchhikers who vanish from moving cars, alligators lurking in New York City sewers, rats that get batter-fried along with the chicken in fast-food outlets, convertibles filled with cement by jealous husbands, housewives caught in the nude while doing laundry, hairdos infested with spiders, pets accidentally cooked in microwave ovens, and so on" (*Choking Doberman* ix). The vivid details in this definition remind the reader of the richness and variety of American legends.

When Brunvand's *The Vanishing Hitchhiker* came out in 1981, hundreds of readers sent him legend texts. He also heard versions of legends during radio and television interviews. Later, when e-mail became common, many readers of Brunvand's books sent him legend material electronically. The rapidly growing popularity of *The Vanishing Hitchhiker* and its sequels increased Americans' familiarity with legend study.

In *The Baby Train*, Brunvand offers the reader a "Type-Index of Urban Legends" (325–47). Type number 10, "Academic Legends," has three subcategories: "Faculty and Research," "Students," and "Blue Book and Other Examination Legends" (345–47). Under each category can be found a list of legend texts, identified by book titles and page numbers. Among the legend variants related to faculty and research, one of the most entertaining texts is the one about the "Trained Professor" (*Curses!* 311–13). This professor's students succeed in modifying his behavior after hours of patient effort. With its neat reversal of the expectation that teachers, not students, will do the training, this legend delights the reader. Other stories in the "Faculty and Research" category include "The Acrobatic Professor" (*Mexican Pet* 192–95), "The Resubmitted Term Paper" (*Curses!* 286–87), and "Dissertation Legends" (*Baby Train* 322–24).

Brunvand's "Students" category is by far the richest, including "Campus Rumor Scares" (*Baby Train* 116–19), "The Roommate's Death" (*Vanishing Hitchhiker* 57–62 and *Mexican Pet* 202–4), and "The Suicide Rule" (*Curses!* 295–98). Medical students' pranks and other hijinks, including some of the legendary exploits of "Caltechies," are included in several books, including *The Baby Train* (293–94 and 315–17). Three student legends not included in this section, "The Dormitory Surprise," "Drugged and Seduced," and "The Gay Roommate," appear in section 5, "Sex and Scandal Legends" (336–38). Two student-generated legends about campus buildings, "Sinking Libraries" and" Switched Campus Buildings," appear in section 7, "Business and Professional Legends" (340–43).

Under the third subcategory, "Blue Book and Other Examination Legends," can be found such piquant texts as "The Unsolvable Math Problem" (*Curses!* 278–83), "The Lesson in Compassion" (*Baby Train* 318–21), and "The Stolen Exam" (*Curses!* 285–86). Some stories, such as "The Announced Quiz" (*Curses!* 284), ruefully acknowledge the cleverness of professors; if a professor announces a quiz in a classified ad, he has, in his own way, told his students what to expect. Others, such as "The Second Blue Book" (*Mexican Pet* 196–98), celebrate the cleverness of students. It is not surprising that legends about students' successful tricks outnumber those about professors' devious strategies. In campus legends, the student is the primary trickster hero.

PSYCHOANALYTIC APPROACHES

Freudian

Alan Dundes, a strong advocate of psychoanalytic folklore studies, analyzes campus legends in his article "On the Psychology of Legend" (1971). Saying that interpretation is more important than classification and indexing, Dundes closely examines several legends told by college students and other adolescents.

According to Dundes, "The Hook," told mainly by teenage girls, expresses girls' fears about their boyfriends insisting on sexual experimentation. This legend follows a double standard for sexual behavior: boys are expected to take initiative, while girls are expected to resist. From the car's radio comes a "conscience-like voice from society," announcing that a sex maniac with a hook has escaped from an insane asylum. Boys, while parking, may act like sex maniacs; they may, in fact, be "all hands." The hook serves as a phallic symbol, representing the girl's fear of what will happen if she loses control (30).

Once the boy gets out of the car and walks around to the girl's side to open her door, he discovers a hook attached to the door's handle. Dundes explains that the girl's insistence on returning home has caused the hook hand to be severed: symbolic castration of the boy, who had hoped to go farther with the girl sexually (30–31).

Dundes also analyzes the legend of "The Cadaver Arm," in which rowdy medical students offer a coin to a toll booth attendant in the hand of a cadaver. Focusing on Americans' fear of coming close to dead bodies, Dundes says it is difficult for medical students to get used to working in a dissection room. Once they have made this adjustment, they belong to a profession that makes others feel uncomfortable. This feeling of discomfort comes from how doctors make their living: "The fact that future doctors use a cadaver arm to pay the toll suggests that they are using the limbs of others, perhaps of victims, to help pay their way in life" (32). By offering the coin in the cadaver's hand to the toll booth attendant, the medical students are reversing the usual roles. Learning to handle cadavers, they are also finding a way to defuse tension between members and nonmembers of the medical profession (32–33).

Another campus legend that has drawn the attention of psychoanalytic scholars is "The Roommate's Death." In his article "Allomotifs and the Psychoanalytic Study of Folk Narratives: Another Look at 'The Roommate's Death'" (1992), Michael P. Carroll examines the plot elements of legend texts from the mid-1960s to the early 1990s. Allomotifs, as defined by Alan Dundes, are plot incidents that perform the same functions in different tale texts. Applying Dundes's approach to legends, Carroll finds that allomotifs in "The Roommate's Death" are symbolically equivalent in the minds of tellers and listeners.

Noting that "The Roommate's Death" is especially popular among young women, Carroll explains that the discovery of the dead roommate's body is the most vivid and important plot element. Phrases from various texts that describe the roommate's body include "bloody and dead," "leg torn off," "arms and legs cut off," and "vocal cords cut out." According to Carroll, young women worry about another event that involves penetration, separation of a body part, and blood loss: sexual intercourse (229). The two young women in the legend represent different aspects of the same personality: the one who suffers pain and death and the other who escapes unhurt. Because one of the roommates stays safe, tellers and listeners can dissociate themselves from fears and anxieties about their sexuality while expressing the presence of those fears and anxieties (230).

Carroll identifies three subtypes of "The Roommate's Death": TRD_1, in which the roommate dies outside the door of her own room; TRD_2, in which the roommate dies in her own bed; and TRD_3, in which a killer breaks into a house where two girls are staying alone, kills one girl, and sits in a rocking chair with the girl's head on his lap. TRD_1 and TRD_2 are the two subtypes most often found on college campuses. As Carroll points out, both of these versions of the story involve massive amounts of blood. Since the roommate dies in bed in TRD_2 and beds are associated with sexual intercourse, the symbolism of the bed supports a psychoanalytic interpretation (231).

Jungian

Elizabeth Tucker's "Ghosts in Mirrors: Reflections of the Self" (2005) analyzes legends told in one residence hall at Binghamton University over a period of five years. Examining 43 narratives about mirror ghosts and related supernatural phenomena, she traces relationships between legend and ritual. Tucker finds that legends about ghostly lovers, gender transformations, suicide, and violent death offer students a quasi-initiatory experience that helps them develop a more complex sense of self.

Tucker explains that both college students and preadolescents have an interest in Bloody Mary, defined by Linda Dégh as "victim, witch, mother, avenger, child abuser, and protector" (*Legend and Belief* 244). Legends about preadolescents summoning a mysterious, witchlike spirit by repeating her name while standing in front of a mirror were first documented by Janet L. Langlois in her article "'Mary Whales, I Believe in You': Myth and Ritual Subdued" (1978). Alan Dundes's "Bloody Mary in the Mirror" (2002) offers an analysis of such legends from a Freudian perspective. The legend tellers in Dundes's and Langlois's studies are preadolescents, but the teller of the "Mary" legend in Dégh's *Legend and Belief* is an 18-year-old male.

Tucker makes the point that college students, as well as preadolescents, summon ghosts in mirrors and tell legends about encounters with spectral beings. She finds three Jungian archetypes, the animus, the anima, and the shadow, appropriate for analyzing college students' legends of mirror ghosts. According to C. G. Jung, archetypes are like the axial structure of the crystal; invisible and inherited, they determine the crystal's structure though they have no material existence of their own. An archetype offers a "possibility of representation" that can become an archetypal image (Jung 13). Jung describes the animus as the female complement of someone who is male, while the anima is the male aspect of the female. The shadow archetype represents the destructive and antisocial impulses that people are trained to suppress.

Using modified Jungian analysis related to Estella Lauter and Carol Schreier Rupprecht's *Feminist Archetypal Theory* (1985), Tucker finds that images of ghosts in mirrors should be interpreted flexibly, with a focus on re-vision. She analyzes three campus narratives: one about a woman seeing a man's face in the mirror of her room, a second about a male resident assistant seeing the reflection of a man in black walking behind him in a hallway, and a third about two female college students seeing and summoning Candyman, the central character of the film by that name in 1992. Finding that the animus/ anima and shadow archetypes apply to all three legends, she notes that these legends make college students aware of their own complexities. While this awareness is serious, ostensive play (lighthearted enactment of legends) makes spirit summoning fun. For college students, summoning Candyman or another spirit usually combines entertainment with exploration of the supernatural.

Sign in the basement of a Binghamton University residence hall. Photograph by Geoffrey Gould.

EXPERIENCE-CENTERED THEORY

In 1976, David J. Hufford published "A New Approach to the 'Old Hag': The Nightmare Tradition Reexamined." The "Old Hag" is what residents of Newfoundland in Canada call a phenomenon experienced by people around the world: waking up at night, seeing or hearing something approach the bed, feeling pressure or strangulation on the upper part of the body, and trying to move or scream but feeling paralyzed (74). In Newfoundland, the "Hag," either male or female, has strong connotations of witchcraft.

Hufford's book *The Terror That Comes in the Night: An Experience-Centered Study of Supernatural Assault Traditions* (1982) shows that the "Old Hag" phenomenon belongs to a cross-cultural pattern of experience, belief, and storytelling. His innovative concentration on the experience itself deemphasizes theoretical interpretation while pointing out that "events accurately observed and reasoning properly carried out are in some cases central in the development and maintenance of folk belief" (xiii). Presenting narratives about supernatural assault traditions, Hufford includes a number of texts from college students and older adults recounting their experiences in college.

Hufford explains the etymology of relevant terms, referring to Ernest Jones's study *On the Nightmare* (1931). Our familiar word "nightmare" combines the Anglo-Saxon "*neaht*" or "*nicht*" (night) with "*mara*" (incubus or succubus). Since the noun "*mara*" comes from the Anglo-Saxon verb "*merran*" (crush), it describes an agent of supernatural assault (*Terror* 53). Instead of using the word "nightmare" for this experience, Hufford uses the more etymologically accurate "*mara*."

In the Middle Ages, Europeans told stories about the incubus, a male demon that pressed itself into women's chests before having sexual intercourse with them. Its female counterpart, the succubus, had intercourse with men. For many years, scholars assumed that accounts of the incubus and succubus were interesting stories with no basis in fact. Hufford's research persuasively demonstrates that these are not just narrative patterns but expressions of common experiences on the borderline between sleep and wakefulness. Some of these experiences seem sexual, as in the incubus and succubus stories, but many involve paralysis and fear with no sexual element.

One of the most riveting texts in Hufford's book comes from a 22-year-old male medical student who had a troubling experience while sleeping in his fraternity house during his senior year in college. Hearing the door to his room slam, he thought his roommate had come in, but no one seemed to be there. Feeling paralyzed, the student felt pressure on his body, then saw a "grayish, brownish murky presence" with "a surrealistic shape." A struggle followed:

This thing was *there*! I felt a pressure on me and it was like enveloping me. It was a very, very very strange thing. And as I remember I struggled. I struggled to move and get out. And—you know, eventually, I think eventually what happened was I kind of like moved my arm. And again the whole thing—the whole thing just kind of dissipated away. The presence, everything. But everything else just remained the same. The same stereo was playing next door. The same stuff was going on (59).

It is interesting to see how closely the narrator focuses on strangeness and sameness. The presence is "very, very very strange." Everything else around the presence stays the same, accentuating its peculiarity. As the narrator continues to describe what happened, he goes into more detail about what he saw: "I would say it was almost kind of gaseous—but *not* gaseous in that it didn't have the transparency that a gaseous kind of thing would have" (62).

These excerpts from the student's story show how much he cared about describing his experience with scientific precision. As a medical student, he understood the importance of detailed observation. His exactitude parallels the level of detail in many other memorates told by college students. When something extraordinary happens, the narrator may feel a need to show the listener what took place by including as many vivid images as possible.

Other folklorists have taken an experience-centered approach, analyzing patterns of belief and self-expression. Gillian Bennett's *Alas, Poor Ghost!* (1999) examines traditions of belief in the stories and conversations of elderly women in Manchester, England. Bennett cites surveys indicating that belief in the supernatural is "higher than one would have thought possible in predominantly rationalist cultures" (11). Her interviews with women between the ages of 60 and 96 show relatively high levels of belief in life after death, telepathy, premonitions, visitations, death omens, and hauntings and somewhat lower levels of belief in fortune-telling and horoscopes.

Bennett identifies five levels of belief and disbelief: convinced belief, some belief, "Don't know," some skepticism, and convinced disbelief. For each, she lists linguistic clues. Convinced belief manifests itself in phrases like "I FIRMLY believe," "Yes, oh yes," and "I've PROOF of that." At the opposite extreme, convinced disbelief emerges in statements like "I don't believe in that" and "I just don't SEE." "Don't know" is indicated in some cases by hesitation, in others by phrases like "I get a bit mixed up about that" (193).

Bennett's lists of words trace the focal points of stories. Asking "Where?," "When?," "In what circumstances?," "What?," "Who?," "How?," and again "Where?," she compiles tables of the words that appear most frequently in her informants' stories about visitations from the dead. The question "In what circumstances?" elicits "dying," "ill," and "wide awake" as the words that appear most often. "Who?" involves a wide variety of responses, including "parent," "husband," "presence," "cat," "smoke," and "flowers."

Although Bennett's study presents data from elderly women, its structure works well in analysis of college students' narratives. The question "Where?" yields answers such as "in my room," "in the hall," and "in the bathroom." Responses to the question "Who?" include "a student who committed suicide," "a girl who died," "Indians," and "the ghost of a slave." Close examination of meaningful experiences, with attention to categories of belief and disbelief, helps the researcher understand complex shades of meaning.

SPECTRALITY

An intriguing interpretation of campus ghost stories emerges in Jeannie B. Thomas's "Pain, Pleasure and the Spectral: The Barfing Ghost of Burford Hall" (1991). Since the publication of Ronald L. Baker's *Hoosier Folk Legends* in 1982, Burford Hall at Indiana State University has been known for its haunted bathrooms. Examining legends in Indiana State University's folklore archive from the 1960s to the early 1990s, Thomas finds that the Burford Hall ghost indulges in a number of activities: laughing, screaming, vomiting, flushing toilets, and turning off alarm clocks. This unusually active ghost behaves like a poltergeist, mischievously playing tricks on students in the residence hall.

Thomas explains that not all Burford Hall legends are about playful and vomiting ghosts; some tell of painful incidents related to periods of tension in American history. For example, a legend from the late 1960s links Burford Hall with a young African American woman who, because of her membership in a black power group, tried to kill a white student. Another legend from the early 1990s identifies Burford Hall as the home of a lesbian ghost who is infuriated by the residence hall becoming coeducational. Thomas explains that both African Americans and lesbians, as well as gays, are liminal figures, "betwixt and between promise and prejudice" (29). Like many other legends, these texts from Burford Hall reflect issues that society is struggling to understand.

Citing Elaine Scarry's *The Body in Pain: The Making and Unmaking of the World* (1985), Thomas argues that legends about painful, traumatic experiences make the past seem real and reinforce the power of certain groups. Some Burford Hall ghost stories warn students about the terrible consequences of opposing social norms. Death, suicide, and vomiting all express pain; eventually, expression of these troubling subjects may make the pain decrease (32–33).

Vomiting ghosts get people's attention, making them want to learn what is going on. Although imagining a ghost vomiting and flushing a toilet may make a person laugh, close examination of the "barfing ghost" reveals its seriousness. As Thomas says, "Following a ghost through its legend versions is challenging and can result in the breakdown of tidy, culturally constructed polarities" (36).

Simon J. Bronner analyzes ghost stories across the United States in *Piled Higher and Deeper* (1995). His categories for supernatural phenomena on college campuses include resident ghosts, suicidal ghosts, lovers' ghosts, and Greek ghosts. New students, Bronner says, find that resident ghosts "personalize the place and underscore its strangeness" (148). He notes that female students "often treat the ghost as a resident guest, albeit a sometimes difficult one. She's often a lost, plaintive soul struck with heartbreak, and thus her antics are understandable, students say" (151). Male students also see ghosts, but the stories told by women place more emphasis on sadness and vulnerability.

Ghosts of lovers who have died tragically are, Bronner says, appropriate to college campuses, where courtship is "a prevalent distraction" (150). Many legends about doomed lovers emphasize parents' and others' prohibitions against getting married as well as wartime suffering. Both texts featured in the "Lovers' Ghosts" chapter of *Piled Higher and Deeper* are related to the Civil War, a frequent setting for college ghost stories in the South. In both stories,

Face in a window of the Jessie Bonstelle Theatre, Wayne State University. Photograph by Elizabeth Tucker.

a young woman and her beloved, a Confederate soldier, die tragically and return to haunt parts of the college campus where they were happy together.

Bronner makes an important point about ghosts of fraternity and sorority houses. These ghosts, he says, tend not to be suicide victims: "Selfishly taking one's life would go against the spirit of brother- and sisterhood prevailing in Greekdom" (153). Many Greek ghosts have died in accidents. Bronner cites an Indiana University legend about Michael A. Frang, a member of Sigma Phi Epsilon in the late 1960s, who was sitting on his fraternity's float during a homecoming parade when a cannon misfired, decapitating him. His ghost inhabits the fraternity house's basement, nicknamed "the swamp," where lights go on and off, doors mysteriously unlock themselves, and objects fly off shelves. Another intriguing fraternity ghost mentioned in *Piled Higher and Deeper* is the spirit of John Henry Frizzell at the Phi Kappa Psi house at Penn State. John Henry, who devoted his life to Phi Kappa Psi, announces his presence by calling the house every morning at 6:40. Each ring represents one of the letters of his beloved fraternity (154–57).

In contrast to legends about the ghosts of loyal, familiar students, legends about the spirits of others outside the campus focus on strangeness and contrast. Sometimes, however, the spectral visitor has a prior claim to the land on which he or she appears. Renée L. Bergland, author of *The National Uncanny: Indian Ghosts and American Subjects* (2000), argues that Native American ghosts "function both as representations of national guilt and as triumphant agents of Americanization" (4). Spectral Indians, Bergland says, appear in many contexts: "They stalk through national history as well as through literary history, and they appear in works by Native Americans as well as those by European Americans" (159). It should, then, be no surprise to learn that Indian ghosts are important characters in campus legends.

In "Spectral Indians, Desecrated Burial Grounds" (2005), Elizabeth Tucker examines rumors and legends about Indian ghosts on the campuses of three universities: Louisiana State University, the University of Wisconsin, and Binghamton University. Finding rumors and legends to be closely entwined, Tucker notes that legends about Indian ghosts often express a sense of injustice. If a campus was built on an Indian burial ground, how much respect was shown for the original inhabitants of the area? College students often welcome the chance to explore important aspects of national history. Ghost stories provide one good way for students to do this while savoring the ambiguity of a ghost that belongs to the campus within a much earlier historical period.

Another kind of spectrality involves conjuration of evil spirits. In his book *Lucifer Ascending* (2004), Bill Ellis analyzes a legend about black magic circulating at Morehead State University in Morehead, Kentucky, in 1972. In this text, several female students consult witchcraft books to find out how to summon evil spirits. Learning that one person should sit before a mirror in a dark room, a member of the group volunteers to let the others tie her to a chair next to a full-length mirror. The others put towels around the door and windows, then stand outside the door. After a while, the woman inside the room starts "screamin' like crazy." When her friends try to enter the room to offer help, they discover that the door is locked from the inside. The dorm mother offers a key, and they hurry in, finding that the woman's face has been "torn to shreds." She is still tied to the chair, and the window is locked. The woman whose face has been shredded dies, and the friend who went in to check on her goes insane (164–65).

Ellis places this legend in the context of mirror witch customs and legends, discussed in the "Psychoanalytic Approaches" section of this chapter. He notes the cautionary message of such legends: if young people fool around with black magic, they can expect frightening consequences. It is significant that students at Morehead State told this legend in 1972, when political unrest and awareness of the Wiccan revival made some people nervous about evil spirits. Soon afterward, in 1973, the film *The Exorcist* gave viewers an unnerving view of an evil spirit possessing the body of an adolescent girl.

Ellis sees the summoning of mirror witches and spirits as a controllable process: anyone who gets too frightened can stop the sequence by leaving

Mohawk Hall, Binghamton University. Photograph by Geoffrey Gould.

the room or turning on the light (167). Within the framework of legend, however, the sequence is inexorable. A young woman dies, her face torn to shreds; she "loses face" because of her recklessness and boldness in toying with the supernatural. As in many other campus legends from the 1960s, there is a strong emphasis on punishment of women who do not follow rules of safe and acceptable behavior.

SUICIDE

Suicide is a painful subject. Overwhelmed by the pressure of college life, some students decide to end their lives. Alert to this possibility, colleges and universities do what they can to prevent suicide attempts. Many departments of residential life train their staff members to watch for signs of impending suicide. A textbook for staff training published in 1995, Gregory Blimling's *The Resident Assistant,* includes a chapter on "Suicide Intervention" with a list of symptoms of suicidal behavior (269–84). This textbook encourages resident assistants to enlist help from troubled students' friends and to consult their campus counseling staff. If all goes well, no suicide attempt takes place.

Sometimes, however, no one can prevent the tragedy of a student's suicide. When a student's life ends in this way, shock waves spread across the campus. Friends grieve, and fellow students ask themselves whether they could ever feel so desperate themselves. In some cases, one suicide follows another. Worried members of the administration may downplay what happened, hoping to keep other students from repeating a tragedy that has recently occurred.

Campus legends do just the opposite: they dramatize suicide, warning students about the dangers of self-destructive behavior. Chapter 3 contains several examples of legends about suicide victims. Often such legends tell of a student living in a residence hall who becomes aware of the ghost of a previous occupant who committed suicide. Other legends describe ghosts that haunt bridges, towers, and other places on campus, waiting to encourage students to end their lives as they did themselves.

Scholarly articles on suicide legends have taken various approaches. William S. Fox's "The Roommate's Suicide and the 4.0" (1990) analyzes a legend that can be summarized in one sentence: "If your roommate commits suicide, you get a 4.0 that semester" (69). Since a "4.0," a perfect "A" average, is the Holy Grail of academe, any promise of such an outcome is bound to get students' attention. Fox explores the legend's variations, finding that some versions include any kind of death, such as death from cancer, while others suggest the possibility of getting straight As if a parent, close relative, or other important person dies. One very specific version explains that if a roommate in a double room dies, the survivor will get a 4.0, but if the tragedy takes place in a suite, all the surviving students will receive a 3.5 (69–70).

To gain further insight into this legend's meaning, Fox conducted two surveys in the spring of 1985: one at Skidmore College, the other at the State University of New York at New Paltz. He discovered that almost three-quarters of the Skidmore students and two-thirds of the students at the state university had heard some version of the legend. Almost all of them had learned the story through oral transmission. The legend circulated more actively among students who lived on campus than among those who lived off campus. Almost half the Skidmore students believed that the suicide policy held true on their campus, while almost five-sixths of the students at New Paltz believed that the policy existed there.

Fox compares "The Roommate's Suicide" to "The Roommate's Death," previously analyzed by a number of other folklorists. In both legends, one of two or more roommates dies tragically. However, "The Roommate's Death," which almost always describes female roommates, emphasizes guilt and responsibility: if the surviving roommate had opened the door after she heard scratching noises, her roommate might have survived. The moral of "The Roommate's Death" is that young women should not stay in a building on their own, vulnerable to the dangers of a violent society. "The Roommate's Suicide" inflicts guilt on no one. Although this legend suggests administrative concern and mysterious grading standards, it does not offer a moral and applies equally well to male and female students (72–74).

Jan H. Brunvand calls the legend of the roommate's suicide "The Suicide Rule." Commenting on Fox's conclusion that the legend reflects no actual grading policies, Brunvand notes that roommates of two students who died tragically—one at Harvard, the other at the University of Chicago—received counseling and grades of "incomplete." Neither of them, however, received a 4.0 average. Brunvand explains that the increasing rate of suicide among adolescents makes this legend worrisome for students. He says, "If there's a college campus in the country that does not have 'The Suicide Rule' legend, I've yet to discover it. And if there's one that does have such a rule on the books, I haven't found it yet either" (*Curses!* 297–98).

Many campus suicide legends remain localized, associated with only one building or outdoor location. In "Joseph E. Brown Hall: A Case Study of One University Legend" (1992), Charles Greg Kelley traces narratives that developed at the University of Georgia after a student hanged himself from a closet door with a belt in 1972. Scrutinizing reports in campus and local newspapers, Kelley finds that newspaper articles influenced oral stories about the hanging. He includes accounts of the hanging from a university police

Corridor in Eigenmann Hall, nicknamed "Suicide Tower," Indiana University. Photograph by Elizabeth Tucker.

officer involved in the case and an English professor, both of whom provide vivid details about what happened.

Especially valuable for folklore studies is Kelley's documentation of this legend's transformation into a ghost story. He points out that the transformation is not surprising "in light of the ambiguous and unusual circumstances surrounding the death" (144). Signs of the student's ghostly presence include footsteps and rearranged furniture, both of which conform to traditional motifs (E402.1.2, "Footsteps of invisible ghost heard," and E599.6, "Ghost moves furniture"). One text from a university archivist who was a graduate student in the mid-1970s raises the question whether Joseph

E. Brown Hall was remodeled because of what happened: "There was some after-the-fact speculation that the building had been modified in an attempt to erase its former usage as a residence hall, but never much speculation beyond that" (146).

After detailed examination of many variants of the legend, Kelley finds a dynamic interrelationship between the news media and oral narrative. He notes that legend composition takes place within the campus community, with dominant features developing over time. Another interesting point concerns the mysteriousness of Brown Hall, which seems to go beyond the legend genre. One custodian at the University of Georgia expresses fear of Brown Hall: "I don't like that building, and I don't *ever* want to go over there!" (150).

CYBERSPACE

The story of computer technology's development has spawned some lively legends. During World War II, the first computers—the British COLOSSUS and the American Mark I—served as code breakers and calculators of ballistic weaponry. John von Neumann, a leader of the Manhattan Project, which built the first atomic bomb, worked on refining the circuitry of ENIAC, a computer assembled at the University of Pennsylvania in 1945. Legends about von Neumann include incidents that illustrate his brilliance and absentmindedness. For example, when von Neumann's wife was sick, he went down to the kitchen to get her a drink of water and rattled around for a while. Going back upstairs without any water, he asked his wife, "Darling, where do we keep the glasses?" Von Neumann alarmed his students at Princeton by erasing equations as soon as he wrote them on the board; he also showed up in class in full evening dress after a night of partying (Jennings 55–56). Comparable legends about Professor Norbert Wiener of the Massachusetts Institute of Technology (MIT), the founder of cybernetics, are discussed in chapter 2.

Other legends tell of students' amazing exploits related to computers. In the early 1970s, students at Dartmouth created an "ANIMAL" virus that rapidly wreaked havoc on the university's entire computer system. This virus's name perfectly matched the folk name for rowdy Dartmouth students: "Dartmouth animals" (see chapter 5). At the California Institute of Technology, informally known as Caltech, a student is said to have used software called "Shiva" (named for the Indian god of destruction) to blow up an IBM computer (Jennings 207–8). One of my own former students tried to cause a more limited kind of damage with a program called "Fiendish." While professors of computer science are often described as being absentminded and otherworldly, some computer-savvy students become known as elusive pranksters with a talent for subversion.

MIT scholar Sherry Turkle explores the relationship between the computer's culture of simulation and people's sense of their own identity. On the Internet, Turkle says, we are "dwellers on the threshold between the real and the virtual, unsure of our footing, inventing ourselves as we go along" (10). This self-invention can involve name and gender changes, as well as other simulations. Just as people can pretend to be something they are not, machines can pretend to be people. One case in point is a MUD (multiuser domain) program named Julia. Julia, who has a "sassy female persona," talks about hockey when any interaction with a human being becomes too complicated. Skilled at repelling flirtatious remarks, she has often been mistaken for a human being (90–93). Given this kind of ambiguity, it is no wonder that the Internet has become a rich domain for legend transmission.

Two of the fastest ways to transmit legends are through e-mail and Instant Messenger. Since the mid-1990s, many people have forwarded "true" e-mail messages that have turned out to be legends in electronic form. Commercial legend Web sites such as the Urban Legend Reference Pages (http://www.snopes.com) and the Urban Legends Research Centre (http://www.ulrc.com) have put enormous energy into determining whether certain narratives are true. Since many people have received e-mail forwards about dangers and horrors and wondered about these reports' veracity, such Web sites have become very popular.

College students may or may not believe e-mail forwards warning young people about dangerous situations. These forwards follow popular legend cycles. For example, a legend about a motorist flashing his car's lights before shooting someone, for the purpose of gang initiation, scared many individuals in the mid-1990s. Once an e-mail forward has entered general circulation, if no danger occurs, the forward becomes less popular.

In the spring of 2004, Jessica Hoesten, an undergraduate student at Binghamton University, designed an experiment to see how easily her fellow students would accept a legend transmitted through e-mail. After deciding what elements constituted a typical e-mail forward—little context, some kind of warning, a near death close to home, and a vulnerable young woman—she sent an e-mail to four close friends. The first part of her e-mail message follows:

DO NOT DELETE THIS EMAIL! Please read this and send it to everyone you know. This is important because someone almost got killed. . . . I never thought that something like this could ever happen at our school. THIS IS NOT A HOAX!

The next few lines describe a female friend of hers who had gone out into the university's nature preserve after dark. The message continues:

They had been drinking and smoking weed and decided to call it a night when her friends thought it would be funny to run off and leave her there when she was a little ways off to go to the bathroom. While on her own, she had seen a tall man dressed in all black hunched over what seemed to be the body of a dead animal. The man saw the girl watching him and came after her. He pushed her to the ground, but luckily she kicked him as hard as she could and managed to escape. She ran from the nature preserve and called 911, but when the police arrived, the man and whatever he was hunched over were nowhere to be seen. It had started to rain so there was no evidence of a struggle. The police told her that unless she could prove that the man really existed, she would have to go home and forget about the incident. Rather than make a huge fuss about it because she knew that nothing would come of it, she told all of her friends to stay out of the nature preserve after dark because she feared that the man was out to rape and/or kill young girls.

Three of the four friends who received this e-mail sent it to at least 10 people; one deleted the message before opening it. Of the three who sent the message on, only one felt certain that the story was true. The others were not so sure, but the possibility of danger made them want to share the story with others. After sending the four e-mails, Jessica sent her story to a fifth friend through AOL Instant Messenger. This student forwarded the message to all her sorority sisters who were online at that time: approximately 50 people. One reason why she sent the message to so many others was to find out whether it was true. When none of her sorority sisters confirmed the story's veracity, she lost interest in it, as did the other friends who had received Jessica's e-mails.

This small-scale experiment neatly demonstrates how easy it can be to get college friends to send electronically delivered narratives on to others. If the story has a familiar setting and dangerous or suspicious characters, it has a fairly high likelihood of traveling farther. Some users of the Internet become proficient at separating truth from fiction, but no one can always be sure where the truth lies. Even professional folklorists have sometimes consulted the Urban Legend Reference Pages (http://www.snopes.com) to determine whether a legend is based on truth. In cyberspace, surreality is more predictable than reliance on fact.

WORKS CITED

Aarne, Antti, and Stith Thompson. *The Types of the Folktale: A Classification and Bibliography.* Helsinki: Suomalainen Tiedeakatemia, 1961.
Baker, Ronald L. *Hoosier Folk Legends.* Bloomington: Indiana University Press, 1982.

Barnes, Daniel R. "Some Functional Horror Stories on the Kansas University Campus." *Southern Folklore Quarterly* 30.3 (1966): 312–31.

Beardsley, Richard K., and Rosalie Hankey. "A History of the Vanishing Hitchhiker." *California Folklore Quarterly* 2 (1943): 13–25.

Bennett, Gillian. *Alas, Poor Ghost! Traditions of Belief in Story and Discourse.* Logan: Utah State University Press, 1999.

Bergland, Renée L. *The National Uncanny: Indian Ghosts and American Subjects.* Hanover: University Press of New England, 2000.

Blimling, Gregory. *The Resident Assistant.* 4th ed. Dubuque: Kendall/Hunt, 1995.

Bronner, Simon. *Piled Higher and Deeper: The Folklore of Student Life.* Little Rock: August House, 1995.

Brunvand, Jan H. *The Baby Train.* New York: Norton, 1993.

———. *The Choking Doberman.* New York: Norton, 1984.

———. *Curses! Broiled Again!* New York: Norton, 1989.

———. *The Mexican Pet.* New York: Norton, 1986.

———. *The Study of American Folklore: An Introduction.* New York: Norton, 1968.

———. *The Vanishing Hitchhiker.* New York: Norton, 1981.

Carroll, Michael P. "Allomotifs and the Psychoanalytic Study of Folk Narratives: Another Look at 'The Roommate's Death.'" *Folklore* 103 (1992): 225–34.

Charriere, Henri. *Papillon.* New York: Pocket Books, 1971.

Christiansen, Reidar T. *The Migratory Legends.* Folklore Fellows Communications 175. Helsinki: Suomalainen Tiedeakatemia, 1958.

Clements, William M., and William E. Lightfoot. " The Legend of Stepp Cemetery." *Indiana Folklore* 5.1 (1972): 92–135.

Crawford, Michael L. "Legends from St. Mary-of-the-Woods College." *Indiana Folklore* 7.1–2 (1974): 53–75.

Dégh, Linda. "The Boy Friend's Death." *Indiana Folklore* 1.1 (1968): 101–6.

———. "The Hook." *Indiana Folklore* 1.1 (1968): 92–100.

———. *Legend and Belief.* Bloomington: Indiana University Press, 2001.

———. "The Roommate's Death and Other Related Dormitory Stories in Formation." *Indiana Folklore* 2.2 (1969): 55–74.

Dorson, Richard M. "The Folklore of Colleges." *American Mercury* 68 (1949): 671–77.

Dundes, Alan. "Bloody Mary in the Mirror." *Bloody Mary in the Mirror: Essays in Psychoanalytic Folkloristics.* Jackson: University Press of Mississippi, 2002. 76–94.

———. "On the Psychology of Legend." *American Folk Legend: A Symposium.* Ed. Wayland D. Hand. Berkeley: University of California Press, 1971. 21–36.

Ellis, Bill. *Lucifer Ascending: The Occult in Folklore and Popular Culture.* Lexington: University Press of Kentucky, 2004.

Fox, William S. "The Roommate's Suicide and the 4.0." *A Nest of Vipers: Perspectives on Contemporary Legend V.* Ed. Gillian Bennett and Paul Smith. Sheffield: Sheffield Academic Press, 1990. 69–76.

Gilbert, Helen. "The Crack in the Abbey Floor: A Laboratory Analysis of a Legend." *Indiana Folklore* 8.1–2 (1975): 61–78.

Grider, Sylvia. "Dormitory Legend-Telling in Progress: Fall, 1971–Winter, 1973. " *Indiana Folklore* 6.1 (1973): 1–32.

Grimm, Jacob, and Wilhelm Grimm. *Kinder-und Hausmärchen* (Children's and Household Tales). Ed. Heinz Rölleke. 3 vols. Stuttgart: Reclam, 1980. Based on the 7th edition of 1857.

Hankey, Rosalie. "Campus Folklore and California's 'Pedro.'" *California Folklore Quarterly* 3 (1944): 29–35.

Hoesten, Jessica. "Rumor Turned Legend: The Source of the Story and Why We Feel the Need to Tell Everyone We Know." Unpublished student paper. Binghamton University, Binghamton, New York, 3 May 2004.

Hufford, David J. "A New Approach to 'The Old Hag': The Nightmare Tradition Reexamined." *American Folk Medicine.* Ed. Wayland D. Hand. Berkeley: University of California Press, 1976. 73–85.

———. *The Terror That Comes in the Night: An Experience-Centered Study of Supernatural Assault Traditions.* Philadelphia: University of Pennsylvania Press, 1982.

Jennings, Karla. *The Devouring Fungus: Tales of the Computer Age.* New York: Norton, 1990.

Jones, Ernest. *On the Nightmare.* London: Hogarth Press, 1931.

Jung, C. G. *Four Archetypes.* Trans. R. F. C. Hull. Princeton: Princeton University Press, 1970.

Kelley, Charles Greg. "Joseph E. Brown Hall: A Case Study of One University Legend." *Contemporary Legend* 2 (1992): 137–53.

Langlois, Janet L. "'Mary Whales, I Believe in You': Myth and Ritual Subdued." *Indiana Folklore* 11.1 (1978): 5–33.

Lauter, Estella, and Carol Schreier Rupprecht, eds. *Feminist Archetypal Theory.* Knoxville: University of Tennessee Press, 1985.

Lecocq, James Gary. "The Ghost of the Doctor and a Vacant Fraternity House." *Indiana Folklore* 6 (1973): 191–204.

Mook, Maurice A. "Quaker Campus Lore." *New York Folklore Quarterly* 17 (1961): 243–52.

Parochetti, JoAnn Stephens. "Scary Stories from Purdue." *Keystone Folklore* 10 (1965): 49–57.

Rollins, Alfred B. "College Folklore." *New York Folklore Quarterly* 17.3 (1961): 163–73.

Scarry, Elaine. *The Body in Pain: The Making and Unmaking of the World.* New York: Oxford University Press, 1985.

Simonsuuri, Lauri. *Typen und Motivverzeichnis der finnischen mythischen Sagen* (Type and Motif Index of Finnish Mythological Legends). Folklore Fellows Communications 182. Helsinki: Academia Scientiarum Fennica, 1961/1987.

Thomas, Jeannie B. "Pain, Pleasure, and the Spectral: The Barfing Ghost of Burford Hall." *Folklore Forum* 24.2 (1991): 27–38.

Thompson, Stith. *Motif-Index of Folk Literature: A Classification of Narrative Elements in Folktales, Ballads, Myths, Fables, Mediaeval Romances, Exempla, Fabliaux, Jest-Books, and Local Legends.* 6 vols. Bloomington: Indiana University Press, 1966.

Till, Gerry Marie. "The Murder at Franklin College." *Indiana Folklore* 9 (1976): 187–95.

Toelken, Barre. "The Folklore of Academe." *The Study of American Folklore.* Ed. Jan H. Brunvand. New York: Norton, 1968. 317–37.

Tucker, Elizabeth. "Ghosts in Mirrors: Reflections of the Self." *Journal of American Folklore* 118.468 (2005): 186–203.

———. "Spectral Indians, Desecrated Burial Grounds." *Voices: The Journal of New York Folklore* 31.1–2 (Spring–Summer 2005): 10–13.

Turkle, Sherry. *Life on the Screen: Identity in the Age of the Internet.* New York: Simon and Schuster, 1995.

von Sydow, Carl Wilhelm. *Selected Papers on Folklore.* Copenhagen: Rosenkilde and Bagger, 1948.

Washburn, Benjamin Earl. "College Folklore at Chapel Hill in the Early 1900s." *North Carolina Folklore* 3.2 (1955): 27–30.

Five

Contexts

POLITICAL PROTEST

At times of political crisis, students on college campuses have often expressed controversial viewpoints. Protests, subversive strategies, and resistance to compulsory military service have resulted in some memorable legends. Material from interviews, books, and campus archives helps us understand how students' legend telling develops in a political context.

A case in point is the telling of legends about students' resistance to the draft for the Vietnam War. In the late 1960s and early 1970s, legends about unusual ways to avoid the draft circulated widely. One legend that I heard in 1972 described a student who ate only potato chips and drank large quantities of water for several days before his Army physical. The salty potato chips raised his blood pressure, and the extra water increased his weight by 30 pounds. For both of these reasons, he received a "4-F" classification and never had to worry about the draft again.

Another Vietnam story told in 1973 described a student who, desperate for a way to avoid the draft, asked a friend what he would recommend. This friend went to his closet and pulled out an old pair of leather sandals. "These are magic sandals," he told the worried student. "Wear them for a while—then you'll be fine." After a week of wearing his friend's magic sandals, the student found that his feet were becoming discolored and sore. When he reported to the Army office for his physical, he was immediately disqualified for military service because of his injured feet.

A legend narrated by a female college student from New York City in 2004 recalls the student who enrolled in medical school courses each semester so that he could avoid the Vietnam War draft. One semester, he forgot to register in time and received a summons from the draft board. Desperately asking friends for advice, he learned that if he dressed up in a nice suit, got a conservative haircut, and came to his draft board appointment early, offering the board members doughnuts while explaining how much he wanted to be a doctor, he might get an exemption. The student got a haircut and a new suit and showed up early, carrying a large box of doughnuts. After explaining how much he cared about becoming a doctor, he received an exemption from the draft.

Arlo Guthrie's popular song "Alice's Restaurant" tells a long, meandering tale of draft resistance (1966): illegal garbage dumping and frenzied mutterings about wanting to kill people result in the singer's freedom from going to war. Long celebrated as a song of counter cultural protest, "Alice's Restaurant" has been a favorite on college campuses for many years. While the story about illegal garbage dumping is specific to the singer's group of friends, encouragement to avoid the draft by acting crazy is the stuff of campus rumors and legendry. Some of these celebrated incidents resemble campus pranks, with their focus on extreme behavior and hilarious exaggerations, but their message is serious.

One of the saddest stories of student resistance tells of the massacre in Tiananmen Square in Beijing, China. On the night of June 3, 1989, Chinese soldiers opened fire on a large group of students holding a peaceful protest against the government's policies. While it is still unclear how many students died, many of them lost their lives in this governmental crackdown. In *Tiananmen Diary: Thirteen Days in June* (1989), Harrison E. Salisbury describes the conflicting rumors and stories that circulated at the time of the massacre. How many tanks rolled through the streets of Beijing? How many students died? Was it true that students took over landmarks in other towns in protest against the government's tyranny? Shocked by what had happened, students around the world mourned what had occurred.

At the turn of the twentieth century, students in tsarist Russia told stories about the genesis of their protest movement. In *Students, Professors, and the State in Tsarist Russia* (1989), Samuel D. Kassow explains how university students followed Lenin's encouragement to protest against the tsarist government on March 4, 1901. Standing in Kazan Square in Saint Petersburg, students raised signs, celebrating their resistance. Some stories describe Cossacks beating students, knocking their hats off, and pushing them against the steps of Kazan Cathedral; others indicate that students started the conflict by hurling rocks at the Cossacks' horses. Kassow says, "Although there were wild rumors to the contrary, no one died or even suffered serious wounds" (129–30).

Legends have also circulated in interesting ways in Third World countries. I had the opportunity to hear some emerging legends at the University of

Abidjan in the Ivory Coast, where I served as a Peace Corps volunteer from 1973 to 1974. In the fall of 1973, 13 years after this West African nation declared its independence from French colonial rule, university students shared stories about an attempted coup that had recently threatened the government's stability. *Fraternité Matin*, the nation's one newspaper, had not reported an attempted coup, but oral narratives described an uprising led by high-ranking officers in the army, saying that when the coup was defeated, the president killed the rebellious officers and ate them. While cannibalism existed in the Ivory Coast at that time, it was difficult to know whether these stories were true.

Other stories told by students at the University of Abidjan from 1973 to 1974 dramatized students' powerlessness to choose their own areas of study and future careers. One student told me the story of a friend of a friend who loved literature and had no aptitude for science. This student had been told to study medicine because the country needed more physicians. Another student said he had heard about someone who had been told to study business although he was terrible at mathematics. Confronted with an impossible career path, the newly designated business major fled to his family's farm. Alarmed by their lack of choice, some of the students asked me to do a campus radio show on the government's mandate to make students' choices for them. Agreeing to organize a show, I asked the students to put their stories on tape. Excitement grew in the student community. However, a few days before the show was scheduled to go on the air, I received a phone call saying that if we went ahead with the show, I would have to leave the country on the next plane. We canceled the show. Looking back on that experience now, I understand that the government saw me as a participant in political protest: an inappropriate role for a Peace Corps volunteer. Since the radio show involved transmission of oral narratives to a large audience, government officials felt threatened by its potential impact.

PSYCHOLOGY

Why do some campus legends flourish while others die out? Each campus has its own unique history, but certain commonalities exist. Chip Heath, a psychologist on the faculty of Stanford's Business School, has conducted experiments to learn what kinds of information people like to share with each other. Working with students, Heath discovered they preferred to share "extreme news" that was either much better or much worse than what their listeners expected to hear. Muggings near campus fell into the "extreme bad news" category, while medical successes became" extreme good news." Hoping to make an impression on their listeners, the students would stretch the truth somewhat. Heath explains, "People do care about the truth of an idea, but they also want to tell stories that produce strong emotion, and that second tendency sometimes gets in the way of the first" ("Ideas That Stick").

Although Heath's study analyzes contemporary rumors and legends, its principles apply to legend patterns from earlier eras. For example, origin legends about intense experiences seem to last longer than legends that provoke only mild emotional responses. Legends about colleges founded in memory of deceased children commemorate tragic loss. Sweet Briar College was founded in honor of Daisy Williams, who died of pneumonia in 1883 at the age of 16. Wellesley College began when Henry and Pauline Smith, who had lost their eight-year-old son to diphtheria, decided to found a seminary to train women as teachers "upon sound Christian principles" (Kendall 58). Of these two origin legends, only one—the story of Daisy Williams—has generated a thriving legend cycle. Sweet Briar College's ghost story Web site (http://ghosts.hbc.edu) presents some of the many legends told by students and faculty members about Daisy's continuing presence on campus.

Many campus legends explore what happens when students undergo extreme stress. Exams, fraternity and sorority hazing rituals, and social pressures test first-year students' adaptive abilities. The central character of "fatal initiation" legends usually dies, displaying the worst-case scenario that freshmen fear. In exam

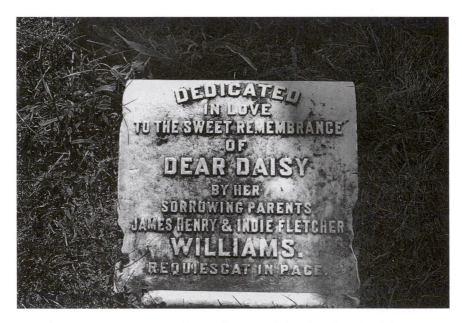

Daisy's grave, Sweet Briar College. Photograph by Geoffrey Gould.

legends, on the other hand, tricky students get the best of their professors by offering quirky answers to challenging questions. Examples of such questions are included in chapters 2 and 3.

Another kind of exam, the personality assessment test, has found its way into campus folklore. Since the early 1970s, many students have taken the Myers-Briggs Type Indicator, often offered in career counseling and residential life staff development. Based on the theories of C. G. Jung, the Myers-Briggs test offers 16 personality profiles. Each type has its own set of letters: for example, "INTJ" means introversion, intuition, thinking, and judging (Quenk). Uncomfortably aware of this assessment process, students have come up with tests such as this one, which circulated in the form of photocopies in 1991:

No-Nonsense Personality Inventory

1. I salivate at the sight of mittens.
2. At times I am afraid that my toes will fall off.
3. As an infant, I had very few hobbies.
4. Some people look at me.
5. I often use the word "feh."

President's house, Sweet Briar College. Photograph by Geoffrey Gould.

6.   Spinach makes me feel alone.

7.   Sometimes I steal objects like medicine balls and ovaries.

8.   Dirty stories make me think about sex.

9.   Cousins are not to be trusted.

10.   Other people's warts don't make me self-conscious.

11.   Sometimes I think someone is trying to take over my stomach.

12.   Often I think I am a special agent of Carl Rogers.

13.   I become homicidal when people try to reason with me.

14.   My teeth sometimes leave my body.

This list's humor comes from its concatenation of bizarre suggestions and criticism. The first item, "I salivate at the sight of mittens," suggests aberrant behavior, but "Dirty stories make me think about sex" classifies a natural response as an abnormal one. Number 13, "I become homicidal when people try to reason with me," brings campus murder legends to mind. In general, such mock tests express students' annoyance with being scrutinized. Skeptical of personality pigeonholing, students enjoy the comic relief of making up tests of their own.

Legends about unusual psychologists have also conveyed students' feelings of discomfort. The best-known legend of this kind is the story of B. F. Skinner, listed on Barbara and David Mikkelson's Urban Legend Reference Pages (http://www.snopes.com). According to this Web site, "Psychologist B.F. Skinner raised his daughter Debbie in a 'Skinner box'; as a result, she grew up psychologically damaged, sued her father, and committed suicide." In various forms, this legend circulated widely in the mid- to late 1960s, showing concern about a scientist unnaturally harming his own child. The legend's central feature was the box in which Debbie Skinner slept and played. People accepted the need for psychologists to train rats in enclosures, but they were outraged by the idea of putting a person into a box. When Internet communication became popular, legends about Skinner continued to circulate. Some Web sites criticize B. F. Skinner, and others defend him; the real Debbie Skinner (Deborah Skinner Buzan) has a Web site of her own. Lauren Slater analyzes the B. F. Skinner legend in depth in her book *Opening Skinner's Box: Great Psychological Experiments of the Twentieth Century* (2004). It is interesting that among the many psychologists who have experimented with human capabilities, only Skinner has provoked a long-lasting campus legend. No matter how much science evolves, comparisons between humans and lab rats do not make listeners happy.

PARAPSYCHOLOGY

One of the most famous American campus ghost stories appears in the annals of parapsychology, a field dedicated to the study of psychic phenomena. "Unfinished Business," an article in the *Journal of the American Society for Psychical Research* (Murphy and Klemme), reports what happened when Mrs. Coleen Buterbaugh, secretary to the dean of Nebraska Wesleyan University in Lincoln, Nebraska, entered the C.C. White Building at about 8:50 A.M. First she smelled a "musty, disagreeable odor"; then she saw a tall, black-haired woman extending one arm to the top of the shelves in an old music cabinet (306). A transcript of Mrs. Buterbaugh's own words explains what happened when she looked out the window: "The street (Madison Street), which is less than a half block away from the building, was not even there and neither was the new Willard House. That was when I *realized that these people were not in my time, but that I was back in their time*" (307).

A staff member at Nebraska Wesleyan thought the ghost of the C.C. White Building might have been Miss Clarissa U. Mills, an instructor in music theory and piano who had died in a room across the hall from the location where the paranormal experience took place. When Mrs. Buterbaugh saw a yearbook picture of the music teacher, she thought this was probably the ghost she had seen. The file cabinet toward which the ghost was reaching contained choral music files from the years before Miss Mills's death in 1936, so the ghost might have been trying to finish work that was not complete. The authors of "Unfinished Business" concluded that the view of the campus as it had been in the past provided "a clear-cut case of retrocognition" (319). While there was some evidence of Mrs. Buterbaugh having neurological abnormalities, this evidence did not seem to cancel out the possibility of paranormal activity.

The story of the ghost and the view through the window has evolved through oral tradition. Storytellers sometimes say that the person who see the ghost and the view of the past is a faculty member, not a member of the dean's staff. Duane Hutchinson's *A Storyteller's Ghost Stories* (1987) correctly identifies Mrs. Buterbaugh as the dean's secretary and calls the ghost "Clara Urania Mills." Hutchinson describes his efforts to find the apartment building where Miss Mills lived. Once he located the building, he talked with a young woman living there who had seen the ghost of a woman with "a big, Afro-like pile of hair on her head" and "funny, pointed button shoes" (34). Internet versions of the Nebraska Wesleyan story have tended to downplay Miss Mills's presence and to focus on the story's main event: an inexplicable view of the past through glass.

While the Nebraska Wesleyan story focuses on smell and sight, some other stories of interest to parapsychologists emphasize sound and perception of cold as well as visual imagery. In the early 1970s, members of Toronto's Society for Psychical Research wrote a description of a hypothetical spirit named Philip. When they tried to contact Philip during a séance, they saw the table move and heard rapping noises (Owen 1976). Almost 20 years later, the professor of an experimental parapsychology class at Franklin Pierce College organized a similar experiment. Choosing six female and two male students who could "suspend disbelief in paranormal activity," the professor invited them to attend meditation sessions and then a Victorian séance. Their meeting room contained a small table covered with a Confederate flag at the center of which was a lighted candle. The students sat on the floor around the table.

At the first meditation session, the students heard a story about "Alexander," an officer in the Confederate army who fell in love with a Yankee woman named Susan. When Susan was killed in a raid on a northern town, Alexander decided to retaliate by spying for the Union army. After the signing of the peace treaty, he told General Lee what he had done. That night, his fellow soldiers heard a single gunshot and found Alexander dead in bed. On his lap was a note that said, "I am sorry for my traitorous acts! At least I shall have peace in knowing I am finally going to join my Susan" (Bourgeois).

Although the students knew that Alexander was an artificial spirit, they had no trouble visualizing him and Susan. During the second session, one of the female students reported that she had dreamed about Confederate army uniforms. Gradually, the experiment produced two main results: unexplained flaring of the candle's flame and strange movement of a basketball-sized cold spot around the room. Some participants also heard knocking on the walls and on the table. Because of these results, the researcher concluded that contact with an artificial spirit could produce psychokinetic phenomena.

Around the turn of the twenty-first century, parapsychologists and interested students made local news headlines by testing college campuses for paranormal activity. Two different groups of researchers spent nights in North Hall at Mansfield University in Mansfield, Pennsylvania, to try to document the presence of Sarah, who had jumped from the sixth-floor atrium when her boyfriend rejected her (Wehrman). Similarly, at the University of Texas at Brownsville, ghost hunters brought recording equipment into the campus library. When one of the researchers felt a supernatural presence staring at him from a hallway, he snapped a picture. The next day, when the pictures were developed, one of them showed a ghostlike figure standing under a light in the hall (Handy).

ANTHROPOLOGY

Anthropology, the study of humankind, overlaps with folklore study in many ways. Both anthropologists and folklorists gather information about human behavior in its social and cultural context. While anthropologists scrutinize people's origins, physical and cultural development, racial features, and social practices, folklorists closely examine the traditions that bring people together in groups. Both folklorists and anthropologists do ethnographies (descriptions of people), and both use similar field recording devices: audiotape recorders, videotape recorders, and cameras.

One bizarre intersection of folklore and anthropology became known as "The Great Ivy League Nude Posture Photo Scandal" when *New York Times* writer Ron Rosenbaum wrote an article about it in the *New York Times Magazine* in 1995. In the late 1920s, Wellesley College started photographing all entering freshmen for the purpose of posture correction. By the 1940s, one of the first requirements for freshmen at Vassar, Smith, Mount Holyoke, Princeton, Yale, and other colleges was a nude posture photo. My mother had her photograph taken in 1942 at Mount Holyoke College. In the fall of 1966, when I got in line for my own posture photo at Mount Holyoke, I was grateful that we were allowed to wear leotards. Posture photos were discontinued in the 1970s at Mount Holyoke, Harvard, Vassar, and Yale as well as on other campuses. In the 1950s and 1960s, students at Yale University told stories about someone breaking into a photography lab in Poughkeepsie, New York, and stealing all the negatives for Vassar's posture photos, then selling them on the black market. Some variants of this story specified that the buyers belonged to Yale's secret society Skull and Bones (Rosenbaum). Naomi Wolf, who graduated from Yale in 1984, describes Dick Cavett's account of the posture photo theft in her book *The Beauty Myth*:

At my college graduation, the commencement speaker, Dick Cavett—who had been a "brother" of the university president in an all-male secret society—was confronted by two thousand young female Yale graduates in mortarboards and academic gowns, and offered them this story: When he was at Yale there were no women. The women went to Vassar. There, they had nude photographs taken in gym class to check their posture. Some of the photos ended up in the pornography black market in New Haven. The punch line: The photos found no buyers (212).

Explaining the devastating effect of this story on the young female graduates, Wolf says, "The speaker had transposed us for a moment out of the gentle quadrangle, where we had been led to believe we were cherished, and into the tawdry district four blocks away where stolen photographs of our naked bodies would find no buyers" (213). Although Cavett wrote a letter to the *New York Times* protesting that his story was a harmless remnant of his years at Yale, it was clear that his narration of the posture photo legend had had an explosive effect on the listeners.

Writing about posture photo legends in 1995, Ron Rosenbaum invoked an even more disturbing possibility: a chain of influence that went back to the eugenics movement of the 1930s and early 1940s. Many photographs of nude Harvard freshmen can be found in W. H. Sheldon's book *Atlas of Men* (1954), which identifies three main body types: ectomorph, endomorph, and mesomorph. Both Sheldon and his predecessor, the Harvard anthropology professor E. A. Hooton, believed that body types held the key to intelligence,

McGraw Tower, Cornell University. Photograph by Geoffrey Gould.

morality, and potential achievement. Hooton's book *The American Criminal* (1939) suggests that criminals have thinner eyebrows, straighter hair, higher nasal bridges, and more protuberant ears than noncriminals have. Correlating body types with age, race, occupation, marital status, and other variables, Hooton tries to prove that body types predict whether a person will commit a crime. Inspiration for Hooton's study came from Francis Galton, social Darwinism's founder, who had proposed a large-scale photo archive for Great Britain.

W. H. Sheldon directed an institute for physique studies at Columbia University and traveled from campus to campus, assembling an archive of students' pictures. Although he dreamed of publishing an *Atlas of Women*, parental outrage at the University of Washington, Pembroke College, and other institutions put a stop to this plan. Rosenbaum asks several probing questions: Was Sheldon a serious scholar or a gatherer of pornography? Were the posture photos intended mainly for posture correction, or was there a hidden agenda of eugenics? Because there are no clear answers, this story is just right for campus legendry, which highlights the unknowable.

LITERATURE

Memoir

Writing about their college years, some authors have vividly described campus legends. Most of these descriptions represent the viewpoint of students, but some come from faculty members and administrators. A warm sense of nostalgia fills many college reminiscences. Some descriptions entertain the reader with humorous details, while others are more serious. The question of belief often arises. Can we trust our memories to tell us exactly what happened? And, if so, will others believe what we experienced?

One of the more lighthearted memoirs is Peter Sammartino's *Of Castles and Colleges: Notes toward an Autobiography* (1972). Sammartino, president of Fairleigh Dickinson University from 1942 to 1967, started its Rutherford, New Jersey, campus when he purchased the Ivison castle, built in 1886. Impressed by the castle's turrets and gables, members of this new university community thought unusual things might happen there. Before long, this proved to be true.

During the college's first year, students told stories about the ghost of Mrs. Ivison, famous in the local community for returning home at midnight, on the anniversary of her death, to seek her husband, whose name was David. Once they had become familiar with this local legend, several students begged President Sammartino to allow them to stay overnight in the castle. Agreeing to let them stay, Sammartino persuaded Julius, a young man on his staff, to hide in a secret passageway on the castle's third floor while the students had a party downstairs. At midnight on the night of the party, Julius tiptoed out of the secret passageway, held a flashlight against a frosted-glass wall, and moaned, "David! David!" Shocked by what they had seen and heard, the students searched the entire castle, finding nothing. When they told President Sammartino what had happened, he replied, "Oh, you were just imagining things" (146). The resulting campus legend continued for some time, and students gave the apparition's name to their literary journal.

The Fairleigh Dickinson students' request to stay overnight in a haunted castle follows the general pattern of the Grimms' folktale "The Youth Who Wanted to Learn What Fear Is" (A-T 326). College students have often planned legend trips in search of ghosts, hoping to find evidence of undeniable supernatural phenomena. What stands out here is the fact that the president himself played a prank, then acted as if he knew nothing about what had happened. Reminiscing about how he came up with his plan, Sammartino says that he and Julius were "like two little boys cooking up a story" (146). In fact, he and his associate acted more like camp counselors than little boys, scaring their charges with a carefully arranged prank that became part of the community's folklore. Fairleigh Dickinson University was relatively small at that time, with friendly relationships among students, faculty, and staff members. It would be difficult to imagine such a prank happening in the twenty-first century, when university presidents' relationships with their students tend to be more formal.

Another memoir related to A-T 326 is Maxine Hong Kingston's *The Woman Warrior: Memoirs of a Girlhood among Ghosts* (1975). Kingston gives the reader a strong sense of her family's supernatural storytelling traditions. Ghost stories provided "good chills" during hot afternoons in the family's laundry (87). These stories of spectral ancestors and other frightening figures convey powerful messages about past tragedies and current social rules.

Chapter 3, "Shamans," tells of Kingston's mother's experiences as a student at the To Keung School of Midwifery in China. The reader gets a glimpse of daily life in a Chinese dormitory for female students, not often familiar to Western readers. Kingston's mother, Brave Orchid, enters the School of Midwifery in her thirties. Older and wiser than the other students, she has no qualms about spending a night in her dormitory's haunted room.

Late at night, Brave Orchid hears "a rushing coming out from under the bed" (68). A Sitting Ghost attacks, pressing against her chest and sapping her strength. Unafraid, she threatens the ghost: "You are a puny little boulder indeed. Yes, when I get my oil, I will fry you for breakfast." She chants her lessons for the next day, then falls asleep and awakens as the other students rush in to see what has happened. "Take my earlobes, please," she tells them, "and pull them back and forth. In case I lost any of my self, I want you to call me back" (71). After classes end, Brave Orchid organizes a ghost hunt that involves burning alcohol and oil in a bucket to fill the haunted room with smoke. Under the bed, the students discover a piece of wood covered with blood, which they burn in a pot.

This dramatic encounter with a Sitting Ghost follows the pattern identified by David Hufford in *The Terror That Comes in the Night* (1982): a ghost presses down on a person's chest, preventing sleep and frightening the victim. As Hufford explains in "Beings without Bodies," the Chinese *bei Guai chaak* is one form of this ghostly attacker known by various names around the world (13).

Another fascinating account of supernatural assault arises in Pascal Khoo Thwe's *From the Land of Green Ghosts: A Burmese Odyssey* (2002). This unusual memoir begins with Thwe's childhood as a member of the Padaung people, for whom ghosts belong to everyday life. The author explains, "Ours is a ghost and spirit culture, and for us the presence of ghosts is as natural as reincarnation is to the Buddhists" (17). Seeing a ghost has little shock value, as spirits from the past constantly interact with the living.

Thwe enrolls at the University of Mandalay, where he lives in a hostel with fellow students and goes to tea shops for simple meals. Having been robbed on arrival, he feels shaky about going outside, but the memory of his tribe's hopes and good wishes makes him venture out to class. He joins a small group of students with an interest in English literature and meets Dr. John Casey, a visiting professor from Cambridge University who likes Thwe's passion for studying the works of James Joyce. Later, Casey sends Thwe a letter inviting him to study in England. Thwe gratefully accepts and eventually becomes the first Burmese tribesman to graduate from Cambridge, dressed in his people's traditional clothing.

Before leaving Burma, Thwe meets a battalion of ghosts. As a member of a student platoon fighting against Burma's military dictatorship in 1989, he goes to Salween to help Karenni fighters. Early one morning, while sleeping, he feels his blanket being pulled away. Suspecting a prank, he awakens his fellow students, but no one admits responsibility for what happened. When they search the area, the students find ghostly figures shivering and groaning. Some wear uniforms; all of them are "soaking wet and grey in colour." When the students point their guns at these specters, they disappear "like smoke" (212). The next day, the students learn that a battalion of Burmese soldiers had died there and had never received proper burial. A combination of Buddhist rites and Christian prayers persuades the ghosts to go away, but sometimes the students hear sounds from the hilltops that suggest further supernatural activity.

Science Fiction

Since the publication of Jules Verne's *Journey to the Center of the Earth* (*Voyage au Centre de la Terre*) in 1864, professors and their students have played major roles in science fiction novels. The term "mad scientist" fits some professor heroes who, longing for scientific achievement, see nothing but their own goals. In some science fiction novels of the nineteenth century, the quest to learn new material involves the study of alchemy: a mysterious pursuit closely linked with medieval legends.

Verne's Professor Hardwigg (known in some editions of *Journey to the Center of the Earth* as Professor Lidenbrock) loves nothing better than learning. Harry, his nephew, irreverently describes him as "a professor of philosophy, chemistry, geology, mineralogy, and many other ologies" (7). Harry cheekily describes his uncle's obsession with knowledge:

He was a very learned man. Now most persons in this category supply themselves with information, as peddlers do with goods, for the benefit of others, and lay up stores in order to diffuse them abroad for the benefit of society in general. Not so my excellent uncle, Professor Hardwigg; he studied, he consumed the midnight oil, he pored over heavy tomes, and digested huge quartos and folios in order to keep the knowledge acquired to himself (8).

In his relentless quest for knowledge, Professor Hardwigg forgets about nourishment and other necessities of life. He is a typical absentminded professor, like Professor Lightbody and other heroes of campus legendry.

Professor Hardwigg resembles Faust, the German legend character who wants, above all else, to learn what holds the earth together. The professor's supreme goal is to gain "*real knowledge of the earth*" through the study of geology and mineralogy (9). Like Faust, he reveres the early philosophers who sought to change base metals into gold. Discovering a parchment from the sixteenth-century professor and alchemist Arne Saknussemm, he struggles to find "profound meaning" in the manuscript's runic letters (15). Suddenly realizing that reading the words *backward* provides the key to their meaning, Harry decodes Saknussemm's message: "Descend into the crater of Yocul of Sneffels, which the shade of Scartaris caresses, before the kalends of July, audacious traveler, and you will reach the center of the earth. I did it" (24). In this exciting way, Harry discovers the key to an arduous but ultimately successful quest.

Almost 50 years before the publication of Verne's novel, Mary Shelley wrote *The Modern Prometheus,* better known to us now as *Frankenstein.* Inspiration for Shelley's novel came from discussion with her husband, Percy Bysshe Shelley, and Lord Byron as well as hours spent reading ghost stories during a rainy summer in a villa near Geneva, Switzerland. Each guest in the villa decided to write a ghost story; Mary Shelley's story came to her during a night of strange dreams during which she saw Frankenstein's monster standing by his creator's bedside.

Shelley's protagonist, Victor Frankenstein, seeks the answers to difficult questions. Even as a child, he expresses a deep desire to learn the secrets of heaven and earth:

The world was to me a secret, which I desired to divine. Curiosity, earnest research to learn the hidden laws of nature, gladness akin to rapture, as they were unfolded to me, are among the earliest sensations I can remember (22).

When he enters the University of Ingolstadt, Victor finds a mentor, Professor Waldman, who tells his students that modern masters of chemistry have virtually limitless powers; "they can command the thunders of heaven, mimic the earthquake, and even mock the invisible world with its own shadows" (33). Resolving to emulate these masters, Victor decides that he will "pioneer a new way, explore unknown powers, and unfold to the world the deepest mysteries of creation" (33). In making this decision, he becomes a Faustian figure with a tragic destiny.

Frankenstein's attempt to create a monster from human body parts is so well known that it hardly requires description. However, there is no substitute for Shelley's own words, known to fewer people than are the scripts of the various *Frankenstein* movies:

I collected bones from charnel-houses and disturbed, with profane fingers, the tremendous secrets of the human frame. In a solitary chamber, or rather cell, at the top of the house, and separated from all the other apartments by a gallery and staircase, I kept my workshop of filthy creation; my eyeballs were starting from their sockets in attending to the details of my employment. The dissecting room and the slaughter-house furnished many of my materials; and often did my human nature turn with loathing from my occupation, whilst, still urged on by an eagerness which perpetually increased, I brought my work near to a conclusion (39).

With obsessive concentration, Frankenstein brings the creature to life. One yellow eye opens, showing that the experiment has worked. From that moment on, disaster develops. The creature kills and destroys, then pursues Frankenstein to reproach him with sadness and anger. What, the creature asks, is the purpose of bringing to life someone who can find no joy and achieve no good purpose? Unable to respond, Victor suffers the emotional devastation that his hasty act of creation has caused. The moral of this story is clear: Faustian meddling with the boundaries of life and death inevitably leads to disaster.

Frankenstein's tragic story has influenced medical school legends, which often feature human bodies and body parts. Although most of these legends have a lighthearted tone, they usually convey the message that people should not treat the human body irreverently. A Berkeley legend of this kind, "Joke on the Janitor," is included in chapter 3.

Almost a century after the publication of Mary Shelley's novel, H. G. Wells published his science fiction masterpiece *The Time Machine* (1895). This novel's protagonist is a time traveler who pursues research on relationships between space and time. Surrounded by friends who represent academic disciplines and positions of civic responsibility—the Psychologist, the Medical Man, the Journalist, and the Provincial Mayor—the Time Traveler tells the group, "You must follow me carefully. I shall have to controvert one or two ideas that are almost universally accepted. The geometry, for instance, they taught you at school is founded on a misconception" (1). Taking the role of an iconoclast, he seeks to prove that old concepts of time and space are wrong.

The Time Traveler believes that people can travel through time to discover a communistic society. With far-reaching scientific imagination, he suggests that "there is no difference between Time and any of the three dimensions of Space except that our consciousness moves along it" (3). Although his friends deny that such a thing can happen, he dares to prove them wrong.

In his reckless determination to break new scientific ground, the Time Traveler is, like Professor Hardwigg and Victor Frankenstein, a "mad scientist." His friends think the Time Traveler is "too clever to be believed"; actions that less brilliant individuals could perform with no objection seem "tricks in his hands" (13). He is certainly a trickster: someone who thinks and moves swiftly, putting his own goals above the needs of others and disregarding society's rules. Paul Radin's *The Trickster* (1969) provides in-depth analysis of such figures. While the Time Traveler is better educated than most tricksters in folk literature, he fits their parameters very well.

Pushing aside his friends' objections, the Time Traveler leaves on a voyage through eras of the past and future. His longest and most memorable trip takes him to the land of the Morlocks, grim creatures of the future who raise innocent young people, the Eloi, to serve as a food supply. The Time Traveler warns readers of perils to come:

I grieved to think how brief the dream of the human intellect had been. It had committed suicide. It had set itself steadfastly toward comfort and ease, a balanced society with security and permanency as its watchword, it had attained its hopes—to come to this at last (97).

While *The Time Machine* has enchanted many readers, it also offers thought-provoking reflections on the mystery of the earth's destiny. If the Time Traveler were not so intent on learning, the book's viewpoint would be very different.

A contemporary best-seller with many similarities to *The Time Machine* is Michael Crichton's *Timeline* (1999), which explores the field of quantum mechanics. One of the book's central characters is Yale professor Edward Johnston, whose archaeological team is excavating ruins of the fourteenth-century French fortress town of Castelgard. At the invitation of the chief executive officer of ITC, a company striving to discover new potential for the use of quantum mechanics, Johnston travels to fourteenth-century France, then finds himself stranded there. Three of his graduate students take the risk of traveling through time to bring their professor home. Medallions around their necks are supposed to help them return, but an accident in the lab makes safe passage impossible.

In a number of ways, *Timeline* resembles the folktale: it has a central hero with three helpers, "magic" medallions, and a quest that is very difficult to achieve. Campus legends have also made their mark on Crichton's novel. The daring, tricky professor obsessed with research and the strange, mysterious lab are familiar ingredients of campus stories. More specifically, legends about tricky archaeologists apply to this novel's characterization and plot. Stories about archaeology professors tricking their students by "salting" excavation sites with objects that don't belong there have become well known in the oral tradition of archaeologists. In some of these stories, students identify the false objects, but in others, the objects become known as amazing finds (Neller).

Professor Johnston, like some professors on contemporary research teams, has the help of several graduate students. Although most of the graduate students are confused and headstrong, they are willing participants in a dark, legendlike drama of uncertain outcome. The conclusion, which is both delightful and surprising, brings this hybrid novel into the realm of fantasy literature: an appropriate twist since quantum mechanics resembles fantasy in its exploration of the unknown.

Mystery Novels

Since the early 1900s, academic mystery novels have drawn some of their best characters from campus folklore. The absentminded professor, the student or professor obsessed with research, and the angry, vengeful colleague all come from the annals of academe. In mystery novels, those who commit—or seem to commit—murder include professors, deans, students, custodians, and other members of the academic community. The sleuth who must identify the murderer may be a professor or someone else who knows the campus well. Readers familiar with academic legend characters understand why professors make such good sleuths. Like Merlin in the cycle of legends about King Arthur, they are farseeing and versatile; like Socrates, they know how to ask important questions. Persistent and devoted, they refuse to deviate from their pursuit of truth and justice.

The academic mystery novel's pathfinder is Dorothy L. Sayers, author of *Gaudy Night* (1936). This novel's setting is Oxford, described as follows:

Students sauntering in pairs. Students dashing to lectures, their gowns hitched hurriedly over light summer frocks, the wind jerking their flat caps into the absurd likeness of so many jesters' cockscombs. Bicycles stacked in the porter's lodge, their carriers piled with books and gowns twisted about their handlebars. A grizzled woman don crossing the turf with vague eyes, her thoughts riveted upon aspects of sixteenth-century philosophy, her sleeves floating, her shoulders cocked to the academic angle that automatically compensated the backward drag of the pleated poplin. Two male commoners in search of a coach, bareheaded, hands in their trousers-pockets, talking loudly about boats (8).

In this idyllic setting, the administrators of Shrewsbury College (a fictitious college for women) discover that a "Poison Pen" is leaving vicious, hurtful notes for others to find. Harriet Vane, an alumna of Shrewsbury who has come back for her college's Gaudy—which American students would call a reunion—discovers that her talent for writing mystery novels has impressed her former teachers. As the Poison Pen's influence becomes more and more troubling, Shrewsbury's administrators beg Harriet to help them find the culprit. Agreeing to stay for a while at Oxford, Harriet confers with Lord Peter Wimsey, who has often asked her to marry him. After the Poison Pen wreaks havoc on the campus, she tries to strangle Harriet. Lord Peter announces that he has determined the identity of the assailant: Annie Wilson, an Oxford servant whose husband committed suicide after a Shrewsbury professor found him responsible for academic dishonesty. Hearing Lord Peter's charge, Annie asks the professor, "You broke him and killed him—all for nothing. Do you think that a woman's job?" (372).

While seriously examining gender issues, *Gaudy Night* combines themes that often come up in the campus legend: suicide, attempted murder, academic dishonor, and preoccupation with research. Sayers emphasizes the importance of scholarly work while bringing *Gaudy Night* to a conclusion that reminds us of the folktale's "happily ever after." Standing on the riverbank with her admirer, Lord Peter Wimsey, Harriet accepts his proposal of marriage with an academically appropriate Latin word: "Placet" (383).

One of the most successful authors of the contemporary academic mystery novel is Amanda Cross, the author of 14 books featuring English professor and amateur sleuth Kate Fansler. "Amanda Cross" is the pseudonym of James Joyce scholar and feminist Carolyn G. Heilbrun, whose scholarly publications include *Writing a Woman's Life* (1988). Cross's love of literature, sense of humor, and familiarity with campus life have resulted in an intriguing series of detective novels.

The first Kate Fansler mystery, *In the Last Analysis,* was published in 1964. "April is the cruelest month," the first line of T. S. Eliot's "The Wasteland," leads the reader into a large Manhattan campus where students, always youthful, make professors feel old. Fansler, a professor of eighteenth-century literature, refers her beautiful student Janet Harrison to a psychoanalyst, Emanuel Bauer. Some weeks later, Janet is murdered on Emanuel's couch, and police discover that his fingerprints cover the knife that killed her. Since Emanuel is her good friend and former lover, Fansler launches an investigation to prove that he is innocent. Interviewing Jackie, a student at her university, she learns that a prank—putting soap in the campus fountain—is a crucial clue. Each glimpse of student life helps Fansler piece together the solution to Janet's murder.

Later mysteries in the Kate Fansler series describe teaching, research, social events, and departmental politics, with an emphasis on feminist issues. In *Death in a Tenured Position* (1982), Janet Mandelbaum, the first woman professor in the Department of English at Harvard University, is found drunk on the floor of the women's room after someone spikes her tea. Determined to find out who wants to discredit this woman, Fansler decides to investigate her colleagues' motives. In this book and others, departmental relations have become so hostile that a sudden fatality raises many suspicions. *Honest Doubt* (2000) begins with the death of Professor Charles Haycock, a woman hater who is detested by the entire Department of English at Clifton University. When Haycock's son insists on exhuming his father's body, it becomes clear that the professor was murdered. Who killed him? Fansler solves the mystery by comparing Haycock's murder to the crime revealed in Agatha Christie's *Murder on the Orient Express* (1974).

Authors of other academic mystery novels have enjoyed referring to novels similar to their own. In Carolyn G. Hart's *A Little Class on Murder* (1989), fifth in the "Death on Demand" series, bookstore owner Annie Laurance agrees to teach a community college class on the "Three Great Ladies of the Mystery": Agatha Christie, Mary Roberts Rhinehart, and Dorothy L. Sayers. After the editor of the college's student newspaper reveals a professor's embezzlement, events unfold with a speed that rivals the tempo of the three great ladies' novels. The embezzling professor commits suicide; someone murders the head of his department, and a bomb destroys the newspaper office, killing a secretary. Laurance, the professor/sleuth, joins forces with her detective husband and her best customer, a "mystery nut," to identify the criminal. With so many crimes happening in rapid succession, this mystery novel offers a difficult puzzle, including a situation sometimes found in academic legends: the suicide of a professor who has fallen into despair at the loss of his academic or personal reputation. Campus legendry focuses more often on students' suicides than on the suicides of professors, but this novel's emphasis on sudden, self-inflicted death, with its reminder of academic and social tensions, follows patterns of college folklore.

Not all academic mystery novels feature professors as sleuths. One popular set of books, M. D. Lake's "Peggy O'Neill Mystery Series," recounts the adventures of a campus policewoman with a talent for finding murderers. In *A Gift for Murder* (1992), a university community goes into shock when successful author Cameron Harris is found dead in a closet with a chapter of his most recent manuscript on his lap. Peggy O'Neill's inquiry into the murder makes some members of the Tower Writers' Collective prime suspects. Since O'Neill has a romantic link to a member of the collective, she knows how to interpret a complicated blend of academic and personal issues. *A Gift for Murder* offers insight into academic life as viewed by the campus police force. It also builds on the "town/gown" disharmony that campus legends have expressed since the battle of Saint Scholastica's Day in medieval Oxford.

Murder becomes multicultural in the novels of Pamela Thomas-Graham, whose sleuth Nikki Chase is the only black professor in Harvard's Department of Economics; Thomas-Graham herself was the first black woman to become a partner at a large company in New York City. In *A Darker Shade of Crimson* (1998), first in the "Ivy League Mystery" series, Chase discovers the body of Rosezella Maynette Fisher, dean of students at Harvard Law School, during a blackout in a classroom building. Learning that Dean Fisher had many enemies in the academic community, Chase enlists the help of the only two people saddened by her passing to solve the mystery. This novel's plot reflects the modern era of electronic communication, as two of the dead dean's computer disks prove to be important sources of information. One of this novel's strengths is its contrast between older Black Americans influenced by the civil rights movement and younger people who are less aware of the importance of the past. With its focus on racial issues within hierarchies of power, Thomas-Graham's novel significantly expands the domain of the academic mystery novel. It also brings to mind important stories of past interracial struggles, some of which have become part of campus legendry.

In *Orange Crushed* (2004), third in Thomas-Graham's "Ivy League Mystery" series, Nikki Chase pays a weekend visit to her brother, a student at Princeton. Her mentor at Princeton, Professor Earl Stokes, is rumored to be considering a move to Harvard now that his book *Color Counts* has become a controversial best-seller. When Stokes dies in a suspicious fire at the construction site of the new Afro-American Studies building, Chase insists on investigating his death, although others warn her not to do so. The results of her investigation threaten to cause difficulties at Princeton and Harvard. For folklorists, the professor's death in a fire at a construction site brings to mind countless academic legends that describe devastating fires and deaths during construction. Because fewer campus buildings had protection from fire in the nineteenth century, many stories from that time period recount catastrophes. Some legends claim that victims of fires remain on campus as ghosts (see chapter 3).

Another recently published academic murder mystery is Mark Cohen's *The Fractal Murders* (2004). As this novel's title suggests, its protagonist is a mathematics professor. Jayne Smyers, a specialist in fractal geometry at the University of Colorado, worries about the fact that three professors who work with fractal geometry have mysteriously died; one committed suicide, and two were murdered Smyers teams up with Pepper Keane, a private investigator and ex-Marine who tracks suspects across Colorado, Mexico, Nebraska, and the East Coast. With his love of Heideggerian philosophy and classic rock music, Pepper Keane entertains and surprises the reader. The novel's blend of murder and suicide on campus brings it into the legend's realm. Fractal geometry's applications, still being discovered, offer exciting prospects for innovation and profit.

Still another novel in which a professor serves as sleuth is Aaron Elkins's *Skeleton Dance* (2000), one of several books in the popular Gideon Oliver mystery series. In this series, the professor is a University of Washington forensics specialist whose skill in identifying old bones has earned him the nickname "Skeleton Detective." At the beginning of *Skeleton Dance,* as he struggles entertainingly with the title of his new book for a popular audience—should it be called *Bones to Pick* or *Bungles, Blunders, and Bloopers?*—Oliver gets a call from police inspector Lucien Joly, who wants help in identifying bones found by a dog at an ancient burial site in a cave near Les Eyzies, France. Accepting the inspector's invitation to travel to Les Eyzies as soon as he can, Oliver learns that the local Institut de Préhistoire is a hotbed of academic rivalries and dangerous secrets. This novel's details mirror the complexities of scholarly study. For example, Jacques Beaupierre is murdered with "an Acheulian cordiform hand ax of the Early Paleolithic variety" (251). Elkins's skill in combining such arcane terms with suspenseful plot development has made his novels appealing to a large number of readers. His focus on old bones reminds the reader of stories about Indian burial grounds and other cemeteries, often told on college campuses.

The most commercially successful academic mystery to date is Dan Brown's *The Da Vinci Code* (2003), which has made millions as a longtime best-seller. Its protagonist, Robert Langdon, is professor of religious symbology at Harvard University. Brilliant but unpretentious, Langdon has become famous through his books on religious paintings and cult symbology (first described in Brown's *Angels and Demons* [2000]). Late at night, after delivering a lecture on pagan symbolism at the American University at Paris, Langdon receives a visit from a police lieutenant with shocking news: an elderly curator at the Louvre has been found dead, with a five-pointed star drawn on his body with his own blood. With the help of Sophie Neveu, a talented cryptologist who is the victim's granddaughter, Langdon starts an investigation to decipher the meaning of the code found near the body. If he cannot solve the mystery in time, an ancient truth guarded by members of the Priory of Sion (whose members have included Leonardo da Vinci, Botticelli, and Sir Isaac Newton) will be lost. A menacing albino monk and other sinister characters reminiscent of the Gothic novel add to this story's suspense. The novel's focus on long-hidden, mysterious dangers reflects the world of the legend, in which perils rooted in the past can arise at any moment. Here, the scholar steeped in ancient legends is the only person who can decipher the secret.

For researchers interested in biblical history and the lineage of the sacred feminine, including goddess worship, Brown's novel offers a fertile field of inquiry. Not long after the book's best-seller status was confirmed, books attempting to distinguish fact from fiction also became very popular. *Breaking the Da Vinci Code* (2004), by Darrell L. Bock, is one of these books. Bock, a specialist in religious history, finds much to criticize. This kind of questioning lies at the heart of the legend: What can we believe? Is there really a conspiracy, or are people just seeking sensationalism and amusement? *The Da Vinci Code* brings academic controversy out of the classroom and into the debates of a diverse readership.

Novels about Student Life

Authors writing novels about college life have covered many facets of academic and extracurricular experience. Sometimes one college student provides the main viewpoint, but in many novels a group of friends absorbs the reader's attention. Some of the best-known novels about college life have a strong connection to campus legends.

Evelyn Waugh's *Brideshead Revisited* (1946) paints a nostalgic portrait of Oxford University in 1923, viewed through the lens of troubling military service in World War II. Waugh's description of Oxford enchants the reader:

Oxford—submerged, now obliterated, irrecoverable as Lyonesse, so quickly have the waters come flooding in—Oxford, in those days, was still a city of aquatint. In her spacious and quiet streets men walked and spoke as they had done in Newman's day; her autumnal mists, her grey springtime, and the rare glory of her summer days—such as that day—when the chestnut was in flower and the bells rang out high and clear over the gables and cupolas, exhaled the soft vapours of a thousand years of learning (21).

Looking back at his Oxford years, Captain Charles Ryder finds them to be as irretrievable as the legendary kingdom of Lyonesse, which sank beneath the sea during the golden age of early Britain. He remembers participating in Eights Week, an intercollegiate rowing event in which "Gilbert-and-Sullivan badinage," choral song, and a ball bring students from different residential colleges together (22). At this point, the story of a remarkable college friendship begins.

Enjoying the company of friends in his ground-floor rooms, Charles suddenly sees the face of Lord Sebastian Flyte, an affluent, eccentric student who always carries his teddy bear, Aloysius. Sebastian appears at Charles's window because, after overindulging in wine, he feels sick. Leaning across the window sill, he vomits, saying, "The wines were too various" (29). The next day, Sebastian sends Charles a roomful of flowers as an apology, and the two students become good friends. Charles learns about the life of the very rich, both in England and abroad, and Sebastian learns what it is like to live in a different sector of British society.

While most of *Brideshead Revisited* describes Charles's visits with Sebastian's family, the initial scenes at Oxford set the stage for a sequence of adventures through which the two central characters mature. Charles explains that all students in the college community must learn to "carry" their wine and to compensate the scout who cleans up after them (29). For young men of the British upper class, Oxford is a proving ground for adult social life and future careers.

Punts on the river at Oxford University. Photograph by Geoffrey Gould.

Mary McCarthy's *The Group* (1963) introduces the reader to eight graduates of Vassar, a Seven Sisters college for women, in the years before World War II. The novel begins in 1933, the year of their graduation, when Kay Leiland Strong marries Harald Peterson, a recent graduate of Reed College. Kay was the first member of her class to run around the table at the Class Day dinner to show that she was engaged to be married. Celebrating Kay's wedding, her group of close friends—Lakey, Dottie, Libby, Pokey, Polly, Priss, and Helena—remember that Kay went through a transformation in college after studying animal behavior with old Miss Washburn, who left her brain to science.

When *The Group* was published, some readers criticized its frankness about women's sexuality. The scene where Dottie Renfrew goes to a doctor to get a birth control device, using her own name instead of a pseudonym, shows how hard it was for upper-class women to break rules of acceptable conduct in the 1930s. Dottie and her friends exchange stories about sexual adventures and misadventures, showing that they know plenty of the rumors and legends that should not be discussed openly in polite society.

Although *The Group* begins with hopefulness and celebration, it ends with the sadness of Kay's funeral. The advent of World War II has made Kay an obsessive observer of the sky: if enemy planes approach, she will sound the alarm. Kay's marriage to Harald has fallen apart, and the political climate is ominous. An unresolved question dominates the last part of the novel: did Kay fall out of a window accidentally while looking for planes, or did she jump? As in many suicide legends, the situation is ambiguous. Members of the Group mourn her passing, remembering their college days when life seemed simpler.

Like *The Group* and other novels, Erich Segal's *The Class* (1986) follows friends through their college years. The author introduces five fictitious members of Harvard's class of 1958, taking them from freshman admission through graduation, careers, and a climactic twenty-fifth reunion.

As might be expected, campus legend patterns influence this novel's development. For example, when freshman Jason Gilbert first locates his room in Straus Hall, he finds a note on the door saying "To my roommate: I always nap in the afternoon, so please be quiet. Thank you. D.D" (23–24). Courteously leaving, then coming back to the room, Jason finds other notes but no visible roommate. Jason's "invisible roommate" reminds us of the legend "The Roommate Who Wasn't There," included in chapter 3. Eventually, Jason meets his roommate, David Davidson, who turns out to be a "roommate from hell": rigid, self-centered, and narrow-minded, with no interests at all except studying. When Jason suggests that they buy a couch for their room, David sanctimoniously replies, "I don't need a couch." Jason says, "Okay, then I'll pay for it myself. But if I ever see you sitting on it, I'll charge you rent" (28).

The Class describes quirky professors, struggling students, and beautiful, enigmatic girlfriends. Since all five protagonists are male, the author looks at campus life from a male viewpoint. One stereotype that he explores is the preppie: a calm, capable student of upper-class background. Both Andrew Eliot and Michael Wiggles worth see themselves as preppies, but sometimes that stereotype proves itself to be wrong. When Michael's girlfriend jilts him, he cheerfully tells one of the cafeteria staff members, "I'm going to kill the Christmas turkey." He pulls a fire ax out of his "baggy, well-worn J. Press jacket," swings the ax wildly, and runs around the cafeteria in pursuit of a turkey visible only to himself. Tables overturn, and people run away. The senior tutor persuades Michael to put the ax down, and doctors from the Health Service offer a ride to the hospital (110–11). This dramatic episode combines two campus legend characters: the well-known "Hatchet Man" and the student who goes berserk because of academic or personal problems. Segal puts an unusual spin on the "Hatchet Man" story by giving a student, not someone from outside the campus, the role of the ax-wielding pursuer.

An even more intriguing group of college friends emerges in Margaret Atwood's *The Robber Bride* (1993). Three women—Tony, Charis, and Roz—gather for the funeral of Zenia, whom they knew at college in Toronto. Both friend and foe, Zenia refuses to leave the women alone. As they eat lunch after the funeral, the ghost of Zenia approaches Charis:

Zenia is coming towards her, and she concentrates all her forces for the moment of impact; but Zenia strides right past them in her richly textured dress, with her long legs, her startling new breasts, her glossy hair nebulous around her shoulders, her purple-red angry mouth, trailing musky perfume. She's refusing to notice Charis, refusing deliberately; she's passing a hand of darkness over her, usurping her, blotting her out (72–73).

A ghost with an angry mouth, Zenia does the same thing she did as a living person: blot out her friends, taking away what they value most. Attractive, irresistible, and enigmatic, she has a talent for destroying friendship. Like the ghost of a destructive roommate in campus legends of haunted rooms, she is impossible to ignore.

As Tony, Charis, and Roz try to resolve their conflicted feelings about Zenia, they remember experiences from the recent and more remote past. Tony, now a college professor, recalls a violent confrontation with a student in her second-year undergraduate survey course who sticks a knife into her desk, shouting, "I need an A!" Tony's diplomatic reply is "I appreciate your directness. Now, why don't you sit down, on that chair right over there, and we can discuss it?" (24). She also remembers her first roommate, who took an overdose of sleeping pills, then disappeared. Before leaving, her roommate had "stayed in bed all day with her clothes on, reading paperback novels and weeping softly" (128). These stories of attempted or possible murder and suicide bring out the darker side of college, both in residence halls and in the classroom.

Jane Smiley's *Moo* (1995) satirizes academic life with a trenchant portrayal of Moo University, an agricultural institution in the Midwest. As the novel begins, sophomore work-study student Bob Carlson makes his way toward the building called "Old Meats" to feed a hungry hog named Earl Butz.

In the tradition of strange, distorted campus buildings, Old Meats has "disappeared from the perceptions of the university population at large" (3). Like the building where he works, Bob has become invisible to the rest of the campus. He exists to feed Earl Butz, who lives in "a sparkling new, clean, air-conditioned, and profoundly well-ventilated Ritz-Carlton of a room" (4).

Earl Butz enjoys a charmed life, eating as much as he can hold, because Dr. Bo Jones wants to figure out how big a hog can grow if allowed to eat without restraint for his natural life span. Jones keeps secret files on the hog's progress, sharing information with others only on a "need to know" basis. His obsession with Earl's diet reminds the reader of other single-minded professors in campus legends. Smiley explains that "Dr. Bo Jones wasn't unlike some of the eccentric farmers you might meet back home. Bob considered that reassuring" (6).

At Moo U, the university's graveyard lies between the Clemson School of Art and Design and the baseball practice field. A ball that falls into the graveyard, called "the ultimate homerun," has to stay in the field until the next Halloween, when new members of the baseball team have to find them at night, using flashlights. Mrs. Loraine Walker, the provost's secretary, finds this to be "a harmless and rather charming tradition" (62). Ironically, Mrs. Walker seems to have more authority over important matters at the university than the provost does. Alert to all new developments, she controls schedules and routines in a kind but firm way. Campus tradition has sometimes made the point that secretaries really keep a college going. In Smiley's book, this tradition proves true.

Another novel rich in humorous observations is Tom Wolfe's *I Am Charlotte Simmons* (2004). While writing this novel, Wolfe spent long periods of time at Stanford University, the University of North Carolina at Chapel Hill, the University of Michigan, and other institutions of higher learning. He also took advice from his college-aged children since some years had elapsed since his earlier novel on youth culture, *The Electric Kool-Aid Acid Test* (1968).

Charlotte Simmons is a brilliant, academically ambitious student from the Blue Ridge Mountains of North Carolina. Entering elite Dupont University as a freshman, she discovers that her fellow students care most about sex, sports, and beer. Although they have excellent academic credentials, most of the students seem indifferent to their course work.

On this fun-filled campus, Charlotte goes through a difficult process of adjustment. Her roommate, Beverly, "sexiles" Charlotte to a futon in another room when a boyfriend visits. Readers familiar with "The Roommate's Death" might expect Beverly to die, but no such tragedy occurs. Students at Dupont accept periodic "sexiling" as a normal procedure.

Wolfe's sensitivity to campus storytelling results in some good dialogue. Toward the beginning of the novel, two male students waving their hands to make urinals flush in the men's bathroom exchange ideas about a female student they know. Is it possible, they wonder, that she has been "re-virginated"? (5). Although students at Dupont have more sexual freedom than college students had 50 years before, who is and is not a virgin stills seems to be a fascinating subject.

Dupont University's landscape gives this novel a sense of authenticity. At the heart of the campus stands a cluster of sycamore trees known as "the Grove." Resembling Plato's grove of Academe, this area connects Dupont to other campus landscapes of the past and present. For Charlotte, who is struggling to get used to college life far from her home in the mountains, the Grove offers badly needed closeness to nature.

At the end of the novel, it is clear that Charlotte has made progress. Watching her boyfriend play basketball, she hears a voice in her head, a "ghost in the machine" that defies description, ask who she really is. "I am Charlotte Simmons," she says firmly (674–75). Cheering her boyfriend on, she seems ready to accept both the joys and the horrors of college life.

FILM

Nutty Professors

Movies about eccentric but likable science professors have appealed to large audiences since the early 1960s, when technology was advancing rapidly. Although the prototype for films about unusual professors is the array of *Frankenstein* movies produced since the 1930s, "nutty professor" films are different. Rather than presenting a grave robber from a dark, mysterious castle, these more recent films introduce mild-mannered, friendly professors whose inventions result in humorous mishaps.

In *The Absent-Minded Professor* (1961), starring Fred MacMurray, Ned Brainard (obviously a brainy individual) accidentally invents flying rubber, "flubber," which bounces high after hitting a hard surface. Brainard puts flubber in his shoes, making amazing jumps that remind the viewer of the folktale's seven-league boots (motif D1521.1). Conflict arises when a corrupt businessman, Alonzo Hawk, tries to get flubber's formula for his own nefarious purposes. The movie's sequel, *Son of Flubber* (1963), shows Professor Brainard coming to grief while working on derivatives of Flubber; helpful students save him from disaster.

Capitalizing on the success of these first two movies, *Chitty Chitty Bang Bang* (1968), starring Dick Van Dyke, presents Professor Caractacus Potts, who invents a flying car. When the professor and his family fly to Vulgaria, the evil Baron Bomburst tries to steal the car. This movie's plot is so similar to that of *The Absent-Minded Professor* that it hardly merits recognition as an original film, but the character of Baron Bomburst, reflecting fear of theft from other countries, takes *Chitty Chitty Bang Bang* in a new direction.

The Nutty Professor (1963) stars Jerry Lewis as Professor Julius Kelp, a nerdlike instructor with a disappointing social life. After a football coach humiliates him in front of his class, Professor Kelp creates a potion that will turn him into a "wild and popular party animal." Since the potion tends to wear off quickly, its effects are very funny. Professor Kelp's sudden changes from nerd to party animal and back are lighthearted analogues of the transformations in *Doctor Jekyll and Mr. Hyde* (1920), starring John Barrymore. In that early movie, the scientist brings out a dark side of himself that causes serious harm. Here the professor liberates his lighter side, the party animal that loves to have fun.

A remake of *The Nutty Professor* in 1996, starring Eddie Murphy, offers a new approach. Instead of wanting to turn himself into a party animal, Professor Sherman Klump feels a deep desire to lose weight. Inventing a chemical that transforms him into a slim but annoying person with the name of Buddy Love, Klump tries to win the admiration of a new female professor at his college. Klump's laboratory research differs from Ned Brainerd's; instead of developing rubber that can help people fly, as befits the "space age" of the 1960s, he searches for a new method of DNA restructuring. In *Nutty Professor II: The Klumps* (2000), Professor Sherman lump's family comes together for his marriage to a faculty colleague. Struggling with his alter ego Buddy Love, Klump tries to extract Buddy's DNA. When the conflict becomes desperate, his family helps him find a solution.

In contrast to movies where professors come up with amazing inventions, *Real Genius* (1985) depicts a community of inventors who are all teenaged prodigies going to college. The most brilliant student, Mitch (Gabriel Jarret), excels at prank playing as well as inventing. In one memorable scene, the teenaged geniuses cut class, leaving tape recorders in their seats to record their professor's lecture; at the professor's place is another tape recorder that plays a lecture for the assembled machines. Based on a campus legend that can be found at http://www.snopes.com, this scene humorously explores the possibility that professors and their students can be replaced by machines. The arch-villain of *Real Genius* is the teenagers' professor, who steals the laser weapon they have invented with the intention of selling it. It is interesting to note that in this movie, the professor is a thief rather than a talented inventor, possibly because, in a comedy where a youthful hero wins, the older mentor must take a different role.

Rowdy Students

Films about wild parties and outrageous pranks on college campuses have been popular since the late 1970s. Drawing material from uproarious student life, filmmakers have created entertaining scenes that have, in turn, influenced campus traditions.

Animal House, starring John Belushi and Karen Allen, achieved almost immediate popularity on its release in 1978. Speculation about the characters' derivation has created an intriguing set of stories. Students on a number of college campuses have claimed that the wild party animal Bluto (Belushi) is based on the life of a graduate of their own institution. Some Dartmouth graduates insist that Flounder (Stephen Furst) portrays an adventurous Dartmouth student whose actual nickname was "Trout." Whether or not those allegations are true, many of us who went to college in the 1960s and 1970s recall that a wild fraternity was often called an "animal house." Since quite a few Dartmouth students took pride in being rowdy, they relished the name "Dartmouth animals." However, Dartmouth certainly had no monopoly on the "no holds barred" behavior that led to many college students' most cherished memories of their undergraduate days.

Animal House takes place at Faber College in 1962, where Dean Wormer (John Vernon) plots to dismantle the uncontrollable Delta House fraternity. Members of a rival fraternity of rich, snobbish young men join the dean in his effort to destroy Delta, but Bluto and his pals manage to save their beloved organization. The film's high points include a toga party, a food fight, and a cornucopia of pranks, most memorably the accidental death of a horse in Dean Wormer's office.

The more recent film *PCU* (1994) is *Animal House* with a twist: an out-of-control fraternity in an era of unlimited political correctness. Droz (Jeremy Piven), a party animal living in the Pit, takes prospective freshman Tom (Chris Young) on a tour of Port Chester University, showing him how the Womynists and other protesters have taken over the campus. Following Droz's lead, Tom dumps many pounds of meat on the heads of vegan protesters dressed as cows, then runs when a crowd of angry students pursues him.

President Garcia-Thompson (Jessica Walter), a paragon of political correctness, threatens to close the Pit unless the students can come up with more than $7,000 in damages. Through a series of hilariously improbable events, the students earn all the money they need by throwing a huge party featuring the reggae band of George Clinton and the Funkadelics. When even this is not enough to save the Pit, Droz and his friends get President Garcia-Thompson fired by showing that she cannot control her students. Garcia-Thompson's unsuccessful pursuit of a whooping crane, the college's endangered mascot, seals her doom as campus president. Port Chester's students decide to give up protesting, and Tom makes the momentous decision to enroll as a freshman the following year.

Still another "animal house" film is *Old School* (2003). Three aging party animals—Mitch (Luke Wilson), Frank (Will Ferrell), and Beanie (Vince Vaughn)—decide to relive their wild youths by starting a fraternity in Mitch's new house near a college campus. Assembling a motley crew of young and older friends, they "party hearty" until Dean Pritchard threatens to evict them. With pleasant but predictable party scenes, this film gives viewers the message "Once a party animal, always a party animal."

Serial Killers

Legends about serial killers on college campuses have been well known since the mid-1960s. "The Hook," "The Roommate's Death," and "Aren't You Glad You Didn't Turn on the Light?" all feature lunatics who delight in murdering innocent victims. Small wonder, then, that college campuses have become familiar settings for "slasher" films, perennially popular with youthful audiences. Starting as straightforward horror movies, these films have evolved into tragicomic killing sprees where the extreme number of deaths provokes more laughter than fear.

The Exorcist (1973), based on the novel by William Peter Blatty (1971), shocked moviegoers and started a wave of campus exorcism legends. Partially filmed at Georgetown University in Washington, D.C., this movie immortalized the "Exorcist Steps" on M Street, down which the character Burke Dennings (Jack MacGowran) falls "with his head turned completely around, facing backwards." The detective investigating Burke's death suspects that he was pushed out of a window by Regan O'Neil, a 12-year-old girl apparently possessed by a demon. An evil-looking medallion excavated in northern Iraq seems to be the source of the trouble. In an intriguing juxtaposition of scenes, *The Exorcist* moves from an excavation in Iraq to an anti–Vietnam War demonstration on the Georgetown campus. Ominous-looking artifacts and student unrest set the stage for the troubling events to follow.

Regan's demon possession begins after she uses a Ouija board, a supernatural game played by many high school and college students. Soon after summoning a spirit called Mr. Howdy, Regan complains that her bed is shaking. Later, after she urinates on her mother's rug, the bed starts to move back and forth wildly. Neither Regan's doctor nor the detective investigating Burke Dennings's death knows what is wrong. Only Father Damien, a sensitive priest, can understand the linkage between demon possession, murder, and desecration of a local church. Father Damien's exorcism of the demon eventually works, though the demon puts up a horrifying fight.

The Exorcist shocked American moviegoers with its graphic depiction of demonic power. On college campuses, this film caused stories about demon possession to spread rapidly. Legends about possessed roommates, mysterious demons, and black masses made the rounds. Whether or not legend tellers believed in demon possession, they found this subject to be compelling. *The Exorcist* provided a sensational view of evil forces that strongly stimulated legend telling.

One year after *The Exorcist*'s release, *Black Christmas* (1974) introduced another horrific situation: serial killings at a sorority house. As the plot develops, murders follow phone calls, and the whole sorority house goes into panic mode. This early example of a "teen slasher" movie preceded *Halloween* (1978) by four years. It also resembles Agatha Christie's popular novel and film *Ten Little Indians* (1946), in which an unknown assailant kills one victim after another.

A later film, *Popcorn* (1991), introduces a murderer who wears others' faces. In a theater that is about to be torn down, college students majoring in cinema stage a horror-movie marathon. Once the show begins, a killer goes after the students, one by one. This movie's facetious tone makes fun of a long string of horror movies: *Halloween* (1978), *Friday the 13th* (1980), *Nightmare on Elm Street* (1984), and their sequels as well as other productions. Films like *Popcorn* offer relief from the tension created by scary movies and frightening legends.

One horror movie of great interest to folklorists is *Candyman* (1992), based on a story by the same name by Clive Barker. This film builds on the popularity of the legend "The Hook," introducing a supernatural antagonist who attacks a series of victims. Folklore graduate student Helen Lyle (Virginia Madsen) and her friend Bernadette Walsh (Kasi Lemons) learn about a vengeful ghost called Candyman while asking a janitorial staff member about a murder near their university in the projects of Chicago. According to local legend, Candyman, once a slave, was punished for falling in love with a client's daughter; he lost his hand, then died in a swarm of stinging bees. The legend also stipulates that anyone can summon Candyman by repeating his name five times while looking into a mirror.

When Helen and Bernadette repeat Candyman's name in front of a mirror, they enact the legend of "Bloody Mary," which says that repetition of a name can bring a vengeful spirit to life, ready to injure the summoner. Why, we might ask, would these two folklore graduate students want to do such a thing? Their need to understand the truth behind the Candyman legend makes them unaware of their need for personal safety. Helen and Bernadette are, to some extent, like absentminded professors who care only about increasing their knowledge base. When their summoning of Candyman leads to a horrific series of murders, viewers learn that rashly dabbling in the supernatural leads to disaster. For folklorists' interpretations of the Candyman/"Bloody Mary" legend/ritual complex, see Janet L. Langlois, "'Mary Whales, I Believe in You'" (1978); Alan Dundes, "Bloody Mary in the Mirror" (2002); Mikel Koven, "*Candyman* Can" (1999); and Elizabeth Tucker, "Ghosts in Mirrors" (2005).

In *Candyman*, a horror legend becomes real. The same thing happens on a grander scale in *Urban Legend* (1998), in which serial killings on a college campus emulate legend patterns. The film's first scene shows a female student from Pendleton University driving down a dark road alone, listening to the radio. When she stops for gas, a station attendant unsuccessfully tries to warn her that someone with an ax is crouching in the back seat of her car. A few moments after she drives away, she becomes a victim of the "killer in the back seat" (analyzed by Jan H. Brunvand in *The Vanishing Hitchhiker*, 52–53).

One of *Urban Legend*'s central characters is a folklore professor who keeps an ax and other strange artifacts in his office. A legend at Pendleton University says that a crazed professor once killed all the students on one floor of Stanley Hall. Wondering whether their own folklore professor is a menace to society, students try to figure out who is responsible for the serial killings on their campus. One by one, students die, following the patterns of the well-known legends "The Babysitter and the Man Upstairs," "The Boyfriend's Death," "The Roommate's Death," and others. Both a campus policewoman and the dean lose their lives while trying to catch the killer. In a surprising plot twist, the killer turns out to be someone that most people would not suspect. The final scene shows a group of students listening to a campus storyteller explain what happened. As the storyteller says, "It's all a legend now."

Urban Legends: Final Cut (2000) introduces a new character, Amy Mayfield (Jennifer Morrison), a student at Alpine University who decides to produce a film on urban legends as a thesis. One by one, members of her film crew fall victim to fatal accidents. Fearing that she may become the next victim, Amy struggles to learn the killer's identity. Very similar in plot to *Urban Legend*, this sequel is not one of the most original horror movies of recent years. However, it plays with the interaction of film and reality in an intriguing way: a film about murders leads to real murders, all of which become part of a film for mass consumption.

Blair Witch

In the summer of 1999, an unusual mass-media campaign introduced *The Blair Witch Project,* a film about three college students. According to the

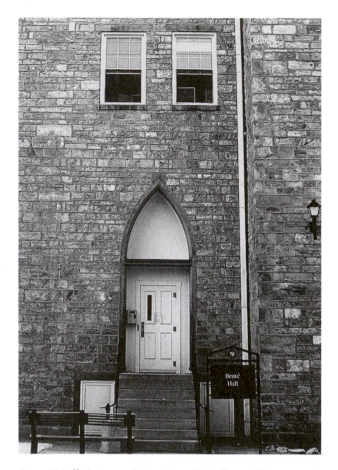

Bruté Hall, Mount Saint Mary's College. Photograph
by Geoffrey Gould.

trailer appearing on many Internet sites, "In October of 1994, three student
filmmakers disappeared in the woods near Burkittsville, Maryland while
shooting a documentary. A year later their footage was found." This "news"
made people wonder whether the students had actually vanished. Burkittsville,
Maryland, was a real place, as was Montgomery College, where the students
had allegedly studied. During the promotional period before the film came
out, the Internet Movie Database (http://www.imdb.com) listed the actors
who played the parts of the three students as "missing, presumed dead." With
this kind of publicity, it was no wonder that many moviegoers, especially
teenagers, had trouble differentiating fantasy from reality.

The plot of *The Blair Witch Project* is simple: three college students, Heather, Josh, and Mike (Heather Donahue, Joshua Leonard, and Michael C. Williams), interview Burkittsville townspeople to collect information about the deaths of seven children in the 1940s, apparently at the behest of the Blair Witch. After completing several interviews, they trudge off into the woods, determined to discover the Blair Witch. Very soon, it becomes clear that they have made a foolish decision. Heather, Josh, and Mike start walking around in circles. Small piles of sticks appear unexpectedly, and then Josh disappears. A bundle of body parts wrapped in his own handkerchief seems to be all that is left of him. The last scene shows an abandoned house where Heather stands in a corner. Her final words, both desperate and sad, sound chillingly realistic.

From the standpoint of campus legends, *The Blair Witch Project* works beautifully. When Heather, Josh, and Mike go into the woods to find the Blair Witch, they are taking a legend trip like those taken by many other college students. The "Blair Witch" legend sounds like an actual folk legend; in fact, its name resembles the name of the "Bell Witch" legend from Robertson County, Tennessee. Before the actors playing Heather, Josh, and Mike started filming the movie, they read a 35-page outline of Blair Witch information that they thought represented real legendry. Deprived of food and sleep, told to ad-lib their lines once they saw what would happen next, the three young actors reacted as other young people their age would react: with fear and alarm. Since most of the events in the film surprised them, their screams and startled looks were genuine.

After *The Blair Witch Project* made the *Guinness Book of World Records* for making $10,931 for every dollar that was spent, moviemakers realized that filming a legend trip could lead to enormous profits. *Book of Shadows: Blair Witch 2* (2000) involves another legend trip, this time to the house of Rustin Parr, the killer of seven children at the Blair Witch's command. When entrepreneurs organize a tour called a "Blair Witch Hunt," several college students decide to take it. After they have camped out at Parr's house overnight, they find that they have lost five hours of memory. This movie did not do as well at the box office as the original *Blair Witch*. Perhaps it was poetic justice that a film about making money from a "Blair Witch" tour did not make quite as much money as its creators had hoped.

Although the *Blair Witch* sequel was a disappointment, a more successful clone of this kind of entertainment was the TV show *MTV Fear*, which showed young people making their way through scary settings such as haunted houses. On college campuses, resident assistants planned programs based on plots from both *Blair Witch* and *MTV Fear*. These programs gave students opportunities to act out their fears in a safe, controlled context.

WORKS CITED

Atwood, Margaret. *The Robber Bride.* New York: Anchor Books, 1993.

Bourgeois, Robert L. "Psychokinesis and Contact with an Artificial Spirit: A Replication of the Philip Phenomena" <http://www.fpc.edu/pages/Academics/behave/psyc/web94–1.htm>.

Brown, Dan. *Angels and Demons.* New York: Simon and Schuster, 2000.

———. *The Da Vinci Code.* New York: Doubleday, 2003.

Brunvand, Jan Harold. *The Vanishing Hitchhiker.* New York: Norton, 1981.

Christie, Agatha. *Murder on the Orient Express.* New York: Penguin Group, 1985.

———. *Ten Little Indians: A Mystery Play in Three Acts.* New York: Samuel French, 1946.

Cohen, Mark. *The Fractal Murders.* New York, Warner Books, 2004.

Crichton, Michael. *Timeline.* New York: Alfred A. Knopf, 1999.

Cross, Amanda. *Death in a Tenured Position.* New York: Ballantine, 1982.

———. *Honest Doubt.* New York: Ballantine, 2000.

———. *In the Last Analysis.* New York: Avon Books, 1964.

Dundes, Alan. "Bloody Mary in the Mirror." *Bloody Mary in the Mirror: Essays in Psychoanalytic Folkloristics.* Jackson: University Press of Mississippi, 2002. 76–94.

Elkins, Aaron. *Skeleton Dance.* New York: William Morrow and Co., 2000.

Handy, John. "Ghost Hunters Sense a Presence at UTB." *Brownsville Herald.* 15 Apr. 2003 <http://www.brownsvilleherald.com/sections/archive/topstoryjmp/5–14–01/News-2.htm>.

Hart, Carolyn G. *A Little Class on Murder.* New York: Bantam Books, 1989.

Heilbrun, Carolyn G. *Writing a Woman's Life.* New York: Norton, 1988.

Hooton, Earnest Albert. *The American Criminal, Vol. 1. The Native White Criminal of Native Parentage.* Westport: Greenwood, 1969 (1939).

Hufford, David. "Beings without Bodies: An Experience-Centered Theory of the Belief in Spirits." *Out of the Ordinary: Folklore and the Supernatural.* Ed. Barbara Walker. Logan: Utah State University Press, 1995. 11–45.

———. *The Terror That Comes in the Night: An Experience-Centered Study of Supernatural Assault Traditions.* Philadelphia: University of Pennsylvania Press, 1982.

Hutchinson, Duane. *A Storyteller's Ghost Stories.* Lincoln: Foundation Books, 1987.

"Ideas That Stick without Advertising Dollars." <http://www.gsb.stanford.edu/news/heath.html>.

Kassow, Samuel D. *Students, Professors, and the State in Tsarist Russia.* Berkeley: University of California Press, 1989.

Kendall, Elaine. *Peculiar Institutions: An Informal History of the Seven Sister Colleges.* New York: G. Putnam's Sons, 1976.

Kingston, Maxine Hong. *The Woman Warrior: Memoirs of a Girlhood among Ghosts.* New York: Vintage International, 1976.

Koven, Mikel. "*Candyman* Can: Film and Ostension." *Contemporary Legend,* new series 2 (1999): 155–73.

Lake, M. D. *A Gift for Murder.* New York: Avon Books, 1992.

Langlois, Janet L. "'Mary Whales, I Believe in You': Myth and Ritual Subdued." *Indiana Folklore* 11.1 (1978): 5–33.

McCarthy, Mary. *The Group.* New York: Harcourt, Brace and World, 1963.

Murphy, Gardner, and Herbert L. Klemme. "Unfinished Business." *Journal of the American Society for Psychical Research* 60.4 (Oct. 1966): 306–20.

Neller, Earl. E-mail communication. 20 Mar. 2004.

Owen, Iris M. *Conjuring Up Philip: An Adventure in Psychokinesis.* New York: Harper Collins, 1976.

Quenk, Naomi L. *Essentials of Myers-Briggs Type Indicator Assessment.* New York: John Wiley & Sons, 1994.

Radin, Paul. *The Trickster: A Study in American Indian Mythology.* New York: Greenwood, 1969.

Rosenbaum, Ron. "The Great Ivy League Nude Posture Photo Scandal." *New York Times Magazine* 15 Jan. 1995. 26–56.

Salisbury, Harrison E. *Tiananmen Diary: Thirteen Days in June.* Boston: Little, Brown, and Co., 1989.

Sammartino, Peter. *Of Castles and Colleges: Notes toward an Autobiography.* South Brunswick: A.S. Barnes, 1972.

Sayers, Dorothy. *Gaudy Night.* New York: Avon Books, 1968.

Segal, Erich. *The Class.* New York: Bantam Books, 1986.

Sheldon, William Herbert. *Atlas of Men: A Guide for Somatotyping the Adult Male at All Ages.* New York: Gramercy, 1954.

Shelley, Mary. *Frankenstein.* New York: Bantam Books, 1991.

Slater, Lauren. *Opening Skinner's Box: Great Psychological Experiments of the Twentieth Century.* New York: Norton, 2004.

Smiley, Jane. *Moo.* New York: Fawcett Columbine, 1995.

Thomas-Graham, Pamela. *A Darker Shade of Crimson.* New York: Simon and Schuster, 1998.

———. *Orange Crushed.* New York: Simon and Schuster, 2004.

Thwe, Pascal Koo. *From the Land of Green Ghosts: A Burmese Odyssey.* New York: HarperCollins, 2002.

Tucker, Elizabeth. Ghosts in Mirrors: Reflections of the Self. *Journal of American Folklore* 118:468 (2005): 186–203.

Verne, Jules. *Journey to the Center of the Earth.* New York: Signet Classic, 1986.

Waugh, Evelyn. *Brideshead Revisited.* Boston: Little, Brown, 1946.

Wehrman, Jessica. "Campus Spooks Abound." *Cincinnati Post.* 30 Oct. 2004 <http://www.cincypost.com/2004/10/30/gcol 103004.html>.

Wells, H. G. *The Time Machine.* New York: Bantam Books, 1991.

Wolf, Naomi. *The Beauty Myth: How Images of Beauty Are Used against Women.* New York: William Morrow, 1991.

Wolfe, Tom. *I Am Charlotte Simmons.* New York: Farrar, Straus and Giroux, 2004.

Glossary

Aarne-Thompson (A-T). *See* TYPE.

Absentminded professor. A professor who seems to be "up in the clouds," unable to concentrate on anything other than scholarly matters. Absentminded professors' behavior has become formulaic so that certain stock features may be included in a narrative whether or not they are actually typical of the professor in question.

Active bearer. Someone who actively shares folklore with other people. This term was introduced by C. W. von Sydow.

Allomotifs. As defined by Alan Dundes, plot incidents that serve the same purpose in different tale texts.

Anaphrodisiac. A substance that diminishes sexual desire.

Aphrodisiac. A substance that increases sexual desire.

Apocryphal. Not authentic or true.

Archetype. According to C. G. Jung, archetypes determine the shape or pattern of images within the human psyche. Common archetypes include the shadow, the animus, and the anima.

Archive. An area, usually in a library, where special collections of books, manuscripts, student papers, sound tapes, videotapes, and other materials are kept safely. Many excellent collections of campus legends are available in college and university archives.

Belief. Certainty that something is true. Legend tellers have different levels of belief, ranging from full belief to skepticism. Although the possibility of belief is important, full belief is not necessary for the narration of a good legend.

Campus. Latin term for "field," first used by Princeton University to designate the grounds of a college or university. Princeton chose this term to distinguish its own land from Harvard's "yard."

Coed. A female student attending a coeducational college or university. This term was commonly used in the early days of coeducation, when female students stood out in a crowd.

Collector. *See* FIELDWORKER.

College. An institution of higher learning. Alternatively, a residential college in which students sleep, eat, and socialize.

Commencement. Graduation ceremony at which students receive their diplomas. Colleges and universities generally use the term "commencement" instead of "graduation" because this ceremony marks the beginning of the graduate's life beyond his or her academic institution.

Contemporary legend. A term for the legend that entered current usage in the early 1990s. Emerging legends and legends in active circulation are covered especially well by this term.

Context. Information related to the collection of a legend text or another kind of folklore: location, circumstances, mood, presence of other people, and any other relevant factors.

Cram. An informal term for rapidly learning course material before an examination. While some college students believe that this method works well, others doubt its reliability.

Custom. A habitual practice. For example, bringing a favorite pen to an exam may become a habit after a student gets a high grade while using the pen.

Cybernetics. The science of designing machines with humanoid intelligence.

Doctoral student. A student who is working on a doctoral degree, such as the Ph.D. (Doctor of Philosophy) or Ed.D. (Doctor of Education).

Don. A professor at a British university.

Dormitory. *See* RESIDENCE HALL.

Eights Week. An intercollegiate rowing event at Oxford University.

E-mail. Electronic communication that lets the sender leave a message to be answered at the convenience of the receiver.

Etiology. Origin or derivation.

Eugenics. The science of improving the qualities of a breed or species through the selection of parents. Application of eugenics to the human race has been highly controversial.

Experience-centered theory. An approach to belief in the supernatural developed by David J. Hufford, author of *The Terror That Comes in the Night* (1982). Those who follow this approach carefully examine traditional narratives to reconstruct the experience that elicits them.

Faustian. Similar to Faust, the medieval German scholar who, according to legend, sold his soul to the devil so he could learn everything he wanted to know.

Fear test. A ritual by which a person proves his or her courage. One well-known fear test consists of spending an entire night in a haunted house.

Festival. A complex ritual or set of rituals, often involving special foods, clothing, and decorations.

Fieldworker. Someone who collects folklore by going out into the "field" of fellow human beings. Fieldworkers may use audiotape recorders, videotape recorders, or electronic communication to record data. They may also take notes, but since note taking is less exact, other methods of recording are favored more.

FOAF. The typical legend teller: a friend of a friend.

Folk. People who share various forms of traditional learning.

Folklore. Coined in 1846 by William J. Thoms, the term "folklore" has been defined in many different ways. Forms of folklore include traditional narratives, songs, customs, beliefs, festivals, crafts, and house types. Often associated with artistic self-expression, folklore helps people articulate their values, needs, and concerns.

Fraternity. An organization of male students, usually identified by two or three letters of the Greek alphabet, for social interaction and mutual support.

Freshman. A first-year college or university student.

Freudian. Characteristic of the theory of Sigmund Freud (1856–1939), the Austrian neurologist who founded psychoanalysis.

Function. The purpose served by an item of folklore.

Genre. A particular kind of folklore, for example, the legend, the folktale, or the joke.

Ghost story. A story about supernatural characters or events. Some ghost stories involve apparitions, while others describe strange sounds, smells, or other sensory impressions. Both folk and literary ghost stories have been popular in the twentieth and twenty-first centuries.

Ghost walk. A tour of haunted sites, typically taking place on or near Halloween. Students and faculty members have offered Halloween ghost walks at an increasing number of colleges.

Greek. Related to a Greek-letter fraternity or sorority.

Halloween. The evening of October 31, when, according to British folk tradition, ghosts walk and mischief reigns.

Hallucinogen. A drug that causes hallucinations, for example, LSD.

Haunted house. Either a house considered to be haunted or a display of frightening exhibits for the entertainment of visitors on Halloween.

Hazing. Abusive or humiliating tricks played on freshmen as part of their initiation into a fraternity, sorority, or another group.

Incubus. According to medieval folklore, a male demon that has sexual intercourse with women while they sleep.

Informant. Someone who shares an item of folklore with a fieldworker.

Initiation. The process by which someone becomes part of a group. College students' initiations take various forms, including fraternity and sorority initiations, which are usually kept secret from nonmembers.

Instant Messenger. Electronic communication that allows people to "talk" with each other in real time.

Irony. An incongruous outcome, different from what might be expected.

Ivy League. An elite group of colleges founded for men's education: Harvard, Yale, Princeton, Brown, the University of Pennsylvania, Dartmouth, Columbia, and Cornell.

Jungian. Related to the theories of the Swiss psychoanalyst Carl Gustav Jung (1875–1961).

Junior. A third-year college or university student.

Land grant. A tract of land given by the government of the United States for the development of a college or university.

Legend. A genre of folk narrative that is closely connected to everyday life. The legend's implied question "Can this be true?" makes listeners eager to learn more about it. Because the legend varies in form and means different things to different people, it is not an easy genre to define.

Liberal arts. A college or university curriculum that includes the arts, humanities, social sciences, and natural sciences. In the Middle Ages, the seven liberal arts were grammar, rhetoric, logic, music, arithmetic, geometry, and astronomy.

Liminal. Literally, "on the threshold": between one thing or state of being and another.

Local legend. A legend that stays in one area.

Ludic. Playful.

Mara. Term introduced by David Hufford in *The Terror That Comes in the Night* (1982) to denote a nocturnal spirit that exerts pressure on its victim's body, causing feelings of paralysis and fear.

Memorate. A first-person narrative based on individual experience.

Metaphor. An implied comparison, for example, "My professor is a psychopath."

Metonymy. A figure of speech in which a part represents the whole.

Midterm. A midsemester examination, usually shorter and less stressful than final examinations.

Migratory legend. A legend that travels from one place to another, regionally, nationally, or internationally. Reidar T. Christiansen's *The Migratory Legends* (1958) was the first detailed legend study of this kind.

Moral. The message conveyed by a legend or another form of folklore.

Motif. A small unit of folklore that can be studied cross-culturally.

Motif index. Stith Thompson's *Motif-Index of Folk Literature,* first published from 1955 to 1958.

Mystery meat. According to some college students, this kind of meat, often served in campus dining halls, is impossible to identify.

Myth. A traditional narrative about gods, demigods, heroes, and creation.

Narrator. Teller of a story.

Oikotype. Regional type, as defined by C. W. von Sydow.

Oral tradition. Tradition transmitted primarily by word of mouth.

Ostension. As defined by Linda Dégh, enactment of a legend or part of a legend in a serious, sometimes harmful way.

Ostensive play. A lighthearted, playful form of ostension.

Parietals. Rules for men's visitation.

Parody. A humorous imitation of a song, story, or other expressive form.

Passive bearer. Someone who knows certain kinds of folklore and may encourage their transmission but prefers not to share them him- or herself. This term was introduced by C. W. von Sydow.

Ph.D. Doctor of Philosophy degree.

Pledge. A student who has expressed the desire to join a particular fraternity or sorority but has not yet been accepted.

Poltergeist. A ghost that makes its presence known by making noise, throwing things, or otherwise causing trouble.

Prank. An outrageous practical joke.

Professor. A college or university teacher. Professorial ranks include assistant professor, associate professor, and professor.

Psyche. A Jungian term for the human mind: both the unconscious and the conscious.

Psychoanalysis. Theories concerning the relationship between the conscious and the unconscious mind as well as treatment of individual patients in relation to those theories.

Quadrangle. An open space surrounded by buildings on a college campus.

Quadrivium. The upper division of the liberal arts in the Middle Ages, with four subjects: arithmetic, geometry, astronomy, and music.

Residence hall. A building where students live while attending college.

Resident assistant (RA). A student who accepts responsibility for the welfare of students in one section of a residence hall. Typically, RAs offer advice, put on programs, and write up disciplinary reports.

Resident director (RD). The head of a residence hall who supervises an RA staff.

Revenant. A ghost that returns from the realm of the dead.

Rite of passage. A ritual involving transition from one state of being to another, for example, commencement.

Ritual. A repeated pattern of behavior.

Roommate. Someone who shares the room of a college or university student. Frequently the victim of murder or self-destruction, the roommate takes an important role in campus legends.

Rumor. An unconfirmed statement, closely related to the legend.

Rumor panic. A rumor that escalates to a wave of fear, as in campus "Hatchet Man" rumors that spread in 1968.

Scout. Staff member at a British university's residential college.

Senior. A fourth-year college student. Students who continue for a fifth year are sometimes called "super-seniors."

Seven sisters. Seven elite northeastern women's colleges: Barnard, Bryn Mawr, Mount Holyoke, Radcliffe, Smith, Vassar, and Wellesley.

Sophomore. A second-year college student.

Sorority. An organization of female students, usually identified by two or three letters of the Greek alphabet, for social interaction and mutual support.

Spanish fly. A preparation of powdered blister beetles, also called cantharides, rumored to be a powerful aphrodisiac.

Specter. A synonym for "ghost."

Structuralism. A form of folklore interpretation introduced by Vladimir Propp in which the sequence of plot elements is analyzed.

Succubus. In medieval folklore, a female demon that has intercourse with men while they sleep.

Studium generale. Curriculum of the medieval university.

Symbol. A representation of something else, either in folk narrative or in other forms of expression.

Town/gown. Conflict between townspeople and students.

Tradition. Material that is passed along from one person to another and from one generation to the next.

Transmission. The process of sharing folklore, either orally or by example.

Trivium. The lower division of the seven liberal arts in the Middle Ages, including three subjects: grammar, rhetoric, and logic.

Type. A pattern of episodes that stays together in tradition. *See* TYPE INDEX.

Type index. Antti Aarne and Stith Thompson's *The Types of the Folktale,* first published in 1928.

Undergraduate. A student who has not yet graduated from college.

University. From the Latin term meaning "a whole," this term has applied to higher education since the Middle Ages. The university brings together students and faculty for the purpose of higher learning.

Urban legend. Often but not always found in urban areas, the urban legend recounts sensational, shocking, and amazing events. This term entered common usage in the early 1980s.

Urform. Original form.

Variant. A text that represents a certain kind of folk narrative (or of another genre of folklore).

Version. Generally synonymous with "variant," although some folklorists have used this term somewhat differently.

Wicca. A nature-oriented religion whose followers worship primarily the Mother Goddess.

Witch. A practitioner of magic and, in some cases, a follower of the Wiccan religion. Medieval stereotypes of witches characterized them as evil individuals who worshipped Satan and tried to corrupt good people.

Witchcraft. *See* WITCH.

World Wide Web. A network of interrelated Web sites available to anyone who has Internet access. The World Wide Web offers many campus legends, but researchers should take care in assessing the authenticity of legend texts found there.

Bibliography

REFERENCE WORKS

Aarne, Antti, and Stith Thompson. *The Types of the Folktale: A Classification and Bibliography.* Helsinki: Suomalainen Tiedeakatemia, 1961. First published in 1928; the original type index, Antti Aarne's *Verzeichnis der Marchentypen,* was published in 1910.

Brown, Mary Ellen, and Bruce Rosenberg, eds. *Encyclopedia of Folklore and Literature.* Santa Barbara: ABC-CLIO, 1998.

Brunvand, Jan H. *American Folklore: An Encyclopedia.* New York: Garland, 1996.

———. *Encyclopedia of Urban Legends.* Santa Barbara: ABC-CLIO, 2001.

Christiansen, Reidar T. *The Migratory Legends.* Folklore Fellows Communications 175. Helsinki: Suomalainen Tiedeakatemia, 1958.

Leach, Maria, ed., and Jerome Fried, assoc. ed. *Funk and Wagnalls Standard Dictionary of Folklore, Mythology, and Legend.* San Francisco: Harper, 1984.

Robbins, Rossell Hope. *Encyclopedia of Witchcraft and Demonology.* New York: Crown Publishers, 1959.

Simonsuuri, Lauri. *Typen und Motivverzeichnis der finnischen mythischen Sagen* (Type and Motif Index of Finnish Mythological Legends). Folklore Fellows Communication 182. Helsinki: Academia Scientiarum Fennica, 1961/1987.

Thompson, Stith. *Motif-Index of Folk Literature: A Classification of Narrative Elements in Folktales, Ballads, Myths, Fables, Mediaeval Romances, Exempla, Fabliaux, Jest-Books, and Local Legends.* Rev. and enl. ed. 6 vols. Bloomington: Indiana University Press, 2000.

LEGEND STUDIES

Baker, Ronald L. *Hoosier Folk Legends.* Bloomington: Indiana University Press, 1982.

Bennett, Gillian. *Alas, Poor Ghost! Traditions of Belief in Story and Discourse.* Logan: Utah State University Press, 1999.

Bennett, Gillian, and Paul Smith, eds. *Contemporary Legend: A Reader.* New York: Garland, 1996.

———. *Monsters with Iron Teeth.* Sheffield: Sheffield Academic Press, 1988.

Bennett, Gillian, and Paul Smith. *A Nest of Vipers.* Sheffield: Sheffield Academic Press, 1990.

Bennett, Gillian, Paul Smith, and J. D. A. Widdowson, eds. *Perspectives on Contemporary Legend, Volume II.* Sheffield: Sheffield Academic Press.

Bronner, Simon. *Piled Higher and Deeper: The Folklore of Student Life.* Little Rock: August House, 1995.

Brown, Alan. *Shadows and Cypress: Southern Ghost Stories.* Jackson: University Press of Mississippi, 2000.

———. *Stories from the Haunted South.* Jackson: University Press of Mississippi, 2004.

Brunvand, Jan Harold. *The Baby Train.* New York: Norton, 1993.

———. *The Choking Doberman.* New York: Norton, 1984.

———. *Curses! Broiled Again!* New York: Norton, 1989.

———. *The Mexican Pet.* New York: Norton, 1986.

———. *The Vanishing Hitchhiker.* New York: Norton, 1981.

Dégh, Linda. *Legend and Belief.* Bloomington: Indiana University Press, 2001.

Dundes, Alan. *Bloody Mary in the Mirror: Essays in Psychoanalytic Folkloristics.* Jackson: University Press of Mississippi, 2002.

Ellis, Bill. *Aliens, Ghosts, and Cults: Legends We Live.* Jackson: University Press of Mississippi, 2003.

———. *Lucifer Ascending: The Occult in Folklore and Popular Culture.* Lexington: University Press of Kentucky, 2004.

———. *Raising the Devil.* Jackson: University Press of Mississippi, 2000.

Glimm, James York. *Flat-Landers and Ridge-Runners.* Pittsburgh: University of Pittsburgh Press, 1983.

Goldstein, Diane E. *Once upon a Virus: AIDS Legends and Vernacular Risk Perception.* Logan: Utah State University Press, 2004.

Goss, Michael. *The Evidence for Phantom Hitch-Hikers.* Wellingborough: The Aquarian Press, 1984.

Hufford, David. *The Terror That Comes in the Night.* Philadelphia: University of Pennsylvania Press, 1982.

Jones, Louis C. *Things That Go Bump in the Night.* New York: Hill and Wang, 1959.

McNeil, W. K. *Ghost Stories from the American South.* New York: Dell, 1985.

Richardson, Anne. *Possessions.* Cambridge: Harvard University Press, 2003.

Roberts, Nancy. *South Carolina Ghosts: From the Coast to the Mountains.* Columbia: University of South Carolina Press, 1983.

Smith, Paul, ed. *Perspectives on Contemporary Legend.* Sheffield: Centre for English Cultural Tradition and Language, University of Sheffield, 1984.

Taft, Michael. *Inside These Greystone Walls: An Anecdotal History of the University of Saskatchewan.* Saskatoon: University of Saskatchewan, 1984.

von Sydow, Carl Wilhelm. *Selected Papers on Folklore.* Copenhagen: Rosenkilde and Bagger, 1948.

Ward, Donald, trans. and ed. *The German Legends of the Brothers Grimm.* 2 vols. Philadelphia: Institute for the Study of Human Issues, 1981.

Whatley, Mariamne H., and Elissa R. Henken. *Did You Hear about the Girl Who . . . ?: Contemporary Legends, Folklore, and Human Sexuality.* New York: New York University Press, 2000.

Yeates, Geoff. *Cambridge College Ghosts.* Norwich: Jarrold Publishing, 1994.

INTERNATIONAL LEGEND COLLECTIONS

Arona, Danilo. *Tutte Storie: Immaginario italiano e leggende contemporanee.* Genoa: Costa and Nolan, 1994.

Bermani, Cesare. *Il bambino è servito: Leggende metropolitane in Italia.* Bari: Dedalo, 1991.

Brednich, Rolf Wilhelm. *Das Huhn mit dem Gipsbein: Neueste sagenhafte Geschichten von heute.* Munich: C.H. Beck, 1993.

———. *Die Maus im Jumbo-Jet: Neue sagenhafte Geschichten von heute.* Munich: C.H. Beck, 1991.

———. *Die Ratte am Strohhalm: Allerneueste sagenhafte Geschichten von heute.* Munich: C.H. Beck, 1996.

———. *Die Spinne in der Yucca-Palme.* Munich: C.H. Beck, 1990.

Carbone, Maria Teresa. *99 Leggende Urbane.* Milan: Mandadori, 1989.

Goldstuck, Arthur. *Ink in the Porridge.* Johannesburg: Penguin Books, 1994.

———. *The Leopard in the Luggage.* Johannesburg: Penguin Books, 1993.

———. *The Rabbit in the Thorn Tree: Modern Myths and Urban Legends of South Africa.* Johannesburg: Penguin Books, 1990.

Klintberg, Bengt af. *Die Ratte in der Pizza und andere moderne Sagen und Grossstadtmythen.* Kiel: Wolfgang Butt, 1990.

———. *Den Stulna Njuren.* Stockholm: Norstedt, 1994.

Renard, Jean-Bruno. *Rumeurs et legendes urbaines.* Paris: Presses Universitaires de France, 2002.

Sempere, Josep, and Antonio Orti. *Leyendas Urbanas en España.* Barcelona: Ediciones Martinez Roca, 2000.

Toselli, Paolo. *Di Bocca in Bocca.* Rome: Stampa Alternativa, 1996.

———. *La Famosa Invasione delle Vipere Volanti.* Rome: Stampa Alternativa, 1994.

POPULAR GHOST STORY COLLECTIONS

All these books contain campus ghost stories. Some have a number of stories from college campuses; others have just one or two.

Adams, Charles J., III and David J. Seibold. *Ghost Stories of the Lehigh Valley.* Reading: Exeter House Books, 1993.

Asfar, Dan, and Edrick Thay. *Ghost Stories of America.* Edmonton: Ghost House Books, 2001.

Colby, C. B., et al. *The Little Giant Book of "True" Ghostly Tales.* New York: Sterling Publishing, 2002.

DeBolt, Margaret. *Savannah Spectres and Other Strange Tales.* Norfolk/Virginia Beach: The Donning Company, 1984.

Grant, Glen. *Obake Files: Ghostly Encounters in Supernatural Hawaii.* Honolulu: Mutual Publishing, 1996.

Hauck, Dennis William. *Haunted Places: The National Directory.* New York: Penguin Books, 1996.

Hutchinson, Duane. *A Storyteller's Ghost Stories.* Lincoln: Foundation Books, 1987.

Mott, Allan S. *Haunted Schools: Ghost Stories and Strange Tales.* Auburn: Ghost House Books, 2003.

Munn, Debra D. *Big Sky Ghosts: Eerie True Tales of Montana.* Vol. 2. Boulder: Pruett Publishing, 1994.

Norman, Michael, and Beth Scott. *Haunted Heritage.* New York: Tor Books, 2002.

Price, Charles Edwin. *Mysterious Knoxville.* Johnson City: Overmountain Press, 1999.

Revai, Cheri L. *Haunted Northern New York: True, Chilling Stories of Ghosts and Spirits in the North Country.* Utica: North Country Books, 2002.

Scott, Beth, and Michael Norman. *Haunted Heartland.* New York: Warner Books, 1985.

Smith, Barbara. *Ghost Stories of the Rocky Mountains.* Renton: Ghost House Books, 1999.

Taylor, Troy. *Ghosts of Millikin: The Haunted History of Millikin University.* Forsyth: Whitechapel Productions, 1996.

Teel, Gina. *Ghost Stories of Minnesota.* Auburn: Ghost House Books, 2002.

Thay, Edrick. *Ghost Stories of Indiana.* Auburn: Ghost House Books, 2002.

Trapani, Beth E., and Charles J. Adams III. *Ghost Stories of Pittsburgh and Allegheny County.* Reading: Exeter House Books, 1994.

Windham, Kathryn Tucker, and Margaret Gillis Figh. *Thirteen Alabama Ghosts and Jeffrey.* Huntsville: Strode Publishers, 1983.

Winfield, Mason. *Shadows of the Western Door: Haunted Sites and Ancient Mysteries of Upstate New York.* Buffalo: Western New York Wares, 1997.

———. *Spirits of the Great Hill.* Buffalo: Western New York Wares, 2001.

COLLEGE/UNIVERSITY HISTORIES

Alberts, Robert C. *Pitt: The Story of the University of Pittsburgh, 1787–1987.* Pittsburgh: University of Pittsburgh Press, 1986.

Alvey, Edward, Jr. *A History of Mary Washington College, 1908–1972.* Charlottesville: University Press of Virginia, 1974.

Bedford, A. G. *The University of Winnipeg: A History of the Founding Colleges.* Toronto: University of Toronto Press, 1976.

Berry, Margaret C. *The University of Texas: A Pictorial Account of Its First Century.* Austin: University of Texas Press, 1980.

Bibber, Joyce K. *University of Southern Maine.* Mt. Pleasant: Arcadia Publishing, 2001.

Bishop, Morris. *A History of Cornell.* Ithaca: Cornell University Press, 1962.

Bogue, Allan G., and Robert Taylor. *The University of Wisconsin: One Hundred and Twenty-Five Years.* Madison: University of Wisconsin Press, 1975.

Brackett, Frank P. *Granite and Sagebrush: Reminiscences of the First Fifty Years of Pomona College.* Los Angeles: Ward Ritchie Press, 1944.

Brubaker, John H., III. *Hullabaloo Nevonia: An Anecdotal History of Student Life at Franklin and Marshall College.* Lancaster: Franklin and Marshall College, 1987.

Callcott, George H. *A History of the University of Maryland.* Baltimore: Maryland Historical Society, 1966.

Clark, Thomas D. *Indiana University, Midwestern Pioneer.* Bloomington: Indiana University Press, 1970.

Cohen, Rodney T. *The Black Colleges of Atlanta.* Mt. Pleasant: Arcadia Publishing, 2000.

Cole, Arthur C. *A Hundred Years of Mount Holyoke College.* New Haven: Yale University Press, 1940.

Conklin, Paul K. *Gone with the Ivy: A Biography of Vanderbilt University.* Knoxville: University of Tennessee Press, 1985.

Coon, Horace. *Columbia: Colossus on the Hudson.* New York: E.P. Dutton and Co., 1947.

Cornelius, Roberta D. *The History of Randolph-Macon Women's College.* Chapel Hill: University of North Carolina Press, 1951.

Coutts, James. *A History of the University of Glasgow.* Glasgow: James Maclehose and Sons, 1909.

Crenshaw, Ollinger. *General Lee's College.* New York: Random House, 1969.

Demarest, William H. S. *A History of Rutgers College, 1766–1924.* New Brunswick: Rutgers College, 1924.

Dyer, Thomas G. *The University of Georgia: A Bicentennial History, 1785–1985.* Athens: University of Georgia Press, 1985.

Elliott, Orrin L. *Stanford University: The First Twenty-Five Years.* Stanford: Stanford University Press, 1937.

Glasscock, Jean, ed. *Wellesley College 1875–1975: A Century of Women.* Wellesley: Wellesley College, 1975.

Griffin, Clifford S. *The University of Kansas.* Lawrence: University Press of Kansas, 1974.

Haglund, Elizabeth. *Remembering: The University of Utah.* Salt Lake City: University of Utah Press, 1981.

Hauk, Gary. *A Legacy of Heart and Mind: Emory since 1836.* Atlanta: BookHouse Group, 1999.

Johns, Walter H. *A History of the University of Alberta, 1908–1969.* Edmonton: University of Alberta Press, 1981.

Kelley, Brooks Mather. *Yale: A History.* New Haven: Yale University Press, 1974.

Loevy, Robert D. *Colorado College: A Place of Learning, 1874–1999.* Colorado Springs: Colorado College, 1999.

Maclean, John. *History of the College of New Jersey.* Philadelphia: Lippincott, 1877.

McFee, Michele. *The Cornerstone: From Breadth through Depth to Perspective: A History of Harpur College.* Binghamton: State University of New York at Binghamton, 2000.

Meiners, Fredericka. *A History of Rice University.* Houston: Rice University, 1982.

Montgomery, James Riley, Stanley J. Folmsbee, and Lee Seifert Greene. *To Foster Knowledge: A History of the University of Tennessee, 1794–1970.* Knoxville: University of Tennessee Press, 1984.

Morison, Samuel Eliot. *The Founding of Harvard College.* Cambridge: Harvard University Press, 1935.

Posey, Josephine McCann. *Alcorn State University: And the National Alumni Association.* Mt. Pleasant: Arcadia Publishing, 2000.

Rudolph, Frederick. *The American College and University: A History.* New York: Vintage Books, 1962.

Seelye, L. Clark. *The Early History of Smith College, 1871–1910.* Boston: Houghton Mifflin, 1923.

Stadtman, Verne A. *The University of California, 1868–1968.* New York: McGraw-Hill, 1970.

Stephenson, Frank. *Chowan College, North Carolina.* Mt. Pleasant: Arcadia Publishing, 2004.

Stohlman, Martha Lou Lemmon. *The Story of Sweet Briar College.* Sweet Briar: Sweet Briar College, 1956.

Taylor, James Monroe, and Elizabeth Hazelton Haight. *Vassar.* New York: Oxford University Press, 1915.

Wilson, Richard, ed. *Syracuse University, Volume 3: The Critical Years.* Syracuse: Syracuse University Press, 1984.

COLLEGE/UNIVERSITY STUDIES

Addy, George M. *The Enlightenment in the University of Salamanca.* Durham: Duke University Press, 1966.

Ashley, Dwayne, and Juan Williams. *I'll Find a Way to Make One: A Tribute to Historically Black Colleges and Universities.* New York: HarperCollins, 2004.

Avorn, Jerry L. *Up against the Ivy Wall: A History of the Columbia Crisis.* New York: Atheneum, 1968.

Betterton, Don. *Alma Mater: Unusual and Little-Known Facts from America's College Campuses.* Princeton: Peterson's Guides, 1988.

Boyer, Ernest. *College: The University Experience in America.* New York: Harper and Row, 1987.

Briscoe, Virginia Wolf. "Bryn Mawr College Traditions: Women's Rituals as Expressive Behavior." Ph.D. dissertation, University of Pennsylvania, 1981.

Brubacher, John Seiler, and Willis Rudy. *Higher Education in Transition: A History of American Colleges and Universities.* Somerset: Transaction Publishers, 1997.

Cantelon, John E. *College Education and the Campus Revolution.* Philadelphia: Westminster Press, 1969.

Carey, James T. *The College Drug Scene.* Englewood Cliffs: Prentice Hall, 1968.

Cobban, Alan B. *English University Life in the Middle Ages.* Columbus: Ohio State University Press, 1999.

Coulter, E. Merton. *College Life in the Old South.* Athens: University of Georgia Press, 1928.

Dixon, Madeline. *Things Which Are Done in Secret.* Montreal: Black Rose Books, 1976.

Duke, Alex. *Importing Oxbridge: English Residential Colleges and American Universities.* New Haven: Yale University Press, 1996.

Emmerson, Donald K. *Students and Politics in Developing Nations.* New York: Praeger, 1968.

Ferruolo, Stephen C. *The Origins of the University: The Schools of Paris and Their Critics, 1100–1215.* Stanford: Stanford University Press, 1985.

Flower, John A. *Downstairs, Upstairs: The Changed Spirit and Face of College Life in America.* Akron: University of Akron Press, 2003.

Gribble, Francis. *The Romance of the Oxford Colleges.* London: Miles Boon, 1910.

Hoffman, Allan M., John H. Schuh, and Robert H. Fenske. *Violence on Campus.* Gaithersburg: Aspen Publishers, 1998.

Horn, Miriam. *Rebels in White Gloves: Coming of Age with Hillary's Class—Wellesley '69.* New York: Random House, 1999.

Johanson, Christine. *Women's Struggle for Higher Education in Russia, 1855–1900.* Kingston and Montreal: McGill-Queen's University Press, 1987.

Kendall, Elaine. *Peculiar Institutions: An Informal History of the Seven Sister Colleges.* New York: G. Putnam's Sons, 1976.

Lavergne, Gary. *Sniper in the Tower: The Charles Whitman Murders.* Denton: University of North Texas Press, 1997.

Mabry, Donald J. *The Mexican University and the State: Student Conflicts, 1910–1971.* College Station: Texas A&M University Press, 1982.

McDavid, Jodi. "We're Dirty Sons of Bitches: Residence Rites of Passage at a Small Maritime University." M.A. thesis, Memorial University at Newfoundland, 2002.

Miller-Bernal, Leslie, and Susan L. Poulson, eds. *Going Coed: Women's Experiences in Formerly Men's Colleges and Universities, 1950–2000.* Nashville: Vanderbilt University Press, 2004.

Pedersen, Olaf. *The First Universities: Studium Generale and the Origins of University Education in Europe.* Cambridge: Cambridge University Press, 1997.

Peterson, Marvin W., et al. *Black Students on White Campuses: The Impacts of Increased Black Enrollments.* Ann Arbor: Survey Research Center, University of Michigan, 1978.

Robbins, Alexandra. *Secrets of the Tomb: Skull and Bones, the Ivy League, and the Hidden Paths of Power.* Boston: Little, Brown, 2002.

Ross, Lawrence C. *Divine Nine: A History of African-American Fraternities and Sororities in America.* New York: Kensington Publishing, 2001.

Schama, Simon. *Dead Certainties: Unwarranted Speculations.* New York: Knopf, 1992.

Sperber, Murray. *Beer and Circus: How Big-Time Sports Is Crippling Undergraduate Education.* New York: Henry Holt, 2000.

Stein, Wayne J., and Maenette K. AhNee-Benham, eds. *Renaissance of American Indian Higher Education: Capturing the Dream.* Mahwah: Lawrence Erlbaum Associates, 2002.

Thelin, John R. *History of American Higher Education.* Baltimore: Johns Hopkins University Press, 2004.

Willie, Charles V., and Ronald R. Edmonds, eds. *Black Colleges in America: Challenge, Development, Survival.* New York: Teachers College Press, 1978.

MEMOIR

Conway, Jill Ker. *The Road from Coorain.* New York: Random House, 1990.

Hannah, John A. *A Memoir.* East Lansing: Michigan State University Press, 1980.

Hart, Benjamin. *Poisoned Ivy.* New York: Stein and Day, 1984.

Kemeny, Jean Alexander. *It's Different at Dartmouth: A Memoir.* Brattleboro: Greene Press, 1979.

Kingston, Maxine Hong. *The Woman Warrior: Memoirs of a Girlhood among Ghosts.* New York: Vintage International, 1976.

Kirkconnell, Watson. *A Slice of Canada.* Toronto: University of Toronto Press, 1967.

Lim, Shirley Geok-Lin. *Among the White Moon Faces: An Asian-American Memoir of Homelands.* New York: The Feminist Press at CUNY, 1997.

Meredith, James H. *Three Years in Mississippi.* Bloomington: Indiana University Press, 1966.

Peacock, Molly. *Paradise, Piece by Piece.* New York: Riverhead Books, 1998.

Sammartino, Peter. *Of Castles and Colleges: Notes toward an Autobiography.* South Brunswick: A.S. Barnes, 1972.

Tennyson, Charles. *Cambridge from Within.* London: Chatto and Windus, 1913.

Thwe, Pascal Koo. *From the Land of Green Ghosts: A Burmese Odyssey.* New York: HarperCollins, 2002.

White, R. J. *Cambridge Life.* London: Eyre and Spottiswoode, 1960.

NOVELS

Atwood, Margaret. *The Robber Bride.* New York: Anchor Books, 1993.

Brown, Dan. *Angels and Demons.* New York: Simon and Schuster, 2000.

————. *The Da Vinci Code*. New York: Doubleday, 2003.

Christie, Agatha. *Murder on the Orient Express*. New York: Penguin Group, 1985.

————. *Ten Little Indians: A Mystery Play in Three Acts*. New York: Samuel French, 1946.

Cohen, Mark. *The Fractal Murders*. New York: Warner Books, 2004.

Crichton, Michael. *Timeline*. Alfred A. Knopf, 1999.

Cross, Amanda. *Death in a Tenured Position*. New York: Ballantine, 1982.

————. *Honest Doubt*. New York: Ballantine, 2000.

————. *In the Last Analysis*. New York: Avon Books, 1964.

Elkins, Aaron. *Skeleton Dance*. New York: William Morrow and Co., 2000.

Hart, Carolyn G. *A Little Class on Murder*. New York: Bantam Books, 1989.

Lake, M. D. *A Gift for Murder*. New York: Avon Books, 1992.

McCarthy, Mary. *The Group*. New York: Signet/NAL, 1964.

Sayers, Dorothy. *Gaudy Night*. New York: Avon Books, 1968.

Segal, Erich. *The Class*. New York: Bantam Books, 1986.

Shelley, Mary. *Frankenstein*. New York: Bantam Books, 1991.

Smiley, Jane. *Moo*. New York: Fawcett Columbine, 1995.

Thomas-Graham, Pamela. *A Darker Shade of Crimson*. New York: Simon and Schuster, 1998.

————. *Orange Crushed*. New York: Simon and Schuster, 2004.

Verne, Jules. *Journey to the Center of the Earth*. New York: Signet Classic, 1986.

Waugh, Evelyn. *Brideshead Revisited*. Boston: Little, Brown, 1946.

Wells, H. G. *The Time Machine*. New York: Bantam Books, 1991.

Wolfe, Tom. *I Am Charlotte Simmons*. New York: Farrar, Straus and Giroux, 2004.

Web Resources

INTRODUCTION

The Internet offers the researcher a feast of information. Those of us who love folklore can count on spending many delightful hours discovering legends, tales, and other material on the World Wide Web. However, we have to remember that not all Web sites are equally reliable. Sites ending with ".com" have a commercial orientation, sites ending with ".org" represent an organization, and sites ending with ".edu" come from an educational institution. Usually the ".edu" sites provide information without underlying commercial agendas. However, it is always wise to think carefully about what Web sites have to offer and how much they can be trusted.

In this electronic age, new Web sites pop up every day, while familiar ones may change or vanish altogether. Because of the Internet's mutability, it is impossible to be sure that resources listed here will always be available. I have listed only Web sites that have been online for some time and seem likely to stay there. If any of the sites seem difficult to find, I recommend looking for them using key words with a reliable search engine. This section is designed to help researchers find full, accurate texts of campus legends as well as contextual information about the folklore and history of colleges and universities. Since there are so many colleges and universities in the world, this is just a selection of the available material. Anyone with Internet access can quickly find more source material using these recommendations as a point of departure.

SEARCH ENGINES

The best way to find electronic resources is to use a search engine of proven reliability. Most search engines do not discriminate between uppercase and lowercase letters. One of the best search engines is Google (http://www.google. com), which has a highly efficient data retrieval system. Google's document retrieval system, Google Scholar (http://www.scholargoogle.com), offers an increasingly large database of full-text articles.

Putting certain key words in quotes can affect a search's efficiency. For example, a recent search for "campus legends" on Google resulted in 523 hits. In that search, only sources that contained the entire phrase "campus legends" were listed. A much broader search for "'campus' + 'legends'" came up with 323,000 hits. Usually it is best to put the whole phrase in quotes so that the search will have maximum efficiency. However, experimentation with different key words and combinations often yields interesting results.

In addition to Google, the following search engines have proven their value:

- Yahoo! (http://www.yahoo.com)
- Alta Vista (http://www.altavista.com)
- Webcrawler (http://www.webcrawler.com)
- All the Web (http://www.alltheweb.com)
- DMOZ (http://www.dmoz.org)
- Excite (http://www.excite.com)

FOLKLORE ARCHIVES

- Brigham Young University Folklore Archives, Harold B. Lee Library (http:// sc.lib.byu.edu/)
- Fife Folklore Archives, Utah State University, Logan, Utah (http://library.usu. edu/Folklo/)
- Folklore Archive, University of California at Berkeley (http://ls.berkeley.edu/ dept/folklore/archive-policy.html)
- Folklore and Mythology Archives, University of California at Los Angeles (http://www.humnet.ucla.edu/humnet/folklore/archives)
- Niagara Frontier Folklore Archives, Buffalo, New York (http://buffalolore. buffalonet.org/archives/FolkloreArchives.htm)
- Northeast Archives of Folklore and Oral History, Maine Folklife Center, University of Maine (http://www.umaine.edu/folklife/index.htm)
- Public Sector Folklore Listserv Archives (http://lists.nau.edu/archives/ publore.html)
- Texas A&M Online Folklore Archive (http://listserv.tamu.edu)

- University of Pennsylvania Folklore and Ethnography Archive (http://www. sas.upenn.edu/folklore/center/archive.html)
- Folklore Archive, Wayne State University Archives of Labor and Urban Affairs, Reuther Library (http://www.reuther.wayne.edu/collections/collections.html)
- Western Kentucky University Manuscripts and Folklore Archives (http://www. wku.edu/Library/disc/)

FOLKLORE JOURNALS

Two of the journals listed here, the *Journal of American Folklore* and *Folklore,* can be accessed through the journal storage Web site JSTOR (http://www. jstor.org). Members of the American Folklore Society (http://www.afsnet. org) can use JSTOR by paying a nominal fee; many libraries offer JSTOR to all members.

- *Contemporary Legend* (http://www.panam.edu/faculty/mglazer/isclr/Contemporary Legend.htm)
- *Folklore* (United Kingdom) (http://www.tandf.co.uk/journals/titles/0015587X. asp)
- *Folklore: An Electronical Journal of Folklore* (Estonia) (http://www.folklore.ee/ Folklore/)
- *Folklore Fellows Communications* (http://www.folklorefellows.org)
- *Folklore Forum* (http://www.indiana.edu/~folkpub/forum)
- *Culture and Tradition* (http://www.ucs.mun.ca/~culture)
- *Journal of American Folklore* (http://www.afsnet.org/publications/jaf/cfm)
- *Journal of Folklore Research* (http://www.indana.edu/~jofr)
- *Newfolk: New Directions in Folklore* (http://www.temple.edu/isllc/newfolk/ journal.html)
- *Voices: The Journal of New York Folklore* (http://www.nyfolklore.org/pubs/ newpub.html)

COLLEGE NEWSPAPERS

To access the Web sites of over 300 college and university newspapers, go to http://www.newspapers.com/college.htm, where you can search for newspapers by state and by title. Many of these newspapers offer online archives of back issues.

SELECTED COLLEGE GHOST STORY WEB SITES

- Emory University, Atlanta, Georgia (http://www.emory.edu/ADMISSIONS/indexa.htm?content_html/dooley)
- Franklin and Marshall College, Lancaster, Pennsylvania (http://www.library.fandm.edu/archives/ghoststories.html)
- Marymount College, Tarrytown, New York (http://www.marymt.edu/~yorke/ghost.html)
- Mills College, Oakland, California (http://www.artsfusion.com/millsghosts/stories.html)
- University of Montevallo, Montevallo, Alabama (http://www.cob.montevallo.edu/StuddardAL/um.htm)
- Nebraska Wesleyan University, Lincoln, Nebraska (http://www.webspawner.com/users/nebraskashauntedcoll/)
- Ohio University, Athens, Ohio (http://geocities.com/Athens/Acropolis/9241/hauntou.html)
- Sweet Briar College, Sweet Briar, Virginia (http://www.ghosts.sbc.edu)
- Wells College, Aurora, New York (http://aurora.wells.edu/~library/ghosts.htm)
- Western Kentucky University, Bowling Green, Kentucky (http://www.wku.edu/Library/disc/GhostStories/Stories/knowmore.htm)

SELECTED COLLEGE HISTORY WEB SITES

- Alcorn State University, Alcorn State, Mississippi (http://www.alcorn.edu/about/history.htm)
- University of California at Berkeley (http://www.berkeley.edu/about/history)
- Bowdoin College, Brunswick, Maine (http://www.bowdoin.edu/about/history/bowdoin_history.shtml)
- Cambridge University, Cambridge, England (http://www.cam.ac.uk/cambuniv/pubs/history)
- Chief Dull Knife College, Lame Deer, Montana (http://www.cdkc.edu/DullKnife/dkmchist.htm)
- Colorado College, Colorado Springs, Colorado (http://www.coloradocollege.edu/welcome/historyofcc/)
- D-Q University, Davis, California (http://www.dqu.cc.ca.us/pages/catalog02–04/general_info/about.html)

- Harvard College, Boston, Massachusetts (http://www.hno.harvard.edu/guide/lore/index.html)

- Howard College, Washington, DC (http://www.howard.edu/Library/HU_History.htm)

- Mount Holyoke College, South Hadley, Massachusetts (http://www.mtholyoke.edu/cic/about/history.shtml)

- Oxford University, Oxford, England (http://www.ox.ac.uk/aboutoxford/history.shtml)

- Sweet Briar College, Sweet Briar, Virginia (http://www.centennial.sbc.edu/history/)

- Vassar College, Poughkeepsie, New York (http://faculty.vassar.edu/daniels/)

- Wayne State University, Detroit, Michigan (http://www.wayne.edu/profiles/timeline.html)

COMMERCIAL LEGEND WEB SITES

- **Urban Legends Reference Pages.** Barbara and David P. Mikkelson are the administrators of this well-known Web site, the purpose of which is to determine the validity of urban legends. Different-colored bullets rate each legend as true, false, ambiguous, unclassifiable, or of indeterminate origin. The "College" section includes nine categories: Administration, Embarrassments, Exam Scams, Hallowed Halls, Homework, Horrors, Medical School, Pranks, and Risqué Business. Detailed bibliographies show familiarity with folklore scholarship. (http://www.snopes.com/college/college.asp)

- **Truth or Fiction.com.** Founded by Rich Buhler, this site devotes itself to tracking Internet e-rumors transmitted through forwarded e-mails with the purpose of finding out whether certain popular rumors and legends are true. The "Education" section includes rumors and legends about college students as well as students at other levels. Other stories about college students, such as the mysterious allegation of "cow-tipping," can be found in the "Humorous Stories" section. (http://www.truthorfiction.com/index-education.htm)

- **About Urban Legends and Folklore.** David Emery's reference pages provide information about the popular legends that have circulated recently, including some legends that involve college students. The site rates legends as "true," "false," or somewhere in between. Different variants of legends, photos, and sources for further reading make this an interesting site to visit. (http://urbanlegends.about.com)

- **The Shadow Lands.** With a plethora of ghost stories organized by state, this Web site offers a treasure trove of material, including many supernatural legends associated with colleges and universities. The site does not analyze legends or give documentation, but it provides interesting leads for further research. (http://theshadowlands.net/ghost/)

Index

About the Author

ELIZABETH TUCKER is Associate Professor of English at Binghamton University. Her work has appeared in such journals as *Children's Folklore Review*, *Journal of Popular Culture*, *Research in African Literatures*, *Western Folklore*, and *Indiana Folklore*.